Sleep Fictions

TOPICS IN THE DIGITAL HUMANITIES

Humanities computing is redefining basic principles of research and publication. An influx of new, vibrant, and diverse communities of practitioners recognize that computer applications are subject to continual innovation and reappraisal. This series publishes books that demonstrate the new questions, methods, and results arising in the digital humanities.

Series Editor
Susan Schreibman

Sleep Fictions

Rest and Its Deprivations in Progressive-Era Literature

HANNAH L. HUBER

© 2023 by the Board of Trustees
of the University of Illinois
All rights reserved
1 2 3 4 5 C P 5 4 3 2 1
⊗ This book is printed on acid-free paper.

Library of Congress Cataloging-in-Publication Data
Names: Huber, Hannah L., 1989– author.
Title: Sleep fictions : rest and its deprivations in
   progressive-era literature / Hannah L. Huber.
Description: Urbana : University of Illinois Press,
   [2023] | Series: Topics in the digital humanities |
   Includes bibliographical references and index. |
Identifiers: LCCN 2023017175 (print) | LCCN
   2023017176 (ebook) | ISBN 9780252045400
   (cloth ; acid-free paper) | ISBN 9780252087523
   (paperback ; acid-free paper) | ISBN
   9780252055003 (ebook)
Subjects: LCSH: Sleep in literature. | Wakefulness
   in literature. | American fiction—19th century—
   History and criticism. | American fiction—20th
   century—History and criticism. | LCGFT:
   Literary criticism.
Classification: LCC PS374.S63 H83 2023 (print) |
   LCC PS374.S63 (ebook) | DDC 810.9/3561—dc23/
   eng/20230622
LC record available at https://lccn.loc.gov/2023017175
LC ebook record available at https://lccn.loc.gov/2023017176

Contents

ACKNOWLEDGMENTS   vii

INTRODUCTION   From Mystery to Medicine:
Diagnosing Sleep in American Literature   1

1   "The Most Restless of Mortals": Patronage and Somnambulism
in Henry James's *Roderick Hudson*   26

2   "A Monst'us Pow'ful Sleeper": Resisting the Master Clock
in Charles Chesnutt's "Uncle Julius" Tales   59

3   "A Great Blaze of Electric Light": Illuminating Sleeplessness
in Edith Wharton's *The House of Mirth*   91

4   "Rest and Power": The Social Currency of Sleep
in Charlotte Perkins Gilman's *Forerunner*   120

CONCLUSION   151

NOTES   163

REFERENCES   167

INDEX   179

Acknowledgments

Many people in all aspects and phases of my life shaped this book into what it is. My fascination with studying sleep began with a narcolepsy diagnosis I received at the outset of my graduate studies, and this book's focus was inspired by an uncannily familiar scene detailing hypnogogic hallucinations in *The House of Mirth*. Cynthia Davis saw the value of such a reading, and after countless rounds of feedback and professional advice, her mentorship carried me through to a fully formed manuscript. Catherine Keyser was unwaveringly enthusiastic about the project and inspired me to create this book's digital companion. David Greven and Mark Smith were instrumental in making the book so deeply interdisciplinary. I presented passages of this book at conferences hosted by the American Literature Association. I am grateful to my fellow literary naturalists for sharpening my focus on literary tropes from the neurasthenic New Woman to the run-down "apostate." I am grateful to my digital humanities family at the University of Illinois Chicago, especially Mark Canuel, whose support and feedback on everything from my book proposal to the digital companion's themed annotations helped facilitate the book's publication.

I want to give immense gratitude to my editor at the University of Illinois Press, Alison Syring, whose reliable timeliness, productive suggestions, and reassuring guidance throughout my first book experience made the process so welcoming and enjoyable. Many thanks to the anonymous reviewers—two experts in literary studies and one in digital humanities—who challenged me to draw clearer connections across chapters and between the book and digital companion. This resulted in a better monograph and a better digital humanities project. I also wish to thank Susan Schreibman, who chose to include this book in the Topics in the Digital Humanities series and whose constructive commentary enriched the book's digital humanities features. The book's colorful text visualizations were made possible by a printing subvention provided by the Center for Southern Studies (supported by the Andrew W. Mellon Foundation) and the Office of the Dean of the College of Arts and Sciences at the University of the South.

Thank you to my dear friends Jennifer and Kedar for all the delicious dinners, glasses of wine, and other homely comforts you provided me during my weekly commutes from Florida to South Carolina. Mom and Dad, no written word can express my appreciation for you and your unconditional love. To Di, mia madrina, thank you, among countless other things, for instilling in that tiny version of me your insatiable appetite for reading and travel. To the parents gifted to me by the love of my life, I am grateful every day that you are my people. To Jacob, whose empathetic nature led to my narcolepsy diagnosis during that second year of medical school, your ambition and adventurous spirit have long been my driving force. Thank you for making this sleepyhead feel safe in our frenzied world and for braving parenthood with me. Waking up to you and our boy every morning is beyond my wildest dreams.

Sleep Fictions

INTRODUCTION

From Mystery to Medicine

Diagnosing Sleep in American Literature

> Edna began to feel like one who awakens gradually out
> of a dream, a delicious, grotesque, impossible dream, to
> feel again the realities pressing into her soul. The physical
> need for sleep began to overtake her; the exuberance
> which had sustained and exalted her spirit left her helpless
> and yielding to the conditions which crowded her in.
>
> —Kate Chopin, *The Awakening*

In Kate Chopin's 1899 novel *The Awakening*, Edna Pontellier grows increasingly sleepless as she confronts the dissatisfaction she feels as a wife and mother. When she discovers that she loves another man, she describes her state of realization as having never been "so exhausted in my life" (73). Eventually, the symptomatic restlessness of her discontent so overwhelms her that she commits suicide. The only refreshing sleep she experiences leading up to her death—and after her "awakening"—is when she collapses into another woman's bed. She pretends to be someone else, a Sleeping Beauty whose love awaits her awakening after a hundred years' sleep. Yet, Edna can only play Sleeping Beauty temporarily: she must return to her husband and suffer the perpetual wakefulness she ascribes to domestic subjugation. At home her sleeping practices grow increasingly unstable. Rather than sleep with her husband, she stubbornly dozes on their porch hammock. Her resting habits conflict with the stereotypical women of her class: ladies of leisure. Edna sees no use for performative rest and instead sleeps only according to her body's needs: "She was not much given to reclining in the hammock, and when she did so it was with no cat-like suggestion of voluptuous ease, but with a beneficent repose which seemed to invade her whole body" (76). Spiting the display of porch leisure, Edna rests simply to restore her energy. Later, she seeks out private spaces for rest, taking daily naps in "many a sunny, sleepy corner . . . to dream and to be alone and unmolested" (149). Only in isolation, away from her husband and children, can she achieve "a sense of restfulness . . . such as she had not known before" (190). By the novel's end, Edna realizes that her only means of attaining unadulterated rest is to escape domestic confinement and familial possession. Her resistance to male control—that of her husband and her sons—results in an "exhaustion [that] was pressing upon and overpowering her" (302). In contrast to the perpetually enervating home space, the sea's "sonorous murmur" beckons Edna (31), and at the novel's end she dies in its lulling and comforting embrace. Ultimately, Chopin's novel details Edna's personal discontent, in which her social identity and personal relationships drive her toward a restless longing for freedom, a condition she finds curable only through death's infinite sleep.

The sleep abnormalities that result from resisting social conformity in *The Awakening* represent a common theme in fin de siècle literature. The long sleep that Edna so desires and ultimately achieves is only available to her through suicide. Restrictions on restorative rest coincide with social modes of oppression, and Edna's pursuit of sleep is portrayed as a rebellious act. I begin with this synopsis of Chopin's work to briefly elucidate my choice of the Progressive Era to study literary representations of US sleep culture. Literature that came before the turn of the century is indeed ripe with sleep themes, motifs, and figures, but the majority of those texts do little to reveal the ways in which sleep circumscribed social agency, particularly for characters already marginalized by race, gender, class, and sexuality.

The antebellum period is often what springs to scholars' minds when I first mention critical sleep studies in US literature.[1] They are quick to reference Edgar Allan Poe, Nathaniel Hawthorne, Charles Brockden Brown, and Walt Whitman (to name a few). In these authors' works, sleep serves as a symbolic conduit or universalizing act. It connects the sleeper either to the supernatural and otherworldly or to nature and humanity. Sleep is, to an extent, commonly portrayed as inviolable. In Poe's case, it preserves feminine sanctity while simultaneously serving as a gateway to a mysterious and often treacherous dream world. His 1831 poem "The Sleeper," for instance, uses sleep as a euphemism to detail the death of a young woman: the lady's beauty and virtue are kept sacred by her everlasting sleep. Hawthorne's "The Birthmark" (1843) also portrays a young woman whose beauty is made everlasting by eternal sleep. Hawthorne's story commingles a mid-century fascination with scientific discovery and the gothic dream world. Aylmer, a scientist, obsesses over the shape of a tiny hand on his new wife's cheek, a blemish that he believes tarnishes Georgiana's otherwise perfect beauty. The notion of ridding her of her birthmark comes to Aylmer in a dream: "The mind is in a sad state when Sleep, the all-involving, cannot confine her spectres within the dim region of her sway, but suffers them to break forth, affrighting this actual life with secrets that perchance belong to a deeper one" (155). Sleep is depicted as a mysterious force that functions beyond the physical realm inhabited by the body. Its "all-involving" powers detach Aylmer from his corporeality and transport him into a dream world. Sleep's mysterious power can infiltrate "actual life," but "actual life" seems powerless to affect sleep in turn. This is confirmed by Georgiana's death at the story's end. Aylmer gives her a tonic that, as she sleeps, removes her birthmark. The powerful "spectres" of sleep both rid Georgiana of her blemish and pull her into eternal rest. In Hawthorne's tale, modern medicine is no match for the spectral persuasions that, channeled by sleep, bewitch Aylmer and claim Georgiana's life.[2] Poe and Hawthorne were clearly influenced by the early nineteenth-century assumption that "sleep was a form of death" (Kryger 6). In his 1830 study *The Philosophy of Sleep*, for example, Dr. Robert Macnish observes that "sleep is an intermediate state between wakefulness and death: wakefulness is regarded as the active state of all the animal and intellectual functions and death as that of their total suspension" (1). Poe's story "The Tell-Tale Heart" (1843) likewise correlates sleep with the supernatural forces of death: the narrator interrupts his victim's sleep by pouncing on and killing him, and Poe suggests that unearthly powers force the old man awake before the attack, propelling his heart to throb "louder! louder! louder! louder!" even after he is dead (359). As Poe's and Hawthorne's fiction suggests, sleep was a gateway between the human world and the mystical realms of the afterlife.

For other antebellum writers, such as transcendentalist Walt Whitman, sleep served as a universalizing force, rather than a symbol of gothic mystery. Whitman's 1855 poem "The Sleepers," for instance, offers a well-known example of sleep's democratizing effect. Jane F. Thrailkill gathers from the poem that "all human beings are alike; moreover, sleep embodies a state of repose in which self-division is muted. The mind and body are, at least momentarily, at peace" (150). Thus, for Whitman, a sleeping person's mind and nervous system are impervious to environmental disruption. He details a series of "antipodes," for which he claims "one is no better than the other" during sleep. Whitman's poem represents what Michael Greaney describes as a discourse "running through western literature . . . in which sleep submits humanity to a biological egalitarianism in which all social differences vanish into an organic sameness" (5). Mid-nineteenth-century medicine also espoused such a notion, describing sleep as the mere result of bodily stasis: a universal "shutdown" state (or "idle mode," in today's tech parlance).[3] This summation led the medical community to largely restrict its interest in somnolent states to *only* abnormal manifestations, such as perpetual drowsiness, sleepwalking, prolonged restlessness, and sleep paralysis. Gothic short stories such as Charles Brockden Brown's "Somnambulism" (1805) and Poe's "The Facts in the Case of M. Valdemar" (1845) exemplify tales in which fantastical sleep abnormalities, such as sleepwalking and hypnosis, are portrayed as unnatural and terrifying.[4] This is not the case with the realist and naturalist texts that later emerged. By the turn of the century, physicians began to question how mundane factors acted on the body in such a way as to elicit the very sleep abnormalities that Brown and Poe rendered purely fantastical. Sleep deprivation was a primary concern. Rather than espouse the value of personal resting time, medical science espoused models for sleep efficiency that would consolidate sleeping hours in an ever-productive society. Scientists also investigated—and attempted to categorize—psychosomatic differences in sleep according to gender, race, and ethnicity. The resultant pseudoscience largely relied on scientific sexism and racism to argue that white women, and non-Anglo-Americans even more so, were less socially evolved than white men and thus suffered most from modernity's wakeful demands.

Bodily Rhythms and the Cultural Clock

This project asks how sleep, as both a quotidian aspect of human life and a hindrance to American proficiency, exposes the complications that modern subjects face within a restless cultural environment. By exploring the circumscription of sleep and social agency in the works of Henry James, Charles Chesnutt, Edith Wharton, and Charlotte Perkins Gilman, I argue that American literature provided a singular response to the turn of the century obsession with wakefulness. From 1875 to 1916—when my chosen texts were written—cultural conceptions, social valuations, and individual practices of sleep were transformed by a range of developments, including the implementation of standard clock time; the mechanization of industrial labor and public transportation; scientific and medical discoveries about the human body; and shifting cultural definitions of sex, race, ethnicity, and class. By complicating the separation of public and private space, the narratives I discuss present characters exhausted by the permeation of the supposedly impervious—or seemingly escapable—aspects of modernity. In other words, sleep is no solace, as respite in the bedroom (if such a space is even accessible) is impeded by artificial light, traffic commotion, and the social pressures of round-the-clock activity. Marginalized figures are the most vulnerable in these narratives, as they are constantly compelled by the cultural clock and stress over their bodily limitations within an increasingly mechanized world. Most importantly, these texts provide psychosomatic portraits of the devastating consequences of sleep disruption and deprivation, thereby countering a popular US cultural confidence at the turn of the century in the body's ability to conquer sleep.

This book builds on Michael Greaney's 2018 study *Sleep and the Novel*, which explores sleep and social agency in European novels of sleep. In the introduction, Greaney argues that "all societies have unwritten rules about when sleep happens, where it happens, when it counts as healthy or natural and when it counts as irresponsible or self-indulgent; when it can be interrupted and when it must be respected; whose sleep is valuable and whose is not. . . . Sleep is a non-negotiable biological inevitability, but the parameters of sleep—when? where? with whom? for how long?—are all open to negotiation" (2). By situating such concerns within the context of US history, the American ideal to master sleep can be traced, as historian Alan Derickson explains, to Benjamin Franklin's mid-eighteenth-century *Poor Richard's Almanack*: "Franklin emphasized the virtues of moderate amounts of sleep, upholding a standard in the range of seven to eight hours a day in a way that balanced rest and wakefulness" (6). Franklin's sleep lessons represent the dawning of an age in which sleep habits were reshaped by the rhythms of industrialism, in which Americans worked throughout the day and took their rest at night. According to anthropologist Matthew J. Wolf-Meyer, "Franklin's recourse to habit—the daily rising at a set hour, leading to the consolidation and timeliness of sleep—is echoed by those who follow him, more properly in the idiom of medicine and sleep. So too are his assumptions about the economic value and efficiency of sleep" (55). By the 1830s, Derickson explains, "sleep practices were expected to complement metronomic regularity in performance on the job" (4). However, it wasn't until the "Second Industrial Revolution," which Lee Scrivner defines as "the influx of new technologies in the period between 1860 and 1910" (215), that sleep became a popular cultural concern and an impediment to be conquered. At this moment in history, wakefulness became universal rather than its opposite.

Sleeplessness across class divides was in many ways due to the widespread installation of electric light at the end of the nineteenth century. Sleep historian A. Roger Ekirch identifies the development of electricity as the turning point in history when sleep "became more compressed . . . and seamless" (334). Whereas two sleeps, stretching over a twelve-to-fourteen-hour period with a wakeful hour or two in the middle, had been common in preindustrial societies, Ekirch found that these disappeared with the emergence of electricity. Sleep specialist Meir Kryger goes so far as to define a specific moment in US history that marks the beginning of a "twenty-four-hour work world": October 1878, the month Thomas Edison requested a patent for his electric light bulb (111). In the opening of his 2017 study *The Mystery of Sleep*, Kryger muses that "despite the thousands of experiments scientists have performed to study sleep, no one has been able to declare with certainty why all lifeforms need sleep; we know only that when animals are prevented from sleeping they eventually die" (5). Kryger concedes what scientists and innovators of the late nineteenth century were unwilling to admit. Instead, figures like industrial-era giants Edison and Frederick Winslow Taylor sought ways to overpower sleep through a round-the-clock work ethic.

Edison, who declared the light bulb the cure for sleep, sought to overrule nighttime rest and bring into vogue a "manly wakefulness" or "heroic wakefulness" (Derickson 5). These terms, coined by Derickson, encompass Edison's argument that the body could be conditioned to exist on little-to-no sleep and that such an effort would lead to economic and social success.[5] Alongside the emergence of his light bulb came the inventor's claims that long bouts of sleep were a thing of the past. Instead, Edison boasted of his ability to thrive off intermittent, short naps throughout the day and night. Wolf-Meyer astutely notes that Edison's particular brand of sleep discipline represents a larger, collective effort to bodily adapt to the demands of capitalism: "At a time when the management of whole populations was necessary for the smooth and orderly advancement of industrial production and exchange, . . . Edison took it upon himself to shape his sleep to his desires. . . . [His] attitudes index . . . qualities of American capitalism that value the flexibility of individuals over that of institutions" (19–20). Historians often align Edison with Taylor, whose widely influential theory of scientific management sought to enhance the output of industrial labor through the minute management of workers' time. In *Insomnia: A Cultural History*, Eluned Summers-Bremner describes Taylor as "a kind of daylight insomniac, obsessed with eradicating every last heartbeat of a worker's unique relation to his body's labour" (121). She defines Taylor's management system as a "worker time-study" that coalesced "with other forms of standardization that govern the modern city," among these Railway Standard Time and electric lighting (121). Insomnia, then, became the zeitgeist of the Progressive-Era industrial complex. According to Greaney, "Insomnia, like

6   INTRODUCTION

sleep, has its own material history, and a shorthand version of its evolution in the modern world would cover the commodification of caffeine and other stimulants; the emergence of a market for pharmacological treatments for sleeplessness; the appearance of the electric light bulb, and with it the ability to banish night-time at the flick of a switch; and the emergence of new technologies of interconnectedness, whether the railway or the telegraph or the telephone that cut across time zones, giving the world the chance to be in ceaseless, unsleeping dialogue with itself" (14). The exhaustion that resulted from these new systems of efficiency and productivity became the object of intense scrutiny and inspired numerous theories about sleep's myriad purposes and mechanisms at the onset of the 1900s.

Physicians Charles Elam and George Miller Beard, in treatises dating from 1869 and 1880, respectively, studied exhaustion-induced sleep phenomena, including somnambulism and neurasthenia, but little sleep research uncovered anything of importance in these latter decades of the nineteenth century. That is until, in a historic 1896 experiment, doctors G. T. W. Patrick and J. A. Gilbert became the first to test sleep deprivation in humans within a twenty-four-hour cycle (Dijk and Schantz). From there, curiosity about sleep continued to increase. A 1903 article in *Popular Science Monthly* summarized the latest findings in sleep medicine: Dr. Percy G. Stiles, evincing precursory thinking to decades-later classifications of sleep cycles, reported that "several physiologists have tested the depth of sleep at different hours of the night. . . . All have agreed that the greatest depth of sleep is reached as early as the second hour" (435). In citing immobility at the second sleeping hour, this observation anticipates later understandings of REM sleep, a vivid-dreaming state in which the sleeper loses almost all muscle tone. The article also questions whether the body's twenty-four-hour sleep cycle is internally regulated, postulating that "what we call natural waking in the morning . . . due to some stimulus from without—light . . . may come from within" (436). However, it wasn't until the 1920s that German psychologist J. S. Szymanski confirmed the hypothesis that humans undergo a rhythmic sleep-wake cycle that spans twenty-four hours (Aschoff), and only in the 1950s did Franz Halberg coin the term *circadian rhythm*, which established the field of chronobiology (the study of biological rhythms in relation to solar and lunar patterns). Despite a capitalist, elitist disregard for—and limited scientific understanding of—sleep's essentiality at the turn of the century, Progressive-Era writers depicted death and near-death experiences as an inevitable result of sleep deprivation, thus using their fiction to articulate ignored and previously unexplored truths about the value of sleep.

Comprehensively, this study explores how characters' relationships to, and alienation from, the individual rhythms of routine rest are shaped by their subtle forms of internalization of—and resistance to—socially constructed linear time. Measurements of time, for example, symbolize one's susceptibility to the demands of the cultural clock. Roderick Hudson, James's sculptor protagonist, is likened to a broken-down clock as he deteriorates under the pressure to produce sculptures routinely and efficiently, and Wharton's main character, Lily Bart, believes she has inherited a compulsion toward servitude due to her father's servility, which was as routine as the swinging pendulum that powered the grandfather clock in her childhood home. Unlike Wharton, Gilman finds moments in which the internalization of the cultural clock can also serve as a means for escaping domestic oppression, yet her white feminist heroes merely eschew domestic work through the scientific management of Black and immigrant workers. This oppressive process is symbolized by the meticulous schedules that the protagonist of *What Diantha Did* (1909–10) uses to track every hour of her employees' daily routine. Chesnutt's work singularly features characters' resistance to linear time that does not necessitate new iterations of oppression. In "A Deep Sleeper" (1893), for instance, the enslaved Skundus cleverly plays on his actual exhaustion through the feigned embodiment of a narcolepsy so severe that it induces a monthlong sleep. He successfully deceives his enslaver, resulting in reforms that benefit all those imprisoned on the plantation. Collectively, this book's chapters reveal how US literature of the late nineteenth and early twentieth century challenged sleep-related pseudoscience by complicating the twinned expectations of wakefulness and sleep deprivation in the modern world. For my chosen authors, sleep is not simply a bygone practice bested by mental effort, physical force, or electrical installation. Instead, each text explores how sleep phenomena function both as an inevitable aspect of humanity and as an affront to an industrialized, time-oriented culture.[6]

Sleeplessness in US Literature at the Turn of the Century

Throughout this project, I measure the extent to which turn of the century social and labor practices restricted rest in ways that twenty-first-century medicine would now deem unhealthy or ineffectual. Moreover, I seek to show how medical studies and scientific theories of sleep, from the contemporary moment to the present, are illustrated in Progressive-Era literary renderings of sleep phenomena. Sleep-related symptoms—ranging from sleep paralysis and lucid dreaming to prolonged wakefulness and sleep deprivation—cohere with contemporary cultural developments. A character's experience of insomnia, for example, is likened to an individual's mind being constantly illuminated by a light bulb. Conversely, a person's subconscious dozing results in the speeding forward of an electrical timepiece, or a character's descent into deep sleep is brought about by a dangerous dose of a chemist's soporific. Historian Anson Rabinbach details how the "human motor [became] a metaphor of work and energy that provided nineteenth-century thinkers with a new scientific and cultural framework" (1). He describes this way of thinking as "modern productivism— the belief that human society and nature are linked by the primacy and identity of all productive activity, whether of laborers, of machines, or of natural forces—[which] first arose from the conceptual revolution ushered in by nineteenth-century scientific discoveries, especially thermodynamics" (3). As characters contend with the demands of a modern social clock, the bodily impulse to rest conflicts with their social compulsion to maintain the steady flow of energy that pulses through the twenty-four-hour culture. These efforts to control and restrict sleep are symptomatic of the coalescence of the United States' long-established Protestant work ethic and the mechanization of industrial advancement.

Amid this, marginalized groups fought to protect their right to rest, something best exemplified by the working-class fight for labor-hour reform. Scientists, meanwhile, remained suspicious of the biological necessity of sleep, and writers used their fiction to complicate dichotomous conceptions of personal hours versus labor time and unconscious sleep versus restorative rest. As Thrailkill observes, the haste of modernity posed a serious mind-body problem for writers, theorists, and scientists of the late nineteenth century. The century's most innovative thinkers "understood the human nervous system to be analogous to, and indeed influenced by, systems of rapid communication and transportation" (22). Given this newfound bodily interaction with modern innovation, Cartesian dualism, premised on an autonomous mind and body, proved an unreliable concept: "The commotion of modernity posed unique challenges to the delicate equilibrium of body and mind, while feelings were understood to provide a crucial conduit, albeit one that was easily damaged or derailed, through which individuals could negotiate a volatile environment" (22). Works of realism and naturalism argue that sleep cannot simply be treated as an on-off mechanism that individuals can activate when ready to take a nap or to settle in for the night. Thus, sleep—as an impregnable, ubiquitous force in an ever-wakeful world—is a persistent theme in fin de siècle US literature.

In the last few decades, literary scholarship—such as Thrailkill's *Affecting Fictions* (2007), Gail Bederman's *Manliness and Civilization* (2008), Jennifer Fleissner's *Women, Compulsion, Modernity* (2004), and Tom Lutz's *American Nervousness, 1903* (1991)—has examined the thematics of perpetual motion in relation to race, class, and gender. These studies form a strong foundation for this project, as they trace the rise of neurasthenia as a diagnosis for the era's emergent sleeplessness. I expand on these studies to show that while neurasthenia certainly does exemplify a challenge modernity posed to sleep, it is not the only means by which sleeplessness might be explored in turn of the century US literature. For instance, Thrailkill uses Whitman's "The Sleepers" as a lens through which to view imagery in Stephen Crane's *The Red Badge of Courage* (1895), particularly the scene in which Henry rests among comrades in contrast to the violent actions of war. Thrailkill derives from Whitman's poem the idea that sleep enables both mind-body cohesion and a unity of individuals. Reading this theme in Crane's novel suggests that turn of the century literature echoed the long nineteenth century's tradition of depicting human bodies in slumber as universally unaffected by modernity. At a time when the nation was rapidly inundated with urban expansion, electrical advancement, and mass consumption, Thrailkill suggests that a reliably rhythmic state of unified, peaceful repose was a welcome counterbalance. While Henry's exhausted body does collapse into the communal slumber of his regiment in *Red Badge*, his sleep is disrupted when he is forced to wake and prepare for battle. As a soldier, he is not entitled to rest when—and for how long—his body wills him to do so. Instead, he is forced to follow the sleeping patterns dictated by his superiors. Rather than find reprieve in restorative rest, Henry is alienated from adequate sleep through his absorption into the industrialized mechanisms of war. Crane's novel, then, revisits the Civil War to evince the beginnings of an individual's assimilation into a labor system that required twenty-four-hour adherence, one that would come to define modern life for working Americans at the turn of the century.

An early exploration of the torturous repercussions of sleep deprivation for the marginalized wartime figure is depicted in E. D. E. N. Southworth's widely successful novel *The Hidden Hand* (first serialized in the *New York Ledger* in 1859 and published as a book in 1888). The novel recounts the adventures of its protagonist, Capitola Black, a tomboy figure who outwits the many men attempting to exploit her for one reason or another. She protects the vulnerable women around her, including her friend Clara, whom she helps escape from the clutches of one of the novel's antagonists, Colonel Le Noir. Le Noir tries to trick Clara into marrying his son, but his plan is foiled by Capitola's ingenuity. Toward the novel's end, Le Noir uses his powerful position in the US military during the Mexican-American War to conspire to kill Clara's lover, Traverse Rock. Le Noir schemes to have Traverse fall asleep at his post by depriving him of rest for four days. In this subplot, Southworth draws from the 1806 Articles of War. Article 46 states that "any sentinel who shall be found sleeping upon his post, or shall leave it before he shall be regularly relieved, shall suffer death, or such other punishment as shall be inflicted by the sentence of a court martial" (US Congress 365). After he is found asleep at his post, Traverse confesses in court that he is guilty of "fatal sleep" (294). He describes his physical state after ninety-six hours without sleep: "'My whole head was sick and my whole heart faint'; my frame was sinking; my soul could scarcely hold my body upright. . . . Sleep would arrest me while in motion, and I would drop my musket and wake up in a panic, with the impression of some awful, overhanging ruin appalling my soul" (295).[7] The suffering he endures from sleep deprivation is immense: "[It] was a night of mental and physical horrors. Brain and nerves seemed in a state of disorganization; thought and emotion were chaos; the relations of soul and body broken up" (295). Southworth dedicates lengthy passages to describing Traverse's gaunt appearance, his "deadly countenance" (293), and his futile attempts to stay awake. The suffering Traverse undergoes due to long-term sleep deprivation—which is inextricably linked to the wartime experience—depicts a theme authors would later explore within the context of modernity's everyday life.

Sleep as a crime for the lowly peon (with its codified war origins) and sleep deprivation as torture are common themes in turn of the century literature. Male characters suffer from newly entrenched and restrictive sleep practices. Jack London's 1906 short story "The Apostate," for example, details the personal reflections and working life of an exhausted, adolescent laborer. Johnny's working day typically begins with his being "torn bodily by his mother from the grip of sleep" (16). The monotony of factory work has a neurasthenic effect: "At night his muscles twitched in his sleep, and in the daytime he could not relax and rest. He remained keyed up and his muscles continued to twitch" (18). Eventually, he collapses from sleep deprivation and misses several days of work. The doctor, seemingly unaware that the boy suffers from prolonged exhaustion, sees nothing amiss. When the boy eventually rebels and achieves a bit of rejuvenating rest, he comes to his own awakening, telling his mother, "I ain't never goin' to work again" (27). He responds to her vehement objections by saying: "I'm plum' tired out. What makes me tired? Moves. I've ben movin' ever since I was born" (27–28). The kinetic haste of modernity has propelled him all his young life, grinding him down to "a twisted and stunted and nameless piece of life" (30). His deformity is a manifestation of a body deprived of restorative rest. Johnny's lifelong sleep deprivation has made him less a human and more a malfunctioning machine. His first act of freedom is to fall asleep under a tree, even as his muscles continue to twitch.[8] In this scene, Johnny is a classic example of a run-down human motor, as described by Rabinbach: "A breakdown of body and mind, fatigue was increasingly identified as a 'modern' disorder of overwhelming social and physical consequence. This perception appears frequently in the poetic literature of exhaustion, which arises almost simultaneously with the medical and scientific literature on fatigue" (40, and see 137–45). The story ends with Johnny sneaking onto a train car, smiling as he lies down to make up for years of lost sleep. The conclusion exemplifies Greaney's claim that "depending on its location and timing, . . . the act of sleep in fiction can involve an assertion rather than an attenuation of personhood" (10). Sleep as an assertive act, an embodied claim to personal time and space, is a common theme throughout my chosen texts.

As I show in my first and third chapters, literary realists Henry James and Edith Wharton were, like the naturalist Jack London, interested in correlations between sleep deprivation, the high-speed transit of an increasingly globalized world, and the body's incessant engagement with industrialized modernity. The plots of character degeneration that track the lives of Roderick Hudson and Lily Bart classify such works as naturalism. Yet, James and Wharton, in general, must be distinguished from most literary naturalist writers due to their realist preoccupation with the privileged upper class. In many ways, the trials and tribulations of Roderick and Lily—while very real and ultimately life obliterating—are teacup dramas compared to the harsh, working-class lives of characters like Johnny.[9] "The Apostate" encapsulates how industrialized labor in the second half of the nineteenth century treated workers like easily manipulated and operated machines. As the efficiency of industrial technology increased, so too were workers expected to train their bodies according to the demands of consumer capitalism. The dreams so emphasized in the sleeping worlds of gothic and transcendental writers die out in a world where individuals have little time for adequate sleep. Ekirch explains that after the emergence of industrialized labor and electric light, "no longer did most sleepers experience an interval of wakefulness in which to ponder visions in the dead of night" (335). An important shift occurred over the nineteenth century, in which nighttime sleeping hours decreased from an average of twelve to fourteen hours across two sleeps "to a new pattern of slumber, at once consolidated and more compressed" (335). Labor practices and workday hours at the turn of the century were key to this "new pattern" of sleeping hours. Henry Ford, for instance, was the figurehead for the eight-hour working day. In 1914, the Ford Motor Company gave in to union cries for "eight hours for work, eight hours for rest, eight hours for what you will" (Reiss 41). As liberating as this may seem for laborers such as London's apostate, a seamless eight-hour sleep schedule allows for little to no flexibility. Benjamin Reiss reveals the inflexibility of these modern sleep practices for the working class: "Eight hours, not four and four with one in the middle for interpreting dreams or making love, or six at night and two after lunch" (41). As I will show, twentieth-century medical discoveries would later prove that restorative sleep practices are unique to every individual. There is no singular number of sleeping hours that can be universally prescribed. Thus, the granting of an eight-hour night's sleep did little to ensure that workers could achieve the adequate rest that best fit their individual needs.

Sleep disparities result from the bodily impact of class-, race-, and gender-related oppression. Alongside the trope of the depleted worker, the New Woman character is another figure for whom restorative rest—and mental clarity, which necessitates the unified calmness of mind and body—is impossible to achieve when at the mercy of an independently reactive nervous system. Theodore Dreiser's *Sister Carrie* (1900) is a prime example. When Carrie Meeber leaves her rural home to seek work in Chicago, she is persuaded by the charismatic salesman Charles Drouet to move in with him. Later, when Drouet accuses Carrie of infidelity, she initially reacts with bravado by pretending to leave him, but the emotional strain depletes her, and she allows Drouet to coax her back inside. Exhausted, she drops into her rocking chair: "The threat of the world outside, in which she had failed once before, the impossibility of this state inside, where the chambers were no longer justly hers, the effect of the argument upon her nerves, all combined to make her a mass of jangling fibres—an anchorless, storm-beaten little craft which could do absolutely nothing but drift" (229). Carrie's inability to act decisively when plagued by exhaustion is again evident when George Hurstwood startles her out of bed with a fake emergency to lure her away from Drouet. Unfortunately for Carrie, she does not fully awaken to her situation until she is already aboard a moving train. Hurstwood's admission that they are leaving Chicago "aroused her in an instant" (275). Carrie's awakening, however, does little to save her from the situation: "She was quite appalled at the man's audacity. This was something which had never for a moment entered her head. Her one thought now was to get off and away. If only the flying train could be stopped, the terrible trick would be amended" (276). Carrie feels herself defeated by the inescapability

From Mystery to Medicine 13

of modern innovation. Although now fully aware of her situation, Carrie cannot halt the means of transportation, which move much faster than her own recognition.

As my opening analysis of *The Awakening* reveals, women suffered under cultural assumptions about the sleeping body. I add to the now-standard treatment of female neurasthenia in turn of the century literary scholarship a concern over the myriad social complications posed by the body's psychosomatic requirement for passive rest, a need that interferes with the perpetual vigilance female characters in realist and naturalist texts feel compelled to exert in an effort to thrive—or, at times, survive—in the modern world. Even as female literary figures fight through fatigue, their efforts are often paradoxical, as their actions rarely achieve their intended results. Fleissner explains that "women's new freedoms [are] inseparable from a growing sense, linking naturalist fiction with the period's burgeoning social-scientific work, that the traditional sense of natural bodily life and a social public sphere must give way to a recognition of all human life . . . and manage the facts of our existence as embodied beings" (*Women* 22). Specifically, Fleissner focuses on female characters' compulsive behavior to show how "naturalism depicts . . . the ongoing negotiations between the [natural and the social] that become most visible and (most forcefully strange) in the elaborations of the smallest details of ordinary bodily upkeep" (22). What Fleissner leaves open for investigation is another routine, physiological requirement: sleep. This aspect of "bodily upkeep" further complicates the ways in which the New Woman navigates modern society.

Sleep via Class, Race, and Gender

Both the frazzled boy laborer and the exhausted New Woman are emblematic of Beard's neurasthenia, a condition that he defined as a modern American disease resulting from an urbanite's overstimulated nervous system. In his 1880 study, Beard declared "one of the most constant symptoms of neurasthenia [to be] wakefulness" (*Practical* 182). He describes the nervously exhausted subject as continually experiencing the vulnerability one feels in those "half-awakened moments at midnight, [when] we are conscious of not having full possession of our powers to meet any attack or danger" (25). More broadly, neurasthenic discourse suggested the frightening possibility of an all-consuming, decentered wakefulness, in which the very fibers of one's nervous system react to environmental stimuli. For Beard and his followers, neurasthenia was most concerning for privileged white people, and the treatment differed according to one's sex. Referring to Theodore Roosevelt's masculinized rhetoric, Lutz details neurasthenic "cures" at the turn of the century: men's cure involved "the exercise of strength and the cultivation of manliness," but for women the cure was to return to the domestic sphere (82). Lutz summarizes Roosevelt's claims: "An elite woman selfishly pursuing a career instead of producing offspring was tantamount to committing suicide, race suicide" (82). The concern that women spread themselves too thin is common in turn of the century literature, in which anxieties about the female nervous system are rooted in the budding professionalization of women.

James's Roderick Hudson—who represents the depleted, adolescent worker—is first introduced via a statue he created of a boy expressing a thirst for some unknown desire. Despite being in his twenties, Roderick is often referred to as a "boy" and is patronizingly treated like an adolescent worker. Whatever desire the boy statuette embodies—success, knowledge, power—it is never achieved, and by the novel's end, Roderick's death symbolizes his failure as a laborer. Wharton's Lily Bart represents the other neurasthenic trope: the New Woman. Like Dreiser's Carrie Meeber, Lily finds that her nervous system reacts independently to modern stimuli as she fails to keep up with the rapid pace of Gilded Age society. The noticeable socioeconomic gap between Carrie and Lily makes little difference in the women's susceptibility to the environmental forces of modernity. Despite Lily's privileged upbringing, she is still required to live dependently on the provisions of others, and like Carrie, she is continuously swept up in—and rendered a victim to—choices made by those with greater social agency. Lily tries countless times to become self-sufficient, yet her narrative ends in her death, a questionable suicide like that of Roderick Hudson. Both Roderick and Lily are relics of a bygone whiteness: fragile, creative types that cannot maintain their stamina within an industrialized, multicultural, modern society. They are defined by what they cannot embody: Roderick is seen by his patron as a failed "blood-horse," always threatening to "stumble and balk" (*Roderick* 129), while Lily is so overwhelmed by fatigue that she is utterly unable to keep up alongside women workers, who remain steadfast day after day, despite their "fagged profiles . . . [and] the unwholesomeness of hot air and sedentary toil" (*House* 219). Disturbingly, the overt absence of nonwhite figures in James's and Wharton's novels suggests that minoritized workers, in contrast to "ideal" (tragically fragile) white characters, are better equipped to function mechanically and can thus better meet the demands of twenty-four-hour productivity.

Chesnutt and Gilman also expose the fragility of whiteness in their texts. Specifically, they reveal how white individuals often rely on Black domestic workers to maintain the sanctity of sleep spaces and to serve as a safeguard over white sleeping bodies. Despite these expectations, Chesnutt shows how African Americans were often portrayed in white culture as sleepy and lazy, while Gilman perpetuates such stereotypes via the treatment of Black workers by her white New Woman characters. Chesnutt suggests that enslaved Black people and later generations of Black laborers played on sleep-related stereotypes to subvert the grueling work schedules that were forced on them by white oppressors. This clever rationing of labor energy and extraction highlights a theme that runs throughout my study: each author, in his or her own way, illustrates how energy and rest can function as modes of social currency and power. Roderick Hudson, for instance, oscillates between supply and withdrawal of his artistic efforts to the dismay of his patron. At times, he stays up for days on end in a flurry of creation, and at others he indulges in long sleeping jags that disrupt his work schedule. In Lily Bart's case, as her financial and social indebtedness increases so too does her exhaustion. When she comes close to independence, she is more restful, but in her phases of social obligation, she grows increasingly exhausted by her patron's incessant demands on her time. Of my chosen authors, Gilman makes most explicit how sleep and energy function as social currency. She instructs white, working- and middle-class women on how to muster enough energy for public work by wringing the maximum amount of labor time out of hired help (explicitly comprising Black and immigrant women). Gilman rationalizes the racism that underscores her vision of domestic industrialization by suggesting that such systems should, over time, educate and elevate Black workers.

Gilman's argument is not far from one espoused by Booker T. Washington, who in the vein of Thomas Edison preached that wakefulness and productivity were a means of Black uplift: in his 1901 memoir *Up from Slavery*, Washington writes that "the ability to sleep well, at any time and in any place, I find of great advantage. I have so trained myself that I can lie down for a nap of fifteen or twenty minutes, and get up refreshed in body and mind" (263). As the title of his memoir suggests, Washington believed that efforts to overpower the body's natural temptation to sleep deeply and soundly for long stretches of time were crucial to Black advancement in a postslavery America. His adherence to Derickson's "heroic wakefulness" may reflect his efforts to counter the stereotypes of Black lethargy that arose during the antebellum period and proliferated into the twentieth century. As Chesnutt reveals, many Black figures of the late nineteenth century internalized stereotypes of Black lethargy and encouraged new generations of Black workers to shed such tendencies. Chesnutt, on the other hand, aligns himself with W. E. B. Du Bois, who suggests in *The Souls of Black*

Folks (1903) that Black workers "cannot see why they should take unusual pains to make the white man's land better, or to fatten his mule, or save his corn" (155). Despite the obvious fact that an enslaved or indentured worker is not incentivized to labor, prominent white thinkers persistently argued that it was in Black individuals' very nature to be lazy. As far back as 1785, Thomas Jefferson observed that enslaved Black people "seem to require less sleep" (148). Later, physician Samuel Adolphus Cartwright would echo such an assumption in his 1851 "discovery" of the disorder *Dysæsthesia Æthiopis*; he claimed that sleepiness was a characteristic of the Black race, an inherent laziness that could only be managed through the prescription of hard labor on slavery plantations (Reiss 139).

Such assumptions about Black working habits resounded in the Progressive Era. In his 1880 work, Beard contrasted neurasthenia—a characteristic of "men and women of intellect, education, and well-balanced mental organizations"—with hysteria: "an excess of emotion over intellect, . . . [common] among the Southern negroes" (*Practical* 103). Capitalizing on such a notion, Theodore Roosevelt made this a core tenet of his particular strain of eugenics. Lutz summarizes Beard's influence on Roosevelt, who garnered from Beard and like-minded thinkers that "inferior races needed protection from . . . their own uncontrollable propensities, and this protection needed to be oppressive" (82–83). Gilman subscribes to this popular notion in her 1908 essay "A Suggestion on the Negro Problem," published in the *American Journal of Sociology*: "Here is potential labor that will not apply itself, and the need for labor unmet. This plan brings the labor to the place where it is wanted, and benefits the laborer in the process. . . . The enlistment would be compulsory. . . . To be drafted to a field of labor that shall benefit his own race and the whole community, need not be considered a wrong to any negro" (85). Here, Gilman advocates for a federally backed reenvisioning of slavery by arguing that African Americans should be conscripted into an industrial army that would train and then assign them to labor posts. As I show in my second chapter, threats of new iterations of antebellum slavery are just what Chesnutt warns against in his writings. In doing so, he shows how anxieties over white fragility and vulnerability, like those that pervade James's, Wharton's, and Gilman's works, were a driving preoccupation in concerns about sleep at the onset of the twenty-first century.

Organization

As I have shown, my chosen authors are uniformly curious about sleep, yet each narrative uniquely explores sleep's role in modern life. James, in his early novel *Roderick Hudson* (1875), provides a limited account of the titular protagonist's restlessness through the eyes of his privileged patron, Rowland Mallet.[10] This method of narrativization underscores the very forces that direct the novel's course of events, which I describe as the social restrictions and cultural demands that exhaust the marginalized figure of Roderick. While Wharton also employs conventions of psychological realism in *The House of Mirth* (1905), her focus on the physiological experience of sleeplessness is what best exposes the limitations of the human body within a modern environment in her novel. For Chesnutt in his "Uncle Julius" tales (1887–1900), motifs of sleep phenomena are woven into the magical realism, southern local color, and regional folklore of his short stories. Fantastical occurrences of sleep—like an enslaved character sleeping through an entire month—are instrumental in Chesnutt's illumination of racial oppression in a post–Civil War South. Gilman, on the other hand, takes a more didactic approach to her depiction of sleep and its purposes in her self-published journal, the *Forerunner* (1909–16). Her fictional treatment of sleep oscillates between utopian visions (where medically guided sleep practices enhance white women's social autonomy and advance modern civilization) and more frightening sociological premonitions (in which female complacency leads to a society metaphorically drugged and stunted).

Sleep Fictions is organized by author and begins with a chapter analyzing James's *Roderick Hudson* to address artistic productivity within the age of American innovation. Reading James's fictional sculptor Roderick Hudson against American innovators of James's own generation such as Thomas Edison, I explore how the novel's understanding of aesthetic production is inflected by a cultural demand for efficiency that was driven by mechanization and twenty-four-hour activity. I refer to late nineteenth-century theorists of social degeneration, such as Francis Galton and George Miller Beard, to historicize cultural arguments that espoused the detrimental effects of industrial and technological advancement on artistic genius. James scrutinizes these theories through the character of Roderick, who considers himself both a product and a victim of his cultural moment, expending incessant energy to keep up with the times. James dramatizes Roderick's deterioration through a thematic tension of kinesis and stasis, in which the artist's active labor produces only immobile figures and the novel's rapid motion culminates in untimely death, highlighting a moment in which American culture drove human bodies to collapse. Taking measure of the late nineteenth-century call for efficiency, the novel forecasts the dangers of a culture that demands constant action.

In the second chapter, I show how Chesnutt's "Uncle Julius" tales correlate popular stereotypes of African Americans as lethargic and indolent with Black efforts to subvert master time schedules on southern plantations. Drawing on the slave narratives of Harriet Jacobs, Frederick Douglass, and Booker T. Washington, I argue that Chesnutt challenges scientific racism by weaving together sleep-themed narratives that detail the harsh labor environments that were the true force behind sleepy Black bodies. I identify Chesnutt's 1893 tale "A Deep Sleeper" as the best example of how enslaved characters in Chesnutt's stories use deception, cunning, and medical discourse to outwit the supposed experts whose role it is to define and diagnose. Moreover, I argue that Chesnutt's stories reveal how drowsy demeanors enable Black laborers to subvert master clock time in the antebellum era and the New South.

The third chapter assesses the pathological restlessness of Lily Bart in *The House of Mirth*. I review the period's limited understanding of sleep to show how Wharton's authentic renderings uncannily precede recent discoveries in sleep medicine. Specifically, Lily's sleeplessness is symptomatic of the twenty-first-century concept of "sleep debt," in which prolonged wakefulness leads one to collapse into undesired sleep states. Wharton exposes this truth through Lily's ongoing resistance to sleep, portraying exhaustion and wakefulness as symptoms of Gilded Age class oppression, in which the incessant social duties forced on Lily are constantly eschewed by the novel's more privileged characters. Furthermore, current sleep studies focus on the implications inherent to American culture's reorganization of time, which values industriousness and technological interaction over an adherence to biological sleep patterns. I argue that Wharton thematizes this concern by employing literary naturalism to reveal the temporal implications of determinism, presenting a social world that will not accommodate the time that Lily needs to rest and restore herself.

The final chapter examines Gilman's portrayal of sleep in the *Forerunner* as paradoxically a social privilege *and* a physiological necessity to reveal how liberation efforts on behalf of the white New Woman were inseparable from the exploitation of ethnic and non-Anglo domestic laborers. Gilman correlates an individual's right to rest with one's capacity for social contribution, competencies very much determined by class, ethnicity, race, and ability. Gilman's treatment of sleep oscillates between utopian visions and sociological premonitions. In her utopian narratives, Gilman draws on lessons of sleep discipline to show how medically guided sleep practices strengthen women's mental and physical capacities. Other stories, meanwhile, express anxiety over poor sleep practices that might culminate in white female complacency and stunted racial evolution. Believing that the body deteriorates under the strain of domesticity, Gilman sought to relegate

From Mystery to Medicine   19

what she viewed as atavistic domestic work to women of racial and ethnic minorities. Throughout the issues of the *Forerunner*, Gilman details the social evolutionary value of brainpower and establishes echelons of labor forms that require more or less repose for renewed energy. While Gilman's theories of brainpower and purposeful repose were clearly intended to empower working women, they are also imbued with problematic doctrines of her day, for she ascribes restorative rest only to those ranked by categories of contemporary social demographics that are better able and more equipped to carry out national progress.

I conclude *Sleep Fictions* with a summary of the connections between sleep phenomena and social compulsion across chapters to reveal a turn of the century literary attentiveness to the constraints that modernity imposes on restorative rest. I then highlight scientific explorations into sleep's myriad purposes, symptoms, and effects on mental and physical well-being to show how such literature anticipated society's ongoing inquiries into sleep, particularly through its anxieties about timelines for ideal sleeping hours and fears over how poor sleep affects individual agency and social contribution. Ultimately, I show how the works in my study expose the complications that have arisen within modern culture, where sleep is a social privilege, while restorative rest regardless of one's social standing remains an enigmatic yet essential component of human life.

Text Visualizations and Digital Companion

When I first began this study, I did not anticipate its evolution into a digital humanities project. But after noticing the obsession that turn of the century authors had with sleeplessness, I began the task of developing a hypothesis for this pattern. Because I was interested in linking these intimate moments in a handful of fictional works to a larger cultural movement, I turned to the Google Ngram search engine (books.google.com/ngrams) to glimpse how sleep-related terminology charted across all texts in Google's English-language corpus during my chosen time period. In doing so, I saw how sleep concerns increased at the turn of the twentieth century. For example, the use of terms such as *sleepless*, *exhaustion*, and *insomnia* spiked during the years between the Civil War and the First World War (figure 1). Obviously, I had no way to contextualize term usage or distinguish between the types of texts in which these terms presented themselves, but I felt that I had sufficient evidence from these early visualizations to form a working hypothesis. From there, it began to make increasing sense to me that I should continue to use digital research methods for this type of project.

FIGURE 1. Google Ngram Viewer provides cursory evidence for how sleep concerns escalated at the turn of the twentieth century. Specifically, the use of terms such as *sleep*, *sleepless*, *exhaustion*, and *insomnia* increased during the years between the Civil War and the First World War.

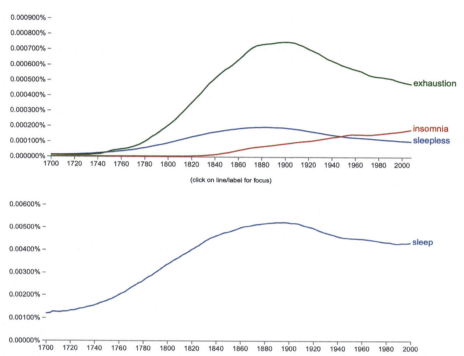

My next step was to employ small-scale textual analysis of my chosen texts, alongside relevant, large-scale searches of popular print culture and scientific publications. I did this by utilizing digital repositories such as Google Books, Project Gutenberg, HathiTrust Digital Library, and more (a full list is provided at this project's digital companion site, sleepfictions.org). The following chapters include text visualizations generated using Voyant Tools (voyant-tools.org), a free-to-use, online tool that allows users to generate from single or multiple texts a range of analytical and visual renderings. To create text visualizations in Voyant, I began with the standard Voyant dictionary for stopwords (i.e., words to exclude) and then added my own as needed (a full list of these is also provided at the digital companion site). In addition to Voyant's standard list of "function words," such as determiners, prepositions, articles, and numerals (that is, high-frequency but low-meaning words), I included as stopwords character and location titles. For the "Uncle Julius" tales specifically, I had to manually input several function words according to the vernacular that Chesnutt employs in his stories. The Voyant visualizations featured in this book enhance my close readings by highlighting the significance of, and connections between, the sleep terms and themes that pervade the primary texts. For example, by charting the use of the very term *sleep* throughout *The House of Mirth*, one can better understand how Lily's insomniac obsession with rest coincides with the plot's most momentous events and suggests that Lily's relation to and alienation from sleep is just as crucial to her deterioration as are the social forces that dictate her situation. Other visualizations highlight common links between sleep-related terms, such the visualization for Chesnutt's story "Mars Jeems's Nightmare" (1898), in which word associations underscore the angst and fear that enslaved characters feel with nighttime rest. Hidden connections such as these are made visible via text visualization and help extend the arguments made in each chapter.

The companion website (sleepfictions.org) is a digital archive and text visualization tool that enables visitors to interact digitally with my research findings and to further explore US sleep cultures from the Progressive Era to today.[11] The website provides a digital archive of the fiction analyzed in this study. Each text is embedded with notes that connect selected passages to a larger corpus of sleep discourse. The site utilizes the tag visualization tool from the open source publishing platform Scalar (scalar.me) to thematize these embedded annotations, and each theme tag highlights a particular sleep-related concern or debate prominently featured in fiction, popular print culture, and scientific publications (figure 2). These themes range from Progressive-Era sleep-related tropes such as the Sleeping Beauty figure, the neurasthenic, and the somnambulist, to twentieth- and twenty-first-century medical terminology such as insomnia, parasomnia, and sleep deprivation. Other concerns represented by theme tags address pseudoscience and scientific racism, as well as issues of soporific addiction, caffeine dependency, time anxiety, and various social conditions within the context of gender, race, class, and disability.

The tags illustrated in figure 2 represent my own interpretation of the texts, as I individually created annotations within Scalar—linked to specific passages within the primary texts—that I then categorized according to my own personalized tagging system. Thus, it is *a* reading (developed through my own reading), not *the* reading (for example, encoded terms from formal discourse analysis), that generates these visualizations. These customized visualizations provide a window into my approach to intertextual readings between the primary texts; while the size of a theme tag's title in figure 2

FIGURE 2. This Scalar-generated visualization shows the thematic tags in the digital companion. The size of each word represents the number of annotations that have been tagged under each particular theme.

represents its prevalence across texts, the theme tags' clustering, as in figures 3 and 4, reveals how these connections occur on a micro level.

Figure 3 shows how the themes *sleeping beauty* and *race* intersect in Gilman's sketch "Improving on Nature" (1912). In the story, Mother Nature, an embodiment of the Sleeping Beauty trope, dozes for an extended period and is then awakened by Man. She discovers that Man has forced women to be "small and weak and foolish and timid and inefficient." The sketch ends as Mother Nature "began to pay attention to business again, rather regretting her nap" (*Forerunner*, vol. 3, no. 7, p. 174). I discuss this story within the context of a "Comment and Review" in the first volume of the *Forerunner*, which criticizes a popular woman's periodical for romanticizing the Sleeping Beauty trope. In a troubling turn, Gilman supports her excoriation of the myth by referencing Edward Lear's 1846 limerick "There Was an Old Man of Jamaica" to illustrate the ills of a contemporary Sleeping Beauty, noting that "sometimes she is married first, and wakes up afterward; like the lady in Lear's limerick" who marries a "Black!" (no. 5, p. 23). By my tagging this story according to its sleep-related themes, visitors interested in an intersection between the Sleeping Beauty trope and race-related subject matter will be directed through these interactive visualizations to Gilman's short story.

Figure 4 provides another illustration of how Scalar's cluster visualization directs users to texts with overlapping themes. In this example, users interested in the intersections between sleep deprivation and class are directed to annotations for two short stories by Gilman and a chapter in James's novel. By clicking on "Deprivation/Debt," users can also gain an understanding of

FIGURE 3. This Scalar-generated image provides a visual of two tags identified in Gilman's sketch "Improving on Nature." The expanded view of those tags, *sleeping beauty* and *race*, reveals the instances in which each theme has been tagged in other texts: the trope of the Sleeping Beauty is tagged in five texts, while broader themes related to race are present in more than forty texts.

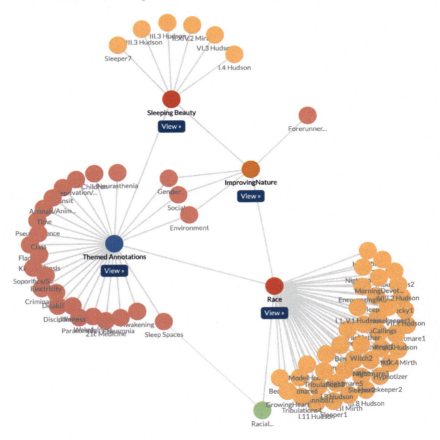

the theme's title. In this instance, the title refers to both sleep deprivation, in which characters are mentally and physically exhausted due to a lack of sleep, and sleep debt, which is defined as long-term sleep deprivation resulting from various forms of social indebtedness. Definitions like these are provided for all themes, along with hyperlinks to relevant cultural and historical resources.

Except for Gilman's *Forerunner*, which by sheer volume was too great to feature in totality on the site (supplemental selections are provided), visitors can go to the website and conveniently access digitized, full-length versions

FIGURE 4. Like figure 3, this Scalar-generated image provides a visual of two expanded tags. In this instance, the visualization reveals three occasions in which texts deal with two themes of similar prevalence: *class* and *deprivation/debt*.

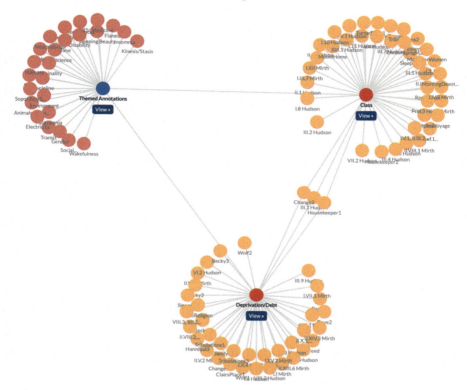

of the works analyzed in the following chapters. Upon perusing these texts, readers will gain a sense of my discovery process: with embedded notes throughout each text, these digitized documents convey to visitors passages in the texts that I found revelatory. These notes, in addition to a reference page, include links to many of the historical, literary, and scientific texts referenced in this study. I also provide hyperlinks to webpages in Voyant Tools that are preloaded with the full-length texts featured on the site so that users may experiment with searching through and across texts as well as creating their own visualizations. It is my hope that the website functions as both a reference tool and an exhibition of literary, cultural, and historical analysis deconstructed from the formal mode of scholarly presentation that occurs here. Visitors can intervene, interrupt, and digress however they see fit and in whatever way their interests in sleep culture direct them.

CHAPTER 1

"The Most Restless of Mortals"

Patronage and Somnambulism in Henry James's *Roderick Hudson*

> There are a great many artists here who hammer away
> at their trade with exemplary industry; in fact I am
> surprised at their success in reducing the matter to a
> virtuous habit: but I really don't think that one of them has
> [Roderick's] exquisite quality of talent. It is in the matter
> of quantity that he has broken down. Nothing comes
> out of the bottle; he turns it upside down; it's no use!
> —Henry James, *Roderick Hudson*

In the final lines of *Roderick Hudson* (1875), Rowland Mallet is deemed by his cousin Cecilia to be "the most restless of mortals" (388). Yet in the novel's opening, Cecilia is wholly unnerved by Rowland's torpid demeanor. She bemoans his lack of social responsibility, advising, "Bestir yourself, dear Rowland, . . . you are expected not to run your course without having done something handsome for your fellow-men" (51). The only passion Rowland can muster is for the arts, so Cecilia facilitates a patronage relationship in which Rowland sponsors the talents of her young friend and aspiring sculptor Roderick Hudson. Rowland is so enthralled with Roderick's work that he promptly arranges for their transport to Europe to begin Roderick's training. As Cecilia is dismayed to discover by the novel's end, it is this very arrangement that results in Rowland's ultimate reduction to perpetual restlessness.

Initially, Roderick seems a cure for Rowland's melancholic longing for self-expression. Upon visiting Cecilia's New England home, Rowland articulates such a concern: "Do you know that sometimes I think I'm a man of genius, half-finished? The genius has been left out, the faculty of expression is wanting; but the need for expression remains" (56). In response, Cecilia offers him the other half of his genius: a young man with the power to express Rowland's devotion to aesthetic ideals. This aspiring sculptor possesses a restless energy that Rowland, who sees himself as "an idle, useless creature" (56), fails to embody. Rowland becomes overseer to Roderick's work and develops a passionate desire to see his investment prosper, through the provision of both productive labor and emotional companionship. While much has been written about the latter—and, more specifically, the homosocial and homoerotic desire that underscores Rowland's patronage (W. Graham; Haralson; Henke; Matheson; Mendelssohn; Person; Rowe; Sofer; Woods)—literary studies calls for a closer look at the bodily repercussions of such an arrangement within the context of late nineteenth-century industrialized US culture.

Rowland aspires to control and direct Roderick's talent in order to profit, personally and monetarily, from his patronage. Wendy Graham explains that unlike with a typical employer, Rowland's speculations about Roderick as a tool for increased financial and cultural capital are subconscious: "Because his passions and worldly interests are insufficiently differentiated, for Rowland the field of commercial endeavor is fraught with temptations that have been sublimated by the culture at large" (106). Rather than view his patronage as a business venture, Rowland sees his act as a contribution to America's aesthetic culture (see also E. Duquette 165). At the same time, however, Graham asserts that "[Rowland] cannot think outside the prison of the American idiom, in which all forms of striving can be reduced to cash value. . . . Though Rowland steadfastly maintains a distance from the means of production and from commercial institutions, he still thinks like a capitalist" (106–7). Rowland as capitalist-entrepreneur is symptomatic of the time when James was writing, in which apprenticeships morphed into positions of wage labor within an increasingly industrialized nation. William Gleason explains that in the era between the 1840s and the 1880s in the United States, there was a "radically transforming shift from a premodern, preindustrial culture—one that emphasized the individual worker and his or her talents for creative productivity—to a modern industrial society that required the anonymous labor of an increasingly undifferentiated mass of workers" (*Leisure* 58). This change transformed the ways in which Americans conceived of hired labor, contributing to what Gleason describes as "the development of new jobs, new workplaces, new hours, and new recreations, [and] American social and cultural values as well" (58). The business relationship established between patron and artist is emblematic of a newfound rejection of a worker's right to free time. Rowland's treatment of

Roderick reflects the directives regarding working hours, recreational activities, and access to periods of rest that were increasingly issued to laborers by their supervisors.

It may seem that Rowland's wealth and Roderick's desire to sculpt fine art, as well as their relocation to Europe, situate their patronage scheme outside the realm of industrial US culture, but I argue against this presumption. Throughout the novel, Roderick is increasingly compelled to work around the clock to create artwork for Rowland, which in turn enhances Rowland's upper-class visibility. In his 1899 study *The Theory of the Leisure Class*, Thorstein Veblen defines masculine displays of "conspicuous consumption" as a turn of the century trend in which a man of wealth and social privilege asserts his status through a "spectacle of honorific leisure which in the ideal scheme makes up his life" (43). By appropriating Roderick's productivity as a means for his own social contribution, Rowland establishes himself as a man of the leisure class. Veblen explains that when not "in the sight of spectators," "evidence [of] leisure . . . can be done only indirectly, through the exhibition of some tangible, lasting results of the leisure so spent—in a manner analogous to the familiar exhibition of tangible, lasting products of the labour performed for the gentleman of leisure by handicraftsmen and servants in his employ" (44). During their stay abroad Rowland reigns over Roderick's time, expecting him to be as productive as a working-class artist while Rowland himself plays the role of leisurely gentleman. Unlike Roderick's apprenticeship at the outset of the novel with the local lawyer Barnaby Striker, Rowland's patronage requires Roderick to take on all the productive labor, while Rowland does no real work. Moreover, Rowland expects Roderick to suppress his own personal ambition so that he may bring to life Rowland's artistic vision. Ultimately, Roderick must keep time according to Rowland's command, diminishing his own agency to that of what James depicts as a reengineered machine.

Rowland requires a steady performance of artistry and comes to treat Roderick as his own mechanical watch, a machine regulated by the owner's hand. At the novel's end, Rowland's arrangement culminates in Roderick's breakdown and his deathly fall from a cliff in the Swiss Alps. As the patronage plot drives the story to its inevitable conclusion, it articulates James's cultural concerns about male artistry as a precarious social identity at the turn of the century. In the novel's first appearance, a serial publication in the *Atlantic Monthly* in 1875, Rowland likens Roderick to "a watch that's running down" ("Provocation" 68). Through Rowland's words, James implies that the indentured nature of the patronage arrangement impedes Roderick's bodily restoration. James portrays the artist as growing increasingly exhausted by his efforts to reconcile Rowland's expectations with his own artistic agency: Roderick aims to unite the cultural and aesthetic ideals of Rowland's extinguishing leisure class with a fierce working-class industriousness, viewing this combination as a means for redefining and invigorating the collective social consciousness of white men in America. In the end, however, Roderick's efforts prove a failure to both the artist and the patron. After Roderick's death, Rowland's attempt to appropriate Roderick's talent—as his own method for social contribution—only results in Rowland's manifestation of the same restlessness that prohibited Roderick from productive labor. This experiment of patronage, which renders Rowland "the most restless of mortals" by the novel's end, underscores the fact that even the most socially privileged were not immune to the repercussions of America's increasing emphasis on twenty-four-hour productivity at the turn of the century.

In this chapter, I ask how the novel's understanding of aesthetic work is inflected by a cultural demand for efficiency, one particularly driven by mechanization and twenty-four-hour activity. In his 1907 preface, James recalls the stress of working on a "book [that] was not finished when it had to begin appearing in monthly fragments." He spent long days in New York City enduring the "experience of difficulty and delay." The pressure to produce pages in so rigid a time frame caused the young writer to feel as if he had "fallen short of any facility and any confidence" (38). The stress of industriousness was symptomatic of the city's urban environment. James recalled the stirrings of bustling productivity when he was just a boy, witnessing firsthand the tumult of the *New York Tribune* office: "That was a wonderful world indeed, with strange steepnesses and machineries and noises and hurrying bare-armed, bright-eyed men" (*Small* 74). Despite this vision of wonderment in his childhood memories, the adult James felt strained by the city's frenetic environment, which had real repercussions for even its highest literary executives in the following decades. For instance, in 1872 the death of esteemed editor Horace Greeley inspired eulogies that bemoaned his lack of "a good night's sleep in fifteen years" and warned that "night work is 'killing our literary men'" (qtd. in Freeberg 105). A round-the-clock commitment to labor practices took hold and infiltrated all social strata of city workers, including the artistic and literary minded, such as Greeley and later James himself. Like journalists who were compelled to keep up with the news, James felt the pressure of staying relevant in an increasingly harried publishing industry.

The emergence of Thomas Edison's electric-powered light bulb only amplified industrialized "night work" and concerns over the dangers of

New Yorkers' newfound electrical lives. In the years surrounding James's composition of *Roderick Hudson*, New York's assiduous atmosphere was exacerbated by an Edisonian model of endurance. Edison, who embodied society's push for innovation, "attracted perhaps the widest attention of the age in the press, journals, and popular books" (Trachtenberg 66). For the white man—working class or social elite—who was nervous about modernity's many advancements, Edison provided a formula for productivity and social success. According to Alan Trachtenberg, "[Edison's] natural genius, flourish[ed] without formal school training, and his instinctual entrepreneurship . . . led him unerringly to . . . marketable inventions" (66). Thus, Edison's eminence erupted from his combination of incessant productivity with "natural genius."

For Roderick Hudson, however, productive labor refuses to be naturally in sync with performative genius. Instead, anxieties of artistry and production plague James's protagonist and do little to synchronize the two components of Edisonian success. James's concern in drafting Roderick's character, as he explains in the 1907 preface, is to depict the young artist as "special, that his great gift makes and keeps him highly exceptional; but that is not for a moment supposed to preclude his appearing typical (of the general type) as well; for the fictive hero successfully appeals to us only as an eminent instance, as eminent as we like, of our own conscious kind" (43). Thus, Roderick as a talented sculptor represents the creative genius of James's generation, failing to survive within a culture plagued by demands for efficiency and productive labor. The novel is embedded with anxieties over the survival of the artist type, a concern common among evolutionary theorists. For instance, Francis Galton, a cousin of Charles Darwin, warned of the dangers that modernity posed to the artist "race" in his 1869 study *Hereditary Genius*: "The Poets and Artists generally are men of high aspirations, but, for all that, they are a sensuous, erotic race, exceedingly irregular in their way of life" (225). Such peculiarity, Galton argues, has led the artist to become a dying breed. He maintains that an artist may only survive if he has "the severity and steadfast earnestness of those whose dispositions afford few temptations to pleasure, and he must, at the same time, have the utmost delight in the exercise of his senses and affections" (227). In Galton's view, the artist type develops out of one's natural ability to evenly pair inspirational pleasures with steady productivity. Edisonian ethics align with Galton's evolutionary standpoint, in which the balance of natural genius with disciplined labor is vital to the success of the modern-day artist.

Exemplifying Galton's dying breed, Roderick fails to balance artistic genius with a working-class mode of production. His deterioration is portrayed through a rapid series of incidents and blunders, a sequence that James criticizes in his reflective preface. James admits, "the time-scheme of the story is quite inadequate" (42). He casts such a failure as purposeful, however, arguing that "Roderick's disintegration" functions as "a gradual process . . . [rather than] the effect of the great lapse and passage, of the 'dark backward and abysm of time'" (43–44).[1] In this way, James cautions his reader against the assumption that some preeminent force initiates Roderick's demise. Instead, James frames Roderick's breakdown as a series of encounters between the individual and his environment: "What I clung to as my principle of simplification was the precious truth that I was dealing, after all, essentially with an Action, and that no action, further, was ever made historically vivid without a certain factitious compactness" (45). James, then, identifies the novel's timeline dilemma as necessary in revealing the "historically vivid" nature of Roderick's undoing.

James's careful charting of Roderick's decline is entrenched in the cultural moment. For instance, the novel prefigures George Miller Beard's hypothesis about artistic genius in his 1881 study *American Nervousness*. Beard argues that "geniuses who are very precocious may be looked upon as the last of their race or of their branch—from them degeneracy is developed; and this precocity, despite their genius, may be regarded as the forerunner of that degeneracy" (263). Roderick's early sculpture the boy statuette is ultimately the greatest of his creations, exemplifying a precociousness that, according to Beard, could potentially result in deterioration and possibly premature death.[2] Thematic destruction, therefore, accounts for the novel's underlying irony: for a work premised on the processes of action (Roderick's continuous attempts to produce noteworthy objects out of artistic genius), James ascribes to his titular character the profession of sculptor, an artistic practice that culminates in a figure forever in stasis. I locate the novel's dramatization of artistic degeneracy in the way the sculptor's active, performative labor produces only immobile figures: just as sculptural processes result in permanent inaction, so too does the novel's rapid motion end in Roderick's stillness after his deadly fall from a mountain, symbolizing a moment in which American culture drove human bodies to collapse.

Tension between kineticism and stasis underscores the questions of bodily control that emerged in the last quarter of the nineteenth century. According to Anson Rabinbach, "The great discoveries of nineteenth-century physics led . . . not only to the assumption of universal energy, but also to the inevitability of decline, dissolution, and exhaustion. Accompanying the discovery of energy conservation and entropy was the endemic disorder of fatigue—the most evident and persistent reminder of the body's intractable resistance to unlimited progress and productivity" (3–4). Fatigue and entropy were exceptions to the increasingly blurred lines between workers and material production, where creators were being conceived of more and more as synonymous with their creations. Echoing the cultural practice of conflating innovator with invention (such as Edison with his electric light bulb), Rowland sees his patronage as a means for possessing both the artist and his artistic creations. In doing so, Rowland reflects Taylorist efforts to deprive workers of any relationship to their own work. According to Eluned Summers-Bremner, such alienation shapes the "unquantifiable, material relation between labourer and task, the discounting of which can certainly affect a worker's ability to sleep at night by making him or her feel discounted and thus frustrated" (121). As a result, Roderick conceives of himself as a victim of circumstance, a cultural product of his age who expends incessant effort to keep up with the times. His entropy is what prevents him from being successful via the production of well-received art. By portraying the myriad ways in which the human body might be halted—by collapsing into exhausted sleep, being shaped into sculpted stasis, or succumbing to the stillness of untimely death—*Roderick Hudson* foresees the dangerous effects of a culture that compels individuals to constant action.

Roderick's Restlessness and the "Right to Be . . . Tired"

Rowland, the reader quickly learns, is a failed flaneur. The narrator explains that he lacks the role's "prime requisite . . . the simple, sensuous, confident relish of pleasure." His Protestant upbringing prevents him from having an "irresponsibly contemplative nature," but neither is his "a sturdily practical one" (58). Rowland feels he is wholly made up of contradictions: "He was forever looking in vain for the uses of the things that please and the charm of things that sustain. He was an awkward mixture of strong moral impulse and restless aesthetic curiosity, and yet he would have made a most ineffective reformer and a very indifferent artist" (58). It is just after these reflections, however, that Rowland expresses nothing short of absolute fascination at the sight of Roderick's artwork. Cecilia presents Rowland with a sculpture Roderick has gifted her. Rowland is enthralled by the figure of a "pretty boy" lustily drinking from a cup, the figure's base etched with the title "Thirst" (59). Through an exchange of dialogue, Rowland and Cecilia conflate Roderick's identity with his bronze creation. Although Roderick is well past twenty, Cecilia and Rowland both conceive of him in adolescent terms, with the former "regard[ing] him as a child" and the latter imagining him to be a "happy youth" (60). In Charles Baudelaire's *The Painter of Modern Life* (1863), he describes the flaneur figure as seeing the world as one does in youth: "The child sees everything as a novelty; the child is always 'drunk.' Nothing is more like what we call inspiration than the joy the child feels in drinking in shape and color" (8). Rowland seeks someone who can channel his own artistic passion. He finds this ideal in the form of a boy drunk off his own sensuous vision of the world. Baudelaire writes that "the man of genius has sound nerves, while those of the child are weak. With the one, Reason has assumed an important role. In the other, Sensibility occupies almost the whole being" (8). Composed of tough nerves, Rowland hopes that the boy behind the sculpture can express what he himself cannot. Before even meeting the sculptor, Rowland is convinced he has met the ideal flaneur, through whose eyes he might see the world with a "sensuous, confident relish of pleasure" (*Roderick* 58).

As he explains to Cecilia, Rowland believes that "true happiness . . . consists in getting out of one's self; but the point is not only to get out—you must stay out" (53). In Roderick, Rowland hopes to invest both his own self-worth and his wealth. He views the boy as someone in need of tending, adhering to Baudelaire's conception of the flaneur as "an artist perpetually in the spiritual condition of the convalescent" (8). In this scene, Rowland sees in the Thirst statuette Roderick's artistic aspirations, his naivete, and his desire for worldliness. In her notes to the novel's 1986 Penguin edition, Patricia Crick notes that the novel's allusive descriptions of the statuette as a "Hylas or Narcissus, Paris or Endymion" (59) serve as "premonitions of Roderick's fate" (390). Most notably, the Endymion myth—an early iteration of the Sleeping Beauty trope—provides insight into the nature of Rowland's patronage. In the tale, the goddess Selene is so taken by the beauty of a young shepherd that she forces him into eternal sleep. In doing so, Selene takes possession of Endymion's body to gaze on as she wishes. Like Selene, Rowland wishes to transform Roderick into a possessable object, as he conflates the sculptor with his Thirst statue and so desires both. As the narrative later reveals, Rowland misreads the passion conveyed in the statue, perceiving Roderick as his own sleeper to control and manipulate.

Rowland's early acts of tutelage aim to elevate Roderick's social status, and he does so by encouraging Roderick to perform great feats of art without making any visible effort. During their first encounter, Rowland assures Roderick that artistic genius is the result of unconscious action: "I read in a book the other day that great talent in action—in fact the book said genius—is a kind of somnambulism. The artist performs great feats, in a dream" (66). Rowland compares creativity to the oblivion of sleepwalking, of one's body functioning outside conscious awareness. James may have derived Rowland's observations from his reading of Frederic Henry Hedge's "Characteristics of Genius," published in the *Atlantic Monthly* in 1868. In this essay, Hedge likens the genius to a somnambulist: "What somnambulism is to ordinary sleep, that genius is to ordinary waking,—a conscious clairvoyance, as somnambulism is an unconscious one. It is a higher waking; it dissolves the dream-band, which in ordinary men interposes between the subject and the object, lifts the heavy lid, and informs with new and sincere perceptions the quickened sense" (155). This description reinforces the perpetual wakefulness that underlies Roderick's artistic efforts. According to Hedge, true genius requires one to dissolve the "dream-band" and lift the "heavy-lid," all while maintaining a "quickened sense." Thus, Hedge's genius-somnambulist defines creative action as an artist's sleepwalker ability to access the dream world while awake. Rowland, meanwhile, puts his own twist on Hedge's genius-somnambulist by warning Roderick: "We must not wake [the artist] up, lest he should lose his balance" (66). Using Hedge's metaphor for his own gain, Rowland implies that Roderick should take on a somnambulist-sleeper state to become a true artist of genius. Furthermore, he sees Roderick as only capable of performing the "childhood" aspects of the artist-flaneur. Baudelaire writes that "genius is nothing more than childhood recovered at will—a childhood now equipped for self-expression with manhood's capabilities, and a power of analysis which enables it to order the mass of raw material which it has involuntarily accumulated" (8). Rowland sees himself as having the "power of analysis" to provide order to Roderick's involuntary bursts of creativity. Thus, sleep for Roderick serves as a catalyst for production, a kinetic force that paradoxically works against sleep's biological function as static, restorative rest.

Roderick takes Rowland's somnambulistic insight to mean that unconscious sleep will bring forth artistic inspiration upon arousal. After their first few months abroad, a complaint from Roderick to Rowland lends insight into the class-related tension between physical labor and artistic creativity that belies genius-somnambulism: "I want to dream of a statue. I have been working hard for three months; I have earned a right to a reverie" (105). Roderick conflates two distinct modes of production, for he expects his productive labor to be naturally followed by unconscious, creative abandon. Rowland, meanwhile, implies that as a genius-somnambulist Roderick need never exhaust himself with conscious effort in the first place. Roderick's conclusion better articulates medical discussions of somnambulism during the period, which stand in opposition to Hedge's genius-somnambulist. In the 1869 study *A Physician's Problems*, Charles Elam defines somnambulism as a physical ailment: "As night and day are united by twilight,—as the two great divisions of organic existences merge into each other . . . so sleep allies itself to waking by *dreaming*, by *sleep-talking*, and by . . . Somnambulism . . . [which] expresses only the activity of one function,—locomotion" (340–41, original emphasis). Elam argues that the activities a body performs while in a somnambulistic state are "mere mechanical repetitions of daily performances" (343) and correlates such a case with working-class men: "It is those acts which are most habitual by day that are most frequently re-enacted by night, and these are sometimes of an extraordinary nature. The simplest are those connected with visiting the various scenes of labor. A young man [for instance] being asleep in the pump-house of the mine in which he worked" (344). Elam enumerates several examples of industrial laborers who in their sleep carry out routinely performed tasks. This supports Roderick's belief that months of labor should lead him to a somnambulistic strain of true genius, for he has studied classical art so intensely that he may continue his efforts in his sleep as do the working men in Elam's study.

Rowland's contradictory requirements—that Roderick train as a productive worker but reserve himself as a man of genius (demanding kinesis and stasis all at once)—anticipate a paradox within *On Vital Reserves*, a pair of essays penned by James's older brother, William. In "The Energies of Men" (1907), the elder James argues that every man has a hidden store of energy that can enable him to overpower fatigue. "The Gospel of Relaxation" (1899), on the other hand, urges its readers to adhere to strict principles of repose. In the former, William James argues that if a man pushes past fatigue, he will find himself "fresher than before, . . . hav[ing] evidently tapped a level of new energy masked until then by the fatigue-obstacle" (*On Vital* 4). The work ethic Rowland envisions for Roderick follows this principle, in which Roderick in a somnambulistic state pushes through fatigue, further utilizing his mysterious fund of energy to channel Rowland's artistic vision. According to the elder James, "our organism has stored-up reserves of energy that are ordinarily not called upon, but that may be called upon: deeper and deeper strata of combustible or explosible material, discontinuously arranged, but ready for use by anyone who probes so deep, and repairing themselves by rest as well as do the superficial strata. Most of us continue living unnecessarily near our surface" (5). Here, James represents what Lee Scrivner explains as a Victorian way of thinking: "Under the influence of thermodynamic ideas, Victorians came to imagine that the forces driving all their thoughts and actions . . . [were] closely linked to 'steam and lightning'; for the forces coursing through Victorians' brains were thought to be essentially indistinguishable from those in the industrial environment of coils and wires and engines—the same technologies that they invented and in which they continued to be invested and involved" (23). Upon meeting Roderick, Rowland is intrigued by the young man's volatility and hopes to harness and conduct his energy into a means of production. Rowland's idea to master Roderick's talent reflects a larger cultural moment, as Scrivner details, "predicated on the metaphor of the human motor and buoyed by a utopian image of the body without fatigue, the search for the precise laws of muscles, nerves, and the efficient expenditure of energy centered on the physiology of labor" (10). Viewing Roderick as a laborer who can carry out his dream of artistic contribution, Rowland hopes to tap into Roderick's "deeper strata of combustible or explosible material" by reconfiguring the artist for ideal efficiency.

Roderick aspires to unstop Roderick's "bottled lightning," a phrase in "The Gospel of Relaxation." William James defines the condition as an "absence of repose" (*On Vital* 59), whereby individuals exhaust themselves through frenzied behavior. The opening descriptions of Roderick convey him as having the two characteristics (a praiseworthy "combustibility" and a condemnable "bottled lightning") that are described in James's pair of essays. Roderick is the very embodiment of a lightning rod, for he is described as a neurotic youth practically buzzing with electricity. Confirming Cecilia's accusation that he does "everything too fast," Roderick elaborates, "I know it! . . . I can't be slow if I try. There's something inside of me that drives me. A restless fiend!" (62). When he first appears, Roderick is the very vision of one dangerously close to electrocution: his opening line, "I'm dripping wet!" implies possible combustion as he ruffles his hair into a "picturesque shock" (62). Jane F. Thrailkill reads Roderick's charged energy as Henry James's attempt to trouble Cartesian dualism, for Roderick's nervous system and physical body have simultaneous and interconnected reactions to the outside world (36). Indeed, Roderick seems to have little control over his nerves' reaction to environmental stimuli. When Cecilia offers him a cup of tea to "restore . . . [his] equanimity," Roderick refutes the calming effects of tea, telling her that it prolongs his wakefulness and forces him to face the following day "with my nerves set on edge by a sleepless night" (63). Roderick's combustible demeanor and overdramatization of tea's detrimental effects underscore the agitative nature of his inner "restless fiend."

William James's essays in *On Vital Reserves* perpetuate a cultural contradiction that his younger brother investigates in *Roderick Hudson*. In kinetic and static contradiction, the elder James pushes men to access their inner "combustibility" while simultaneously denouncing "bottled lightning" as a "characteristic national type," one defined by the "intense, convulsive worker

[who] breaks down and has bad moods so often that you never know where he may be when you most need his help,—he may be having one of his 'bad days'" (*On Vital* 60–61). Such a description illustrates Roderick's character throughout the novel, whereas Rowland is a model for William James's ideal of repose and relaxation (that is, until Roderick's death). The elder James best articulates this paradox of simultaneous kinesis and stasis through the following conjecture: "I suspect that neither the nature nor the amount of our work is accountable for the frequency and severity of our breakdowns, but that their cause lies rather in those absurd feelings of hurry and having no time, in that breathlessness and tension, that anxiety of feature and that solicitude for results, that lack of inner harmony and ease" (62). In *Roderick Hudson*, such feelings are far from "absurd." Roderick depends on successful patronage to provide for his mother and his fiancée in New England. Unlike Rowland he cannot rely on inherited wealth to make his way in the world or sit idly by while others do work for him. This lack of financial stability instills in Roderick deep anxieties, a freneticism that can be resolved neither through a newfound work ethic nor through a blind allegiance to Rowland's worldview.

Rowland, meanwhile, cannot see past his wealthy position to anticipate such obstacles. Instead, he naively speculates on Roderick's electrified demeanor. First, he notes that the young artist is physically akin to a rod: "The fault of the young man's whole structure was an excessive want of breadth. The forehead, though it was high and rounded, was narrow; the jaw and the shoulders were narrow; and the result was an air of insufficient physical substance" (64). Rowland notices that Roderick seems constantly overcome by some internal power source: "Mallet afterwards learned that this fair, slim youth could draw indefinitely upon a mysterious fund of nervous force, which outlasted and outwearied the endurance of many a sturdier temperament. And certainly there was life enough in his eye to furnish an immortality!" (64). This last observation implies that Roderick's incessant energy might be siphoned away, and Rowland aspires to teach Roderick how to balance his nervous energy with the self-control necessary for artistic production. The younger James then lends a preemptive, case-study response to his brother's call for "a topography of the limits of human power . . . a study of the various types of human being with reference to the different ways in which their energy-reserves may be appealed to and set loose" (*On Vital* 39). Rowland's efforts and subsequent failures do indeed expose the limits of appealing to and setting loose another's "energy-reserves."

As the first syllable of Roderick's name implies, he serves as a bearer of energy that Rowland hopes to wield for his own benefit. Likewise, the etymological connotation of "Rowland's cognomen—Mallet," as Michèle Mendelssohn explains, "is indicative of his role as creator, as a human incarnation of a sculptural tool. Roderick is created by Rowland insofar as he owes his identity as an artist to Rowland's patronage" (530). Paradoxically, Rowland is racked with guilt for being what he considers "an idle useless creature": "He had sprung from a rigid Puritan stock, and had been brought up to think much more intently of his duties of this life than of its privileges and pleasures" (*Roderick* 54). As Mendelssohn observes, "Rowland is aware . . . that action and production are fundamental elements of life." Yet, Rowland is "able neither to act nor to produce, [so he] resolves to search outside himself for happiness. . . . Patronage provides a pretext for the realization of his own dream" (517). Without Rowland having to lift the mallet himself, his wealth and cultural capital afford him, through Roderick's labor, a conduit for artistic expression. In short, Rowland remains in stasis while Roderick is forced into a state of perpetual freneticism.

Roderick's New England sculptures express the artist's fears of objectification and allude to his self-perception as a marginalized member of society. Before seeing Roderick's studio, Cecilia provides Rowland with a detailed account of Roderick's life, depicting him as a young man oppressed by his schismatic personhood. As the son of a timorous New England girl and a Virginian enslaver who drank himself to death, Roderick has in his bloodline both the Protestant work ethic of industrial northerners and the stereotypical lethargy of landowning southerners. While his formative years took place on a slavery plantation, he was relocated to his mother's New England home after his father's death. By experience and by blood, Roderick is a mingling of contradictory American identities. Whereas his father lived licentiously on his inherited estate, his mother came from a "Massachusetts country family" (67). As a descendant of both southern gentry and working-class New Englanders, Roderick sees unity only in the "whiteness" of both sides. Thus, he relies on race to reconcile his contradictory lineage and, as the novel later shows, to provide a desperate means of affirming his own agency.[3]

James's foreshadowing is evident when Roderick walks Rowland through his makeshift New England studio. As Leland S. Person notes, "Surveying Roderick's early sculptures reveals an interesting range of male figures with obvious roots in the historical moment" (127). The pieces represent various forms of objectification that Roderick has witnessed or experienced in his own life: "One was a colossal head of a negro tossed back, defiant, with distended nostrils; one was the portrait of a young man whom Rowland immediately perceived by the resemblance to be his lost brother; the last represented . . . the vivid physiognomy of Mr. Barnaby Striker" (72–73). The first piece is a remnant of Roderick's earliest memories, for it depicts a facial expression that Roderick must have imagined from his childhood as the son of "an owner of lands and slaves" (67). Despite the figure being of "colossal" proportions and looking "defiant," implied skin color nevertheless relegates the bust's subject to enslavement. Roderick cannot see the indentured nature of Rowland's proposed patronage; he has internalized whiteness as the ultimate exemption from enforced servitude.

I am not arguing that Roderick's patronage experience is anything compared to the conditions of Black enslavement in the US South. In fact, I am proposing the opposite: the "Negro" sculpture stands in stark contrast to Roderick's self-conception, suggesting that whiteness serves as a blinder to social injustice. Historian David R. Roediger explains that for white workers in the United States in the mid-nineteenth century, "the pleasures of whiteness could function as a 'wage.' . . . That is, status and privileges conferred by race could be used to make up for alienating and exploitative class relationships, North and South. White workers could, and did, define and accept their class positions by fashioning identities as 'not slaves' and as 'not Blacks'" (13; see also Gleeson; Hild and Merritt). Furthermore, Roderick's whiteness prevents him from achieving an authentic work ethic that could potentially enable his success under Rowland's patronage. As Roediger summarizes, W. E. B. Du Bois "argued that white supremacy undermined not just working class unity but the very vision of many white workers. He connected racism among whites with a disdain for hard work itself, a seeking of satisfaction off the job and a desire to evade rather than confront exploitation" (13). Throughout the course of the novel, this is exactly what Roderick does. As the enormity of his obligation to Rowland looms ever larger, Roderick refuses to negotiate with Rowland to improve his working conditions. Instead, he grows increasingly unproductive: he flaunts the social privilege afforded by Rowland's patronage, without doing any real work. He opts to live akin to Veblen's pecuniary gentleman, in whom the "substantial canons of the leisure-class scheme of life are a conspicuous waste of time and substance and a withdrawal from the industrial process" (334). Roderick eventually refuses to merely bolster Rowland's lifestyle of conspicuous consumption and instead aspires for his own life of leisure.

Class oppression—a force that Roderick simultaneously ignores and resists—is embodied in the second bust: a rendering of his deceased brother, coupled with a "small model design for a sepulchral monument" (72). Having "New England blood [that] ran thicker in his veins than the Virginian" (67), his brother, Stephen, died fighting for the Union. Roderick portrays his brother as forever at rest, yet he still clutches his weapon: "The young soldier lay sleeping eternally with his hand on his sword" (72). The sleeping figure is a fine representation of the novel's thematic paradox of stasis and kinesis. Although the soldier is in a permanent sleep, his hand remains on his sword as if ever ready to swing into action. Through contrasting descriptions of the brothers, Cecilia reflects, "Stephen, the elder, was [their mother's] comfort and support. I remember him . . . [a] practical lad, very different from his brother . . . a very fine fellow." Whereas Stephen held allegiances to nation and home, Roderick was "horribly spoiled" (67). In adulthood, Roderick resents his brother's passing, as it compels him to provide for his mother. He complains to Rowland: "She would fain see me all my life tethered to the law like a browsing goat to a stake. In that way, I am in sight" (76). With characteristic histrionics, Roderick perceives his familial indentureship as something from which only Rowland can rescue him. Rather than be like his sworn protector of a brother, Roderick envisions himself as a fair creature in need of rescue and tutelage.

Roderick's melodramatic vision of himself as a shackled creature forced to act at the behest of his mother lends insight into the oppressive nature of the third bust. It is modeled after the lawyer Mr. Striker, who tells Rowland he is a "self-made man, every inch of me!" (89). Espousing Galton's definition of a successful artist, Mr. Striker preaches to Rowland: "The crop we gather depends upon the seed we sow. [Roderick] may be the biggest genius of the age; his potatoes won't come up without his hoeing them. . . . Take the word for it of a man who has made his way inch by inch and doesn't believe that we wake up to find our work done because we have lain all night a-dreaming of it; anything worth doing is devilish hard to do!" (89). Mr. Striker is the opposite of the idly refined Rowland. The latter hopes to flee to Rome, where he can partake in an "idealized form of loafing; a passive life . . . [that] thanks to the number and the quality of one's impressions, takes on a very respectable likeness to activity" (53). In Roderick's eyes, Rowland provides an escape from the pressures of US industriousness as embodied by Mr. Striker. Richard Henke observes that by setting "passivity . . . against the activity of the masculine other," James's early works feature a doubling of male characters that "challenges a singular conception of masculine identity" (257). In *Roderick Hudson*, the productive power of masculine activity is called into question. Rowland, a man of wealth and privilege, knows only a decorum centered on idleness and leisure. Roderick, on the other hand, feels compelled to behave in a similar fashion while also working to fulfill his commitment to sculptural production.

As Roderick's "catalyst," Rowland is perturbed by any expression on Roderick's part of inaction or exhaustion. Rowland premises Roderick's artistic capacity on the number of sculptures the artist produces under his patronage, paying him in advance for twelve statues. In this way, Rowland sees Roderick's physical body as a vehicle for production and a "financial investment" (Mendelssohn 518). Through such a relationship, class status determines Rowland's role as incentivizer and Roderick's as creator. Mendelssohn points out that "as Roderick's patron, Rowland essentially serves as a catalyst. He goads Roderick into action while remaining inactive himself; . . . being a catalyst, is not in itself an action, but it generates action" (518). Even as Rowland remains in stasis, he forces Roderick into frenetic labor by moderating his time and behavior, placing trust in Roderick's mysterious "divine facility" (*Roderick* 114).

When Roderick appears drowsy, Rowland fears for the longevity of his investment. In an early instance after Roderick informs Rowland of his betrothal to Mary Garland, Rowland notes that Roderick's "climax was a yawn" (102). Eroticized disappointment implies that Rowland feels romantically rejected (whether by Mary or by Roderick, it remains unclear) and highlights Rowland's frustration with Roderick's lack of transparency. Naomi Z. Sofer accounts for Rowland's obscure romantic desire and, more importantly, identifies Rowland's fear of disconnection from Roderick's artistic performativity (193). Once in Rome, after perusing a vast trove of classical art, Roderick responds to their explorations by "throwing himself back with a yawn" and complaining of "an indigestion of impressions" (*Roderick* 103). Rather than garner energy and inspiration from the legendary art that surrounds him, Roderick is alarmingly fatigued. Each time Roderick displays weariness where there should be stamina, Rowland frets over Roderick's appreciation for the classics and his potential for mastering their reproduction.

To Rowland's disappointment, being deprived of hands-on work has an enervating effect on Roderick. Rather than passively consume art, Roderick longs to create it. For Rowland this is problematic to his investment. He expects Roderick to learn the skills of leisure-class art consumption so that he may then emulate the classics in his sculptural work. Roderick fails to respect this stipulation of Rowland's patronage, telling him: "The other day, when I was looking at Michael Angelo's *Moses*, I was seized with a kind of defiance—a reaction against all this mere passive enjoyment of grandeur" (104). Roderick's response is underscored by a working-class sentiment, a desire to rebel against the passive privilege of aesthetic culture. Roderick argues that to truly appreciate art one must attempt its creation. For Roderick, mere artistic consumption is tiresome, while aesthetic creation is a source of invigoration. This offends the sensibilities of Rowland, who expects Roderick's industry to serve as an expression of his own artistic sentiment. Veblen's discussion of conspicuous consumption details the intentions underscoring Rowland's education of Roderick:

> The tendency to some other than an invidious purpose in life . . . , the purpose of which is some work of charity or of social amelioration . . . , proceeds . . . [from] the motive of an invidious distinction. . . . This last remark would hold true especially with respect to such works as lend distinction to their doer through large and conspicuous expenditure; as, for example, the foundation of a university or of a public library or museum; but it is also, and perhaps equally, true of the more commonplace work of participation in such organizations. These serve to authenticate the pecuniary reputability of their members, as well as gratefully to keep them in mind of their superior status by pointing the contrast between themselves and the lower-lying humanity in whom the work of amelioration is to be wrought. (339–41)

Rowland's efforts at "an invidious purpose in life" derive, as Veblen describes, from "the motive of an invidious distinction." In the opening pages of the novel, the narrator concedes, "that Mallet was without vanity I by no means intend to affirm" (52). While conversing with Cecilia, Rowland feels "gently wooed to egotism," as he muses on his "own personal conception of usefulness": "He was extremely fond of all the arts, . . . [and] there prevailed a good deal of fruitless aspiration toward an art-museum. He had seen himself in imagination, . . . in some mouldy old saloon of a Florentine palace, turning toward . . . some scarcely-faded Ghirlandaio or Botticelli, while a host in reduced circumstances pointed out the lovely drawing of a hand" (52). Rowland quickly views Roderick as the real-life replacement for his imagined "host in reduced circumstances"—in Veblen's words, a man of "lower-lying humanity"—whose labor will provide Rowland with the classical art that he may then claim as his gift to the world.

In keeping Roderick's company throughout the day, Rowland expects him to behave as a man of leisure outside his working hours. Thus, he celebrates Roderick's incessant labor and late-night social calls as "the happiest *modus vivendi* betwixt work and play" (114). The late-night calls represent social activity (masked by idleness) within the leisure class. Rowland's constant surveillance of Roderick, even during times of "play," is characteristic of the ways in which work and play became antitheses to be moderated by overseers within American industry. Gleason explains, "one of the most striking results of the mid-century shift from the more seasonal work rhythms of preindustrial agricultural toil to the day-in, day-out wage-driven shifts of American industrial society was stricter and stricter separation of

42   CHAPTER 1

'work' and 'play' hours" (*Leisure* 45). Therefore, Roderick's successful "play" represents his assimilation into Rowland's leisure class. Roderick's efforts at "work and play," however, leave him no time for sleep. In his creation of the Adam and Eve sculptures, for instance, Roderick spends "a month shut up in his studio; he had an idea and he was not to rest till he had embodied it" (111). Roderick feels compelled to avoid rest until his sculpture is complete. He succeeds in maintaining a persistent wakefulness as he earnestly follows Rowland's timeline of production, providing his patron with a sculpture after his first three months abroad (107). To Rowland's delight, Roderick manages to balance his daytime labor with long nights of social activity: "[Roderick] wrestled all day with a mountain of clay in his studio, and chattered half the night away in Roman drawing-rooms. . . . He enjoyed immeasurably . . . the downright act of production. He kept models in the studio till they dropped with fatigue" (114). Yet, nothing in the novel implies that Roderick is anything more than human. Therefore, as foreshadowed by the models who "dropped with fatigue" during his early days of inspiration, Roderick's body too must eventually succumb to exhaustion.

Rowland fails to acknowledge Roderick's reliance on routine rest, for he believes that Roderick contains infinite energy. This accounts for Rowland's surprise when, after completing the Adam and Eve statues, the sculptor feels exhausted. With a "somber yawn," Roderick tells Rowland he is at a loss for inspiration. Rowland is surprised by Roderick's need for rest, reflecting that "he was in a situation of a man who has been riding a blood-horse at a steady elastic gallop, and of a sudden feels him stumble and balk" (129). Mendelssohn likens Rowland to "a successful stockholder whose investments make money and thus work for him so that he does not have to, [and who] understands patronage to mean that the artist works, creates, and (re)produces for his patron" (518). Rowland's association of Roderick to a thoroughbred, a "blood-horse," emphasizes that Roderick is an object of speculation and investment. Moreover, Rowland feels that his patronage is so powerful that he can control Roderick's access to rest. "Because Rowland sees Roderick as action incarnate," explains Mendelssohn, "Rowland comes to believe that his role is 'to render scrupulous moral justice' to Roderick" (518–19). Under the constraints of Rowland's charge, Roderick does not feel in control over his ability to rest. Later, Roderick details his artistic genius likewise through an equestrian frame, but in his conception an exhausted horse only means that he must bear his burden on his own back: "Nothing is more common than for an artist who has set out on his journey on a high-stepping horse to find himself all of a sudden dismounted and invited to go his way on foot" (196). In this scenario, Roderick allots himself much less agency than Rowland allows himself. The passive voice in Roderick's observation leaves the reader pondering what force dismounts the "artist." Rowland's reflection, on the other hand, places him in control of both the reins and the horse's pace. He need only allow his horse a moment of rest before returning it to its "steady elastic gallop."

From the outset of his patronage, Rowland invests in both Roderick's artistic production and his physical body, treating the young artist like his own tool and instrument. In Rowland's mind, Roderick's figure is as aesthetically valuable as his sculptures: "Rowland vaguely likened him to some beautiful, supple, restless, bright-eyed animal, whose motions should have no deeper warrant than the tremulous delicacy of its structure, and be graceful even when they were most inconvenient" (69). That Roderick's movements "should have no deeper warrant" than to display his "structure" distinguishes his importance in Rowland's eyes from a valuation based solely on his artistic creation. Mendelssohn defines Rowland's "socially and contractually sanctioned justification for watching his ward" as his "right to sight" (514). Rowland presumes that Roderick's "motions" merely function to flaunt his handsome structure. Therefore, one can reason that for Rowland, Roderick's body possesses the power to create but lacks the faculties to carry out such tasks effectively and efficiently. Like the subjects of Roderick's early sculptures who are scrutinized around the clock (the enslaved man and the Union soldier), Roderick is rendered perpetually vulnerable to Rowland's watchful gaze. Moreover, Roderick's "bright-eyed" quality recalls the "hurrying bare-armed, bright-eyed men" that James witnessed as a boy, carrying out the orders of newspaper executives in the *New York Tribune* office (*Small* 74).

For Rowland, Roderick's abilities are so innate that any notion the young man has of his artistic purpose is misguided and requires redirection. Roderick reconciles Rowland's all-commanding patronage by trying to merge both of their artistic aspirations within a shared whiteness. However, as the narrative progresses, Roderick's efforts fail and his endeavors to mimic Rowland's classical ideals deprive him of inspiration. To celebrate Roderick's first sculptures abroad, Rowland hosts a party of fellow artists. At the party, Roderick parrots his patron, making a passionate appeal for uniquely American art. His speech is rife with evocations of industrial masculinity, nativism, and social Darwinism: "We stand like a race with shrunken muscles, staring helplessly at the weights our forefathers easily lifted. But I don't hesitate to proclaim it—I mean to lift them again! I mean to go in for big things; that is my notion of art. I mean to do things that will be simple and vast and infinite" (123). Roderick's words reflect the beginning of

44   CHAPTER 1

a middle-class trend that Gail Bederman describes as "a cult of the 'strenuous life'" seeking to revitalize white male power: "Between 1880 and 1910, . . . middle-class men were especially interested in manhood. Economic changes were undermining Victorian ideals of self-restrained manliness. Working-class and immigrant men, as well as middle-class women, were challenging white middle-class men's beliefs that they were the ones who should control the nation's destiny" (11, 15). Roderick's declaration reflects a post-Reconstruction anxiety among working-class men over modernity's destabilization of class, gender, and racial identity. Roderick's internalized elitism runs its course through his artistic overtures. As the son of a white enslaver, he implies that his ancestors maintained a racial superiority that his generation has failed to uphold, so he intends to channel his restless energy and aesthetic effort into uplifting the white racial spirit. Sara Blair explains that "James entertains the romance of cultural exhaustion in numerous texts of travelogue in order to reconstitute the *données* of 'race and instinct' as aesthetic or imaginative resources, through which the enterprise of 'general culture'—of Spencer's 'civilization'—can be renegotiated and redeemed" (29). Roderick's pleas to his dinner companions reflect his longing to reaffirm his white masculinity and class identity through art.

Meanwhile, Rowland continually rejects Roderick's efforts to infuse his work with *his* (the artist's) "notion of art." He dismisses Roderick's commitment to "fling[ing] Imitation overboard" to achieve a "National Individuality" (70). Rather than take the young man seriously, Rowland reimagines Roderick as having the self-awareness of a "restless, bright-eyed animal" (69). As Sofer articulates, Rowland's patronage comes with specific stipulations that direct Roderick's actions:

> According to the terms of Rowland's proposal, Roderick will be entering into a relationship with a "friend" who is willing to pay in advance for future works, clearly a mark of great faith. However, when Roderick exclaims, "You believe in me!" Rowland hastens to "explain" that his belief in Roderick is actually contingent on a large number of "ifs" and that Roderick will be held to Rowland's standards from what constitutes acceptable levels of "struggle" and the exercise of "virtues." . . . It is, in fact, a business relationship: a contractual agreement in which Rowland has . . . purchased an interest in Roderick's life and behavior, something that Rowland clearly understands and attempts to convey to Roderick. (190)

Given that Roderick feels limited, bound, and antagonized by his life in New England, he settles for Rowland's conception of the ideal sculptor and the provisions of their verbal contract. Eventually, though, Roderick deteriorates under this agreement, in which he labors at the command and benefit of his patron. This occurs most pointedly when Roderick finally admits to Rowland his feelings of enervation. Rowland is taken aback by Roderick's confession, but because of his recent productivity Rowland deems Roderick to be deserving of rest. Roderick takes Rowland's observation as permission to be exhausted and asks self-consciously, "Do you think I have a right to be [tired]?" (129). Rowland's acknowledgment of Roderick's fatigue hinges on his power to monitor Roderick's behavior. Therefore, when Roderick proposes that he separate from Rowland in his pursuit of restoration, Rowland grows agitated, a response that leads Roderick to confess: "I have a perpetual feeling that you are expecting something of me, that you are measuring my doings by a terrifically high standard. You are watching me. I don't want to be watched! I want to go my own way; to work when I choose and to loaf when I choose" (130). Roderick articulates the exhaustive nature of being under constant surveillance. Rowland tentatively approves Roderick's request but, after a month passes, grows frustrated. In Rowland's eyes Roderick is only deserving of restorative rest when it serves as compensation for his labor, and he has no way to measure Roderick's proficiency when the artist is out of sight. Rowland's efforts to keep an eye on Roderick increase throughout the course of the novel. Moreover, as I explain in the next section, Rowland's perception of Roderick's body as an instrument transforms from metaphors of animality to those of mechanization as he seeks further control over Roderick's time and labor.

The Pendulosity of Genius: From Somnambulist to Sleeping Beauty

Roderick does indeed benefit from restorative rest while away. He strolls through Switzerland like a flaneur, loafing from town to town and lazily observing local customs. In his first letter to Rowland, he writes, "I was walking twenty miles a day in the Alps, drinking milk in lonely chalets, sleeping as you sleep, and thinking it was all very good fun" (135). Thirdly in his enumeration, Roderick emphasizes the natural rhythms of sleep. Rather than see his body's capitulation to unconscious rest for what it is—a necessity—Roderick views sleep as a holiday lark. Meanwhile, his time away culminates in further indebtedness to Rowland. Thus, James implies that Roderick is compelled by Rowland's power of patronage to put in more work for taking personal time away.

Self-control, or the balance necessary to maintain one's productive powers, is framed in *Roderick Hudson* as a masculine strength. Amid meanderings Roderick is coerced into traveling to Baden, where he forfeits much of Rowland's money to gambling. Upon his return, Roderick promises Rowland another sculpture in two months' time. As Roderick grows increasingly anxious over his artistic agency, he considers himself to be less of a man: "Six months ago I could stand up to my work like a man, day after day, and never dream of asking myself how I felt" (162). Eric Haralson argues that "*Roderick Hudson* establishes a set of concerns for masculine potential, variety, and relationships" (31). More specifically, the novel questions whether a male artist might still maintain his masculinity if he fails to hone his craft. As Rowland observes to Cecilia at the novel's start, balance and control are essential to artistic masculinity: "When a body begins to expand, there comes in the possibility of bursting; but I nevertheless approve of a certain tension of one's being. It's what a man is meant for" (81). Rowland's emphasis on a "certain tension of one's being" represents conflicting states of kinesis and stasis that resonate with Alan Derickson's definition of "manly wakefulness" (2). In tracing the historical connections between masculinity and wakefulness, Derickson notes that nineteenth-century innovators like Edison did not devalue sleep completely. Instead, they believed in sleeping only as long as was required to continue with one's work. It was the indulgence in "unproductive rest" that equated to unmanliness (5).

James looks back to Nathaniel Hawthorne to investigate the effeminacy of the idle artist. In *The Marble Faun* (1860) women must be in constant action, fully frenetic. Otherwise, they are at risk of a "dangerous accumulation of morbid sensibility," something akin to a perilous electrical charge: "The slender thread of silk or cotton keeps [women] united with the small, familiar, gentle interests of life, the continually operating influences of which do so much for the health of the character, and carry off what would otherwise be a dangerous accumulation of morbid sensibility. A vast deal of human sympathy runs along this electric line. . . . And when the work falls in a woman's lap, of its own accord, and the needle involuntarily ceases to fly, it is a sign of trouble, quite as trustworthy as the throb of the heart itself" (33). Women are safe from an electrified hysteria as long as they remain busy in their adherence to productive output. Miriam, one of the artists in *The Marble Faun*, suffers when her paintbrush "involuntarily ceases to fly" (33). Like Roderick, she is plagued by inner fiends. When she notices Donatello perusing her sketches, she cries, "I did not mean you to see those drawings. They are ugly phantoms that stole out of my mind; not things that I created" (37). Akin to Roderick's early statues, Miriam's artwork is inspired by her inner anguish. Her method of art composition is a stark contrast to

James's masculine mode of art production. Like a lightning rod, men should have the masculine ability to harness and moderate their artistic energy. The inability to control artistic flow, Hawthorne implies, is a feminine trait.

Despite Rowland's encouragement, Roderick, like Hawthorne's Miriam, cannot master his art through self-control. As Sheila Teahan points out, the enigma of artistic intention becomes the focus of the second half of James's novel: "The questions of originality and belatedness that *Roderick Hudson* inherits from *The Marble Faun* are (at least thematically) evaded altogether; the novel swerves in mid-course from an inquiry into what it means to be an American artist in the late nineteenth century to an allegory of the problem of the will" (160). The allegory that Teahan elucidates is framed in gender-specific terms. The will is a problem insofar as its possessor embodies transgressive gender traits. Rowland, for instance, proposes a seemingly easy remedy for Roderick's anxieties. He tells the artist to be "stronger in purpose, in will." To this Roderick replies: "The will, I believe, is the mystery of mysteries. Who can answer for his will? who can say beforehand that it's strong? There are all kinds of indefinable currents moving to and fro between one's will and one's inclinations. People talk as if the two things were essentially distinct; on different sides of one's organism, like the heart and the liver. Mine I know are much nearer together. It all depends upon circumstances. I believe there is a certain group of circumstances possible for every man, in which his will is destined to snap like a dry twig" (138–39). Roderick admits his lack of strong resolve. He cannot discern will from inclination, which, like Hawthorne's "electric line [of human sympathy]," comprises "indefinable currents moving to and fro." The image of flowing electricity connects the "different sides of [Roderick's] organism" and recalls the reader's first image of an electrified Roderick, drenched in sweat with his hair standing on end. Unlike Rowland's vision of manly control over one's inner tension, Roderick's body is overwhelmed by an internal energy that threatens his masculine composure.

After his return from Baden, Roderick increasingly suffers fits of emotional breakdown, and Rowland is devastated to find that Roderick cannot balance his electrical feminine energy with a masculine work ethic. As the stress of producing new artwork weighs on the artist, Roderick grows increasingly emotional: "He was discontented with his work, he applied himself to it by fits and starts, he declared that he didn't know what was coming over him; he was turning into a man of moods" (142). Failing to find inspiration in self-discipline, Roderick hopes to achieve creative revelation while dreaming. He asks Rowland, "Is this of necessity what a fellow must come to . . . this damnable uncertainty when one goes to bed at night as to

48   CHAPTER 1

whether one is going to wake up in an ecstasy or in a tantrum?" (142). Ironically, by fretting over the possibility of waking without inspiration, Roderick deprives himself of the calm necessary for bodily repose. He seeks out moments of rest where he can find them, declaring at one point, "I shall take a nap and see if I can dream of a bright idea or two" (197). In this scene, Rowland does his best to guide Roderick toward a masculinized work ethic, telling him, "If you have work to do, don't wait to feel like it; set to work and you will feel like it." Roderick, however, refuses to set "to work and produce abortions!" (197) and instead passively hopes for genius to strike (197).

As Rowland oversees Roderick's nap time he notices the approach of Christina Light, a beautiful young woman who fascinates Roderick. Her name denotes illumination, indicating that she, like Roderick, carries some mysterious, internal energy. Like a light bulb, Christina illuminates and compounds Roderick's electrified agitation. Rowland grows increasingly weary of her interactions with the artist, fearing her encouragement of Roderick's impetuousness. In an earlier scene, Christina tells Rowland, "[Roderick] seems to have something urging, driving, pushing him, making him restless and defiant" (184). In Rowland's eyes, Christina aggravates Roderick's inner fiend and is a distraction to his work. Indeed, upon her arrival, she immediately awakens Roderick from his slumber. When Rowland tries to stop her, she refers to him as "Mr. Hudson's sheep-dog" (199), while her companion, Prince Casamassima, deems Roderick a "Sleeping Beauty in the Wood" (199). In perceiving the pair as Sleeping Beauty and devoted male guardian, the prince and Christina assign Roderick an effeminate role. Whereas Rowland seems comfortable with the homosocial intimacy of providing vision to his personal somnambulist, he seems, at least subconsciously, to fear a heterosexual mutation of such a relationship, in which he plays sheepdog protector to a helpless(ly useless) Sleeping Beauty. Such a transformation would release Roderick from the constraints of masculine productivity and deprive Rowland of his promised artwork. Moreover, this metamorphosis would reverse the roles of stasis and kinesis, forcing Rowland to labor while Roderick rests.

To counteract Christina's influence, Rowland does his best to redefine his patron status and regain control over Roderick's time. Midway through the novel, he begs Christina Light to leave Roderick alone. Her influence, according to Rowland, is detrimental to Roderick's productivity: "Hudson, as I understand him, does not need, as an artist, the stimulus of strong emotion, of passion. He is better without it; he is emotional and passionate enough when he is left to himself. The sooner passion is at rest therefore the sooner he will settle down to work" (231). Rowland implies that the only "stimulus" Roderick needs to work productively is that which Rowland provides. He also hints that Roderick should put his desires to sleep, so that he may perform according to Rowland's directives. Any excess "passion" inspired by Christina would only push Roderick's restlessness toward morbidity. This scene completes Rowland's conception of a somnambulist Roderick, one whose personal desires are put to rest while his body labors in the creation of Rowland's vision.

Christina replies by accusing Rowland of treating Roderick like a watch of his own making. Comparisons of Roderick to a mechanical timepiece reoccur often in the novel's second half and reinforce Rowland's power over the young artist. Christina sees Rowland's expectation of Roderick's perpetual freneticism as tied to both movement and time. Christina astutely perceives Rowland to be the winder of the clock, setting the time by which Roderick should mechanically tick. In this way, the motion of timekeeping for Roderick represents both how he registers Rowland's command of time and how he futilely attempts to overcome it.

In discussing mechanical clock culture after 1870, Michael O'Malley writes: "The design of American clocks and watches, in the advertising and publicity they generated, consistently reiterated a few basic themes. Mechanical timekeepers stood for getting control—gaining power over the confusing and potentially hostile world of schedules, appointments, and standard time, or gaining power over unruly employees. But they also encouraged a strange merger of personal authority, of identity, between timekeeping machines and their owners. Clock time, machine time, savored unmistakably of discipline, surveillance, and control in both the design of the objects themselves and the discourse surrounding them" (151). O'Malley captures the discursive treatment of Roderick as clock in the novel, for Roderick keeps time according to Rowland's command. Rowland replies to Christina's question—"If I leave him alone he will go on like a new clock, eh?"—in the affirmative, telling her that because of her company, Roderick is "like a very old clock indeed" (231). Unwittingly, Rowland foreshadows similarities between the young artist and Christina. When Rowland encounters the young lady at Mass, she confesses her envy of Rowland's entitlement to rest. He challenges her with being too young to say such a thing. She contradicts him by speaking of her mother's absolute control, which has psychologically aged Christina far beyond her years: "I was a little wrinkled old woman at ten" (227). Christina's confession calls to mind Edith Wharton's image of Lily Bart in *The House of Mirth* (1905). Looking in the mirror, Lily frets over the increasing worry lines across her face, and she spends countless nights stressing over the possibility of leaving unfulfilled her mother's dying wish that she marry into wealth. James renders Christina's premature aging more figuratively, suggesting that youthful indulgence in sleep is unattainable for a girl whose mother intends to sell her off to the highest bidder. Mendelssohn explains that "Rowland, through his gaze, reifies Roderick. Rowland is in effect acquiring creations as well as a creator, a person who can produce for him. In this respect, Roderick becomes one of Rowland's creations, in the same sense that Christina Light is the product of her mother's efforts and a work of art saleable on the marriage market" (527). Like Roderick, Christina exhibits her own form of genius throughout the novel. She is intuitive and highly intelligent. She exemplifies the precocity of genius that, according to Beard, is often morbid and prematurely aging in its excess. Therefore, the metaphorical renderings of these two marginalized characters—Christina Light as (albeit invisibly) prematurely aged and Roderick as deteriorating clockwork—emphasize the bodily strain of social indentureship.

Roderick frets over his lack of self-control and increasingly believes that his susceptibility to exhaustion is the source of his failure. He sees a night's bed rest as a risk, at least figuratively, to his genius. He internalizes Rowland's perception of him as clockwork, asking: "What if the watch should run down, . . . and you should lose the key? What if you should wake up some morning and find it stopped, inexorably, appallingly stopped?" (195). By correlating weakness with the unconscious abandon of deep sleep, Roderick imagines that his genius, as a machinelike apparatus, might break down overnight. O'Malley suggests that "efficient machines became analogous to the 'survival of the fittest' in human society. Would men and women have to become like machines—amoral, running with mechanical regularity—in order to survive an industrial society?" (178). Here, O'Malley draws a correlation between two conceptions of time passing. The first are micro units of time, in which the machinery of the human worker grows overtaxed by the industrial working day. The second are macro units of time, represented by the evolutionary scale that, according to eugenicists like Galton, tracks the deterioration of the white race. Sleep as a bodily impediment is a danger to both the steady automation of Roderick's creative genius, and the ongoing existence of the artist type in US culture.

Try as he may, Roderick cannot overcome his impulse toward rest, and he suffers from increasing exhaustion. He muses on this conundrum when he observes to Rowland, "The whole matter of genius is a mystery. It bloweth where it listeth and we know nothing of its mechanism. . . . If it gets out of order we can't mend it; If it breaks down altogether we can't set it going again" (196). For Roderick, remaining ever vigilant to one's creativity is necessary. Yet, he views genius as both autonomous and mysterious, so he has no sure means of keeping it up. Thus, he is left to anguish over his body's physical limitations and his mind's failure at self-mastery. Rowland stresses over Roderick's impending breakdown, reasoning that "[Roderick's] beautiful faculty of production was a double-edged instrument, susceptible of being dealt in back-handed blows at its possessor" (190–91). While the "possessor" in Rowland's reflection is left unspecified, it is apparent that he hopes to possess Roderick artistically and bodily and feels betrayed when Roderick's behavior does not accord with him.

After Rowland blames Christina for Roderick's languishing effort, Roderick chafes under Rowland's possessiveness. The sculptor responds with rancor: "When you expect a man to produce beautiful and wonderful works of art you ought to allow him a certain freedom of action, you ought to give him a long rope, you ought to let him follow his fancy and look for his material wherever he thinks he may find it! . . . In labour we must be as passionate as the inspired sibyl; in life we must be mere machines" (192). According to Graham, this passage represents Rowland's perception of Roderick "as a better class of servant in whom clockwork regularity is prized. . . . For Rowland, Roderick is merely a mechanical difficulty that can be corrected through reengineering" (121). Roderick's response articulates the oppressive nature of ticking away according to Rowland's conception of labor time. Rowland refuses him the personal freedom to explore artistic inspiration, while at the same time expecting him to produce artwork in an automaton fashion. Even for someone as restless and energetic as Roderick, his round-the-clock performance as Rowland's somnambulist pushes him toward bodily collapse.

Roderick begins to resent his innate genius, viewing it instead as a dangerous, external force that is controlled through Rowland's mesmeric mastery over his somnambulist self. For Roderick his artistry becomes an oppositional force that places his own agency in peril. He contends, "If I'm to fizzle out, . . . let me at least go out and reconnoitre for the enemy, and not sit here waiting for him, cudgeling my brains for ideas that won't come!" (192). In his defiance of masculine self-composure, Roderick's expectation that he will "fizzle out" forecasts his deterioration: "I'm prepared for failure. It won't be a disappointment, simply because I shan't survive it. The end of my work shall be the end of my life" (196). In this sense, Roderick accepts his embodiment of Rowland's broken-down timepiece. Because it is up to Rowland to control his impetuous nature, a task at which the patron has failed, Roderick describes himself as his own maker's doomsday clock: "'I have a conviction that if the hour strikes here,' and he tapped his forehead,

52   CHAPTER 1

'I shall disappear, dissolve, be carried off in a cloud! For the past ten days I have had the vision of some such fate perpetually swimming before my eyes. My mind is like a dead calm in the tropics, and my imagination as motionless as the phantom ship in the Ancient Mariner!'" (196). So thoroughly the (self-destructive) clock of Rowland's making, Roderick tics off the seconds as he taps his forehead, tracking the time that passes without his producing a thing.

A Voyant-generated visualization chart helps make clear the persistence of Rowland's watchfulness over Roderick's productivity. The graph in figure 5 tracks the prevalence of the term *watch* (encompassing both the act of watching and a timekeeping instrument) and variations on the root word *produce* in *Roderick Hudson*. I included both forms of *watch*—as a verb and a noun—due to the recurring comparison of Roderick to a broken-down timepiece, as this analogy goes hand in hand with the watchful gaze that observes him as such. The parallel trend lines of the terms *watch* and *produce* throughout the novel highlight how Rowland's watchful gaze—and his treatment of Roderick as if he can manufacture artwork as efficiently as a ticking clock—is most evident when Roderick's productive efforts are brought into focus. The terms are in near-perfect alignment for much of the book, with their wavelike structure demonstrating how Rowland's watchful gaze does, for a time, efficiently direct Roderick to produce artwork. The ebb and flow underscore the reward system that Rowland establishes, where

FIGURE 5. This Voyant-generated "Trends" graph charts the prevalence of terms *watch** and *produc** throughout *Roderick Hudson* (the asterisk includes terms with the same root word).

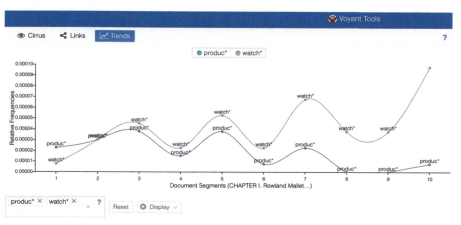

Roderick is granted playtime following a successful sculpture. As time goes on, Rowland again begins to push Roderick toward labor, and the latter continues to work accordingly. But this parallelism only occurs to a certain point, and then the terms completely diverge.

This striking divergence represents Roderick's full capitulation to idleness. At the midpoint of the novel (around segment 5 in figure 5), Roderick's productivity never recovers its previous glory. Fittingly, it is at this point in the novel that Roderick is sculpting the "lazzarone lounging in the sun; an image of serene, irresponsibile, sensuous life." To Mr. Leavenworth's critique that "sculpture should not deal with transitory attitudes," Roderick retorts: "Lying dead drunk is not a transitory attitude! Nothing is more permanent, sculpturesque, more monumental!" (240). For Roderick, one's collapse into idleness and debauchery is irreversible: the ability to produce is irrevocably lost. The pressure to carry on only entrenches Roderick's desire for stasis. Like the lazzarone, whose rest is fashioned by Roderick's hands specifically to be gazed on, Roderick offers up his body to be seen as irrevocably broken down.

Rowland reacts to Roderick's morbidity by internally wishing that the sculptor "had more of little Sam Singleton's vulgar steadiness" (197). He longs for Roderick to imitate Singleton's version of the American male artist, one who follows a steady, working-class methodology. At first, Rowland values the turbulence of Roderick's true genius over his working-class counterpart Singleton, but after struggling with Roderick's failure to steadily produce he comes to appreciate those artists who sell their artwork like any other household ware. This change in sentiment is foreshadowed during the earlier dinner party scene, in which Rowland celebrates Roderick's Adam and Eve statues. Rowland describes the guests he has invited by emphasizing both their Protestant work ethic and the marketplace value of their artistic labors. After years of "indefatigable exercise," for example, Gloriani perfected his "very pretty trade in sculpture of the ornamental and fantastic sort" (117). Sam Singleton, a painter of small watercolor landscapes, was first noticed by Rowland through a display of his artwork in a storefront window. Rowland reflects that Singleton's "improvement had come . . . hand in hand with patient industry" (118). The third artist, Miss Blanchard, was a woman "not above selling her pictures," whose flower paintings were "chiefly bought by the English" (119). Toward the novel's end, Roderick contrasts himself to Singleton, whose name implies a simplistic, singular focus on work and industry. Roderick tells him, "You remind me of a watch that never runs down. If one listens hard one hears you always—tic-tic, tic-tic" (361). Adhering to the model of Edisonian success, Roderick associates the productive artist with routine output. However, his nervous impulses dictate his behavior and deprive him of the self-control necessary for such a rhythm. He is left only to rely on unconscious abandon to create his art and is ultimately condemned by his inability to master control over his own body.

Conclusion

Eventually, Roderick's emotional distress overwhelms him. Bereft of Christina's company, Roderick finds new ways to escape artistic labor and affirm his own social agency. What results from Roderick's distress is his desire to affirm his social agency in other ways, particularly through his embodiment of whiteness. He befriends a "fantastic jackanapes"—a Central American emissary to the pope—and enmeshes himself within a circle of "very queer fish" flanked by "negro lackeys" (222). Roderick describes the evening with his "Costa Rican envoy" as "awfully low," telling Rowland, "All of a sudden I perceived it, and bolted. Nothing of that kind ever amuses me to the end: before it's half over it bores me to death; it makes me sick" (223). Although Roderick hopes for Rowland to see the contrast of Roderick's fine tastes against those of the "awfully low" Costa Rican crew, Rowland only perceives, as Eli Ben-Joseph puts it, "Roderick's weakness [as] adorned with distasteful ethnic nuances" (43). James borrows here from Hawthorne; as David Greven observes, "one of the chief themes to emerge in Hawthorne's work is the powerful linkage he establishes between sexual otherness and racial otherness" (150). In *Roderick Hudson*, James uses this linkage to reveal how Rowland, in judging Roderick according to his "exotic" company, comes to sees Roderick as transgressively effeminate.

Bursting into Rowland's room at four in the morning, Roderick "flung himself into an armchair and chattered for an hour" (223). Roderick behaves as the classic flaneur, staying up all night and wandering the streets, lording his aristocratic superiority over those forced to labor during the day. He espouses the role that Rowland admired Roderick for embodying at the novel's start, yet Rowland now views such behavior as the result of a horrific transformation: "[He was] willing to wait for Roderick to complete the circle of his metamorphoses, but he had no desire to officiate as chorus to the play." Rowland refuses to engage, declaring: "Allow me to say I am sleepy. Good night!" (224). Roderick prattles on, nonetheless. Rowland fails to send Roderick away and is deprived of nighttime rest. Roderick's recent changes represent a dangerous turning point ("the circle of his metamorphoses") for Rowland, who is becoming personally depleted by Roderick's unrest. In the beginning he was enthralled by Roderick's flaneurisms, but now he has come to see the economic and bodily repercussions of such behavior. In a letter to Cecilia following the incident, Rowland writes, "He's too confoundedly all of one piece; he won't throw overboard a grain of the cargo to save the rest. Fancy him thus with all his brilliant personal charm, . . . his look as of a nervous nineteenth-century Apollo, and you will understand that there is mighty little comfort in seeing him in a bad way" (238). Rowland implies that he is endangered by Roderick's deterioration. By viewing himself as the single witness to Roderick's "metamorphoses," Rowland acknowledges the role reversal at play. This transformation reflects Georg Wilhelm Friedrich Hegel's master-slave dialectic, in which a longing for social and personal recognition results in the master's taking on the very class-conscious characteristics that make the "slave" his "other" (see D. Duquette). Through his efforts to police Roderick's behavior and enforce his own masterly role, Rowland discovers that the patronage arrangement has eventually caused a reciprocal effect, in which Roderick's restlessness deprives Rowland of bodily restoration. Figure 6 charts the use of the words *sleep* and *restless*, along with any suffix variations, throughout *Roderick Hudson*. The terms are more prevalent at the matching points throughout the narrative, suggesting that as Roderick grows more restless both the sculptor and his patron become increasingly fixated on achieving restorative rest. I created this visualization after drafting this chapter, and it provides a bird's-eye view

FIGURE 6. This is another Voyant-generated "Trends" graph that tracks the use of *sleep** and *restless** throughout *Roderick Hudson* (asterisk includes terms with the same root words).

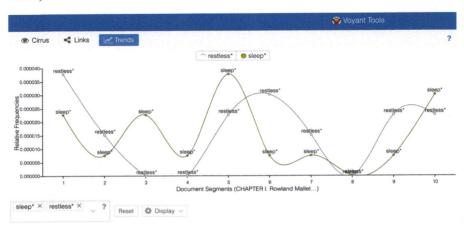

56   CHAPTER 1

of my close reading. The two terms are at high points at the novel's opening, middle, and close. In the beginning, only Roderick is restless and concerned about his loss of sleep, which is reflected in the line for *restless* being slightly higher than that for *sleep*. At the midpoint of the novel, Roderick has gone to Baden, where he is frivolous in his indulgence in sleep. Upon his return, as the graph reflects, Roderick grows increasingly restless again. It is only at the story's end that his restlessness grows to such extent that both he and his patron match one another in their insufferable exhaustion.

Upon his death, Roderick finally achieves stasis, forcing Rowland to assume the freneticism he has avoided throughout the novel. Rowland's reception of this transmission of restlessness is evinced by the pleasure he experiences in protecting Roderick's helpless, inanimate corpse. The events of Roderick's death, suggestive of a fall from a cliff, are indirectly rendered: the reader learns of the death only after Rowland and Singleton discover the artist's dead body lying at the bottom of a ravine. In an action that recalls his sheepdog protection of napping Roderick in the park, Rowland watches over Roderick's corpse while Singleton goes for help. During this time, Rowland notices that "the eyes were those of a dead man, but in short time, when Rowland closed them, the whole face seemed to awake. Roderick's face . . . looked admirably handsome" (386). At last Rowland gains control over Roderick's vision, which enables him to look "admirably" on the young man's masculine representation. This image anticipates the fin de siècle scenery that appears in such novels as *The House of Mirth* (as when Lawrence Selden reflects upon seeing the dead Lily Bart).

Halfway through James's novel, Rowland reinforces the implications of his patronage, telling Roderick, "Whatever happens to you, I am accountable. You must understand that" (189). Roderick replies, "That's a view of the situation I can't accept. . . . I know all I owe you; I feel it; you know that! But I am not a small boy nor an amiable simpleton any longer, and, whatever I do, I do with my eyes open. When I do well the merit's my own; if I do ill the fault's my own!" (189). Roderick resists the temptation to embody, for Rowland's pleasure, the Thirst statuette or an Edenic Adam. He proclaims that he must see the world through his own eyes and be full beneficiary—or failure—of his own work. This metaphor opposes Rowland's vision of Roderick as his own somnambulist. This experiment, as Roderick later explains, is one that will have inescapable repercussions for Rowland: Roderick asks, "What am I . . . but an experiment? Do I succeed—do I fail? It doesn't depend on me" (196). Months later, as Roderick's inert body is made fully vulnerable to his possessor, Rowland acknowledges his role in Roderick's death, reflecting on the ordeal as a deeply personal failed investment: "Roderick's passionate walk had carried him farther and higher than he knew. . . . He had made the inevitable slip. . . . Now that all was over Rowland understood how exclusively, for two years, Roderick had filled his life. His occupation was gone" (387). Rowland cannot leave his patronage unscathed, for Roderick's death has left Rowland with nothing to show for his efforts. Thus, restlessness acts as a contagion that infects Rowland for having failed in his patronage. He accepts the burden of perpetual freneticism that he once forced on his now-dead patron.

Despite his privilege, Rowland is unable to secure a reliable mode of production that exists beyond his own bodily effort. Roderick's death, therefore, is a precursor to Peter Quint's demise in James's 1898 novella *The Turn of the Screw*, a character whose "fatal slip, in the dark" from some steep slope results in a deadly head wound (66). Like Quint's ghost, Rowland emerges from Roderick's passing as a spectral version of his tutelage. Whereas Quint's implied pedophiliac relationship with his young student leads to a ghostly haunting, Rowland's conflation of patronage and possession prompts a spectralized slippage from his former self into a frenetic embodiment of the young artist. As he incessantly wanders between the homes of Mrs. Hudson and Cecilia, he haunts the spaces that Roderick formerly inhabited, becoming, as Cecilia professes in the novel's final lines, "the most restless of mortals" (388).

CHAPTER 2

"A Monst'us Pow'ful Sleeper"

Resisting the Master Clock in Charles Chesnutt's "Uncle Julius" Tales

> So long as we have laws determining, by standards of race or complexion, whether or not a man shall vote, where he shall eat or *sleep* or sit, where he shall be taught and what; and so long as we have social customs fixing, by the same standards, what trade he shall follow, what society he shall be received in, what position he shall be permitted to attain in life, just so long will the race question continue to vex our republic.
>
> —Charles Chesnutt, "A Plea for the American Negro"

In the previous chapter, I discussed Charles Elam's 1869 theory of working-class somnambulism, in which exhausted laborers repeat in nighttime sleep the same mechanical actions of their previous day's work. In this chapter, I will focus on similar conjectures made in earlier decades by physicians in the US South who argued that repetitive habits were innate among enslaved African Americans. Physician Samuel Adolphus Cartwright, who was employed by the Medical Association of Louisiana to document health conditions among the enslaved, wrote in 1851 of his newfound "medical discovery": *Dysæsthesia Æthiopis*. This racialized "ailment" caused persons of African origin to behave "like a person half asleep, that is with difficulty [being] aroused and kept awake" (Reiss 132). Cartwright held a belief common among antebellum doctors that African bodies required less sleep than their Anglo counterparts, assuming enslaved people only needed enough rest to make it through a day's labor. At the same time, however, he claimed that the enslaved, if given the chance, would spend all their time in repose.

Historian Benjamin Reiss details these findings, which were as fascinating as they were horrifying: "Afflicted slaves . . . would 'wander about at night, and keep in a half nodding sleep during the day,' mindlessly disrupting their communities like a 'faulty automaton or senseless machine'" (132). Reiss's summation of Cartwright's diagnosis calls to mind Elam's description of a sleep disorder symptomatic of overwork. Yet unlike Elam, who identified environmental factors as the reason for working-class somnambulism, Cartwright asserted that the very bodies of the enslaved were at fault. For Cartwright, *Dysæsthesia Æthiopis* was a race-specific affliction—an inherent laziness—that could only be managed through the prescription of hard labor.

Cartwright's contradictory summation—that enslaved Black people survived on little-to-no sleep while also suffering from an innate inclination toward perpetual drowsiness—echoes theories put forth decades earlier by Thomas Jefferson. In *Notes on the State of Virginia* (1785), he proposed that enslaved workers "seem to require less sleep. A black, after hard labour through the day, will . . . sit up till midnight, or later, though knowing he must be out with the first dawn of the morning." Yet in the same passage, Jefferson notes that "their existence appears to participate more of sensation than reflection. . . . An animal whose body is at rest, and who does not reflect, must be disposed to sleep of course" (148–49). Jefferson ignores any connection between enforced labor and sleep deprivation, opting instead to present the enslaved as animalistic creatures capitulating to sleep only when dormant, rather than humans whose bodies require the restorative sleep. Jefferson's paradoxical reasoning reflects a poor attempt to justify overworking enslaved people, yet his speculations were codified in later scientific works: his assertions were reprinted in Francis Bowen's 1854 revision of Dugald Stewart's 1792 volume *Elements of the Philosophy of the Human Mind* (190–91), as well as in Bruce Addington's 1915 study *Sleep and Sleeplessness*. The latter references Jefferson to argue for the childlike "feebleness of . . . inferior intellectual development" among African Americans (23–24), reflecting a larger effort to promote fears of Black hysteria, which, as I explain in the introduction, became a core tenet of Theodore Roosevelt's particular strain of eugenics. In this way, Roosevelt echoed Jefferson's validation of enforced labor, carrying such notions well into the Progressive Era.

In the "Uncle Julius" tales, penned between 1887 and 1900, Charles Chesnutt disrupts a postwar cultural mythos linking Blackness with somnolence and originating in the antebellum South.[1] John, the tales' narrator, is a white northerner who moves to a North Carolina farm to improve the health of his wife, Annie, and capitalize on affordable land and labor. While John's commentary typically commences and concludes each story, the tales themselves comprise recollections by the formerly enslaved Julius McAdoo. Through Julius's storytelling, Chesnutt aims to subvert the era's scientific racism, suggesting that "racial" characteristics attributed to African Americans actually evolved out of the deprivation of enslaved individuals' most basic needs for sleep, food, and familial connection. Across the "Julius" tales, Chesnutt highlights the reciprocity of needs within systems of slavery, in which enslaved people were forced to substitute one for the other. The tale within a tale structure reveals how the "advancements" of Reconstruction merely led to new labor systems where Black workers suffered from the same lethargy, starvation, and social isolation endured by previous generations.

In their fight for personal time, enslaved people subverted plantation time in ways that were echoed by their descendants, who resisted the "master clocks" of mechanical timekeeping. According to Michael O'Malley, turn of the century electrical clock systems depended on a "master clock" to maintain correct time. By the 1880s, companies like the Western Union were using telegraphic signals that "linked 'slave' . . . clocks with a single, more accurate 'master clock' located many miles away" (153). As I explained in the previous chapter, O'Malley argues that the management of others' time became a mark of "authority, . . . [and] savored unmistakably of discipline, surveillance, and control" (151). O'Malley's claim supports my reading of Henry James's *Roderick Hudson* (1875), in which Roderick internalizes Rowland's treatment of him as a mechanical means of production. The characters in Chesnutt's stories, meanwhile, thwart white demands for routine labor. Whereas Roderick is inhibited by his internalized whiteness and therefore depends on Rowland for affirmation and support, Chesnutt's Black characters resist slaving to master plantation time, an overtly oppressive force built into the very structure of the South. As the "Uncle Julius" tales demonstrate, the Reconstruction and post-Reconstruction eras did little to save the formerly enslaved and their progeny from exploitation at the hands of wealthy landowners and northern carpetbaggers like John, who displaced onto Black bodies white anxieties felt nationally about the industrial productivity imperatives of the Gilded Age. Therefore, this chapter builds on existing readings of Chesnutt's stories to highlight the continuities of sleep and energy between the body politics of slavery and those of the Reconstruction moment to reveal how characteristic sleepiness became a rhetorical tool for subverting master clock time within nineteenth- and early twentieth-century US southern culture.

Master Clock Time and the Antecedents of CPT

Chesnutt's stories are rife with Black characters who, while still suffering from want of sleep, perform symptoms of sleep deprivation to their advantage. In this way, they play on the racial stereotype of what eventually became known as Colored People's Time, or CPT. Etymologist Barry Popik traces the emergence of the derogatory initialism CPT to 1912, and historian Mark Smith locates CPT's nonpejorative antecedents in the nineteenth-century South: "CPT is a useful shorthand to describe how African Americans as a class of laborers resisted planter-defined time during and after slavery. CPT was an intuitive intellectual and social construct serving to repudiate the demands of time-conscious southern agrarian capitalists, old and new" (130). According to Smith, white southerners assumed that their Black captives were inept at comprehending clock time, but it "may well have been a clever ploy [by the enslaved] . . . to manipulate white time definitions and racial stereotypes by feigning ignorance and causing, for want of a better phrase, temporal inconveniences" (143). Julius and his progeny, hired to work on John's vineyard, often embody Smith's description of CPT's antecedents. Julius's grandson, Tom, for example, is called out by John for being, "very trifling, and I was much annoyed by his laziness, his carelessness, and his apparent lack of any sense of responsibility" (91). While John finds pleasure in the "almost sabbatic [town] in its restfulness" and the leisurely distraction of Julius's oration (4), he detests any evidence of lethargy among the indentured Black workers on his new plantation. Thus, John's contradictory sentiments about the South—as both a sleepy region for repose and a frenetic site of industrial growth—are embedded within the framed construction of the tales.

As Chesnutt reveals, Black southerners took advantage of contending conceptions of time and gained minor forms of power by subverting the CPT stereotype. In the opening pages of Chesnutt's first novel, *The House behind the Cedars* (1900), he describes the town of Patesville, a fictionalized version of Fayetteville, North Carolina, where he came of age. At the center of both the fictional and real town sits the Market House. Built in 1838, Fayetteville's town hall and marketplace is described in the novel during the era of Reconstruction. As John Warwick approaches the building, he observes that the "four-faced clock, rose as majestically and uncompromisingly as though the land had never been subjugated." He marvels at the incongruity of the "red brick, long unpainted," with a clock tower that continues "to peal out the curfew bell, which at nine o'clock at night had clamorously warned all negroes, slave or free, that it was unlawful for them to be abroad after

62   CHAPTER 2

that hour, under penalty of imprisonment or whipping" (3). He wonders whether the constable of his childhood still rings the bell but notices "a colored policeman in the constable's place—a stronger reminder than even the burned buildings that war had left its mark upon the old town, with which Time had dealt so tenderly" (4). This passage suggests Reconstruction's potential for advancing Black southerners, yet Warwick soon witnesses his sister, Rena, stoop "to pull a half-naked negro child out of a mudhole and set him upon his feet" (9). Despite a Black citizen's control over the bell's tolling, the clock still rings out "as though the land had never been subjugated." The child's descent into the mudhole represents a new generation of freed Black people rendered vulnerable to the racial oppression of a Jim Crow culture. Such subjection, Chesnutt shows, exists both spatially and temporally, as portrayed by the mudhole itself as well as the clock's uncompromising position in the town. The opening chapter of *Cedars* questions whether a Black man's new reign over the town clock—his adherence to standard time—symbolizes real progress: how can one be truly free in a labor system ruled by standard time's dictation of every waking, and sleeping, hour? This question is in the foreground of Chesnutt's "Uncle Julius" tales, which look back to slavery to understand the circumscription of embodiment and social constructs of linear time.

Chesnutt's earliest tale, "The Goophered Grapevine," written in 1887 and featured first in the 1899 *Conjure* collection, opens with John's description of the town center: "There was a red brick market-house in the public square, with a tall tower, which held a four-faced clock that struck the hours, and from which there pealed out a curfew at nine o'clock" (3). The town clock's persistent representation of "planter-defined time" is merged during the Jim Crow era with the standard clock time that developed at the turn of the century. O'Malley explains that master time and its dictation of a slave time became the standard for industrialized and electrified clock time, and Smith adds that "because slave masters could not force slaves to internalize time, slaves helped open a window of resistance to planter-defined time, and it was a window which [laborers] used when they could" (130). CPT became a way to counter white regimes of labor time and complicate white southern restfulness. Julius's storytelling represents an effort to impose one's own sense of time onto white elites. In doing so, Julius represents the freed people Smith discusses, who, "rather than accept the premise from which planters operated and engage in negotiations about the length of time to be worked and thereby accept the legitimacy of clock-defined labor, . . . often refused outright to even debate the merits of planters' definitions of fair compensation for their labor power" (165). Thus, John's fraught employment of Tom

"A Monst'us Pow'ful Sleeper"   63

can be understood through Smith's description of Black workers, whose "careful withdrawal and rationing of their labor power" was interpreted by their employers as "lethargy" (165). As Jolene Hubbs explains, the *Conjure* stories reflect how this "withdrawal" and "rationing" occurred both before and after the abolition of slavery: "'The real-life Uncle Julius'—the ex-slave laborer in the 1890s South—was more likely to be employed as a tenant farmer than a coachman. Chesnutt's conjure tales represent . . . workers—'farm-hands' who live in cabins on John's land—in order to shine a light on the relationship between antebellum enslaved farm labor and postbellum economically entrapped tenant farming" (23). Little does John know that Julius, as the stories suggest, is teaching Tom how to ration his labor by playing on John's misguided notions of race.

Julius's lessons may reflect Chesnutt's response to concerns expressed by formerly enslaved writers like Booker T. Washington, who worried over Black youths' susceptibility to internalized stereotypes of Black enervation. In *The Future of the American Negro* (1899), Washington explains that "the Negro, it is to be borne in mind, worked under constant protest, . . . and he spent almost as much effort in planning how to escape work as in learning how to work. Labour with him was a badge of degradation. . . . Out of these conditions grew the habit of putting off till to-morrow and the day after the duty that should be done promptly to-day" (88–89). Philip Alexander Bruce makes a similar observation in his 1889 autobiography *The Plantation Negro as a Freeman*: "As laborers, the members of the new generation . . . have a marked disposition to doze and sleep" (184). These testimonies evince Black writers' internalization of white fears that indolence was an epidemic among Black workers. By contrast, Chesnutt's stories are reticent to validate such stereotypes of Black youth. Instead, his sardonic plantation fiction calls into question Black people's "marked disposition to doze."

Chesnutt aligns himself with W. E. B. Du Bois, who writes in *The Souls of Black Folk* (1903) that while forced labor has made African American boys the "personification of shiftlessness," "they are not lazy." Du Bois explains that convict labor—as a new form of enslavement—has resulted in a particular behavior among Black youth: "They'll loaf before your face and work behind your back with good-natured honesty. . . . They are improvident because the improvident ones of their acquaintance get on about as well as the provident. Above all, they cannot see why they should take unusual pains to make the white man's land better, or to fatten his mule, or save his corn" (155). Du Bois's commentary provides two important revelations about the "Uncle Julius" tales. First, Du Bois condones "squatter" tendencies, in which Black inhabitants pilfer from white landowners; and second,

64   CHAPTER 2

he implies that there is a futility—even a danger—in being a "good" Black worker. Chesnutt explores these Du Boisian concepts by portraying as distinctly perilous both the Black "squatter" (represented in the outer tales by Julius, whose shrewd bargaining with John over time and space seems all consuming) and the hardworking Black laborer (an ill-fated trope woven into the inner tales of Julius's storytelling).

This latter figure is explored in several of Julius's stories, beginning with "The Goophered Grapevine." Critic William L. Andrews has dubbed the story's protagonist, Henry, "the indefatigable worker" whose hard work unjustly leads to his being circulated from plantation to plantation (62). Henry's body eventually gives out under the strain of labor: "Henry . . . des went out sorter like a cannel. Dey didn't 'pear ter be nuffin de matter wid 'im, 'cep'n' de rheumatiz, but his strenk des dwinel' away 'tel he did n' hab ernuff lef ter draw his bref" (*Conjure* 13). Being exhausted to death is Henry's ultimate "reward" for being an ideal worker. Analyzing the titular character in "Po' Sandy" (written in 1888 and published as the second story in the *Conjure* collection), Richard H. Brodhead notes that "in slavery the more capable one is, the more others desire to own his labor; . . . to be a slave means to be at someone else's disposal, literally not to be able to be where one wishes to be" ("Chesnutt's Negotiation" 311). As Du Bois explains, Black laborers resisted taking "unusual pains to make the white man's land better" because they understood that hard work merely led to further exhaustion and exploitation. These efforts, it is important to note, were not the source of the CPT stereotype but rather mere plays on an already developing white, racist conception of the "lazy" African. Thus, the enslaved and their descendants developed strategies for avoiding objectified labor through subversions of plantation time, a cultural phenomenon that played on stereotypes of Black somnolence.

Sleepy Subversion in the "Uncle Julius" Tales

Chesnutt plays on stereotypes of Black somnolence and laziness to chart the tug and pull of time control between white landowners and Black inhabitants before the Civil War and after. The parallel of pre- and postwar subversions of master time is best illustrated in the story "A Deep Sleeper" (1893), one of the "'non-conjure' conjure tales" excluded by Houghton Mifflin from the 1899 collection *The Conjure Woman* (Chesnutt, *Conjure* 45). The tale cleverly upends cultural assumptions about Black lethargy and, as Bruce Blansett astutely observes, critiques the era's medical pseudoscience: "'A Deep Sleeper' is an overt satire [both of] *Dysæsthesia Æthiopis* and of the belief in black persons' propensity for sloth" (97). While Blansett argues that "A Deep Sleeper" questions the legitimacy of white medicine, he does not consider how it might serve as a lens through which to read the remaining "Uncle Julius" tales. By understanding how sleep is used subversively in this particular text, readers can begin to discern other, subtler moments in which sleep functions as a medium for social exchange in the stories.

"A Deep Sleeper" opens with John's measurement of time: "It was four o'clock on Sunday afternoon, in the month of July . . . [in] the Sabbath stillness" (*Conjure* 42). John notices Julius returning from his service as deacon of his community church and orders him to deliver a watermelon. Rather than respect Julius's Sabbath, John expects him to subscribe to his own "master" schedule. Julius responds by sabotaging John's Sunday plans, forcing his own measurement of time on his employer. As William Gleason notes, both the inner and outer tales reveal "acts of black resistance to planter-defined space" ("Chesnutt's Piazza" 46). Beyond this resistance to white spatial control, however, Chesnutt's tale also poses a challenge to planter-defined time. While Skundus pretends to be asleep, for instance, he claims his own sense of time through his secret meetings with Cindy in the swamp. In the outer tale, John's desire for a watermelon—from a patch long tended by Julius and his kinfolk—represents, as John Edgar Wideman explains, a "system of black-white power relationships in the South, [and] the struggle to establish personal space and territorial rights" (65). By distracting John with his tale of a "monst'us pow'ful sleeper" who once "slep' fer a mont'" (*Conjure* 44), Julius wins a battle—as he has his supposedly sleepy grandson steal the watermelon—in his war with John over "territorial rights." Claudine Raynaud reads Skundus's tale as a "slave tale variation on the theme of 'Sleeping Beauty': the male slave escapes and tricks the master through a pretend deep sleep. Sleep means subtracting oneself from the reality of slavery, i.e., not working" (698). Julius guides Tom through a similar reenactment: he has the boy feign sleepiness and steal the watermelon, therefore abstracting himself (Julius) from John's command. Through such a process, Julius simultaneously plays on and reinforces John's racist assumptions about Black lethargy. Just as Skundus maintains his own sense of time and space through a feigned narcoleptic fit, Julius uses time to his advantage by distracting John while Tom lays claim to the watermelon patch.

Julius's wordplay also suggests the ways in which enslaved people took advantage of white assumptions about Black somnolence. A prime example is when Skundus's assumed narcolepsy enables him to marry his sweetheart, Cindy. His trickery is so masterful that the doctors themselves conclude that Skundus "had be'n in a trance fer fo' weeks" (*Conjure* 49). The hired physicians diagnose Skundus with "a catacornered fit" (49) and instruct Dugal to prevent future episodes by granting Skundus and Cindy cohabitation. Critical accounts by Blansett and Robert B. Stepto note the ambiguity surrounding Julius's use of "catacornered" rather "catatonic," with the latter observing that "with the neologism 'catacornered fit,' Julius conflates the sense of a cataleptic fit with that of an oblique or slanted (catacornered) act. The malapropism suggests that 'deep sleeping' could be a cover for other activity (in Skundus's case, sneaking off to linger in the swamp by Cindy's new plantation, or in Tom's, stealing the watermelon) as well as a biological condition" (Chesnutt, *Conjure* 49n3). Stepto's explanation supports Blansett's argument that "by not only demonstrating a slave's capacity for subversiveness, but also showing how the white master's belief in the science of the day makes him more susceptible to this type of deception, ["A Deep Sleeper"] functions as a satire on the science of the white community" (97–98). Just as Skundus subverts the notion of the deep-sleeping enslaved individual, Julius purposely plays on the word *catacornered*, suggesting that Skundus anticipates such a diagnosis and elicits the doctors' prescription. Thus, implicit in "A Deep Sleeper" is a historical practice in which enslaved people used deception, cunning, and medical discourse to "conjure" the supposed experts whose role it was to define and diagnose.

The story of Skundus influences Tom, whose half-asleep demeanor shields him from exploitation. The outcome of such a disposition stands in stark contrast to the fate of the hard worker. Consequently, Julius advocates for the "squatter" mentality described by Du Bois, in which Black people "loaf before your face and work behind your back." This is just what Julius instructs Tom to do in "A Deep Sleeper." Moreover, Julius plays on John's perception of dialect—as a reflection of Black laziness—to force patience on his listener. In doing so, Julius entrances John, leaving him temporarily spellbound and vulnerable to Julius's control over time's passage. Wideman explains that "Black speech, the mirror of black people's mind and character, was codified by dialect into a deviant variety of good English. Negro dialect lacked proper grammar, its comic orthography suggested ignorance, its 'dats' and 'dems' and 'possums' implied lazy, slovenly pronunciation" (60). John associates Julius's storytelling with popular stereotypes of southern Blackness: for John, Julius's speech represents poor intellect and a lethargic demeanor. Yet despite such assumptions, John, Annie, and her sister, Mabel, are eager to play audience to Julius's tales. Mabel loves hearing stories and "spent much of her time 'drawing out' the colored people in the neighborhood" (*Conjure* 42). Mabel's eagerness alludes to the common practice among privileged white people to demand entertainment from poor Black people. In this way, storytelling became a prime avenue for subtly imparting lessons of Black strife and correcting white assumptions about Black identity. Bill Christophersen, for instance, reads "A Deep Sleeper" as a story that "concerns the subtle, even ritualized forms of resistance in which Skundus, Julius, Tom, and Southern blacks in general were of necessity well-versed, and implicates John as the deep sleeper par excellence for his naïve underestimation of his fellow blacks" (212). Thus, Chesnutt uses the tale to defy white assumptions about the intellectual inferiority of African Americans. Using wit to play on stereotypes of Black sloth, Julius, Skundus, and Tom outsmart their unsuspecting white oppressors.

Figure 7 provides a visualization of term links in "A Deep Sleeper." This web of word associations illuminates terms and phrases associated with stereotypical, racist caricatures of the sleepy Black person. Words in blue are keywords used in my search, and those in orange are words that appear in proximity to the key terms. Notice that with different forms of the word *sleep* come different clusters. *Sleeper* and *sleepers* are connected to titles of lineage—*uncle, grandfather,* and *gran'daddy*—underscoring the long-standing tradition of adopting traits of sleepiness as a means of subversion. Reversely, the act of sleeping—*sleep'n, sleepin,* and *slep*—is connected to

FIGURE 7. This Voyant-generated visualization uses the "Links" feature to explore linkages between specified words (in blue) and autogenerated related words (in orange) in "A Deep Sleeper."

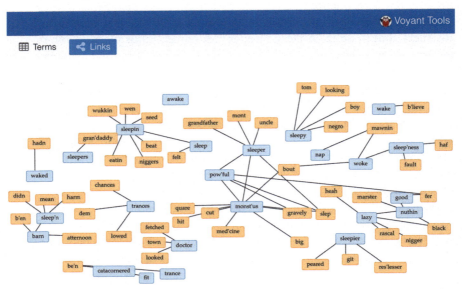

words that suggest danger, such as *beat, harm,* and *gravely.* Other words highlight how sleep-related descriptors are used to berate Black characters, for *lazy* connects to *good fer nuthin* and *rascal.* Likewise, *sleepy* points directly to descriptions of Tom, highlighting his role in embodying (albeit for devious means) the sleepy Black stereotype. These words form the foundation of this reading, as they represent the stereotypical traits that white people projected onto sleep-deprived Black bodies. I produced this visualization in the midst of drafting this chapter, and it was this visual that led me to further investigate the violence that resulted from these stereotypes. For instance, the "harm" done by "sleep'n"—and oversleep being a "gravely" undertaken act—underscores how dangerous it could be to simply sleep while enslaved. Violence then became a focus in my reading of other tales, particularly, as I will discuss, in "Mars Jeems's Nightmare."

Through his enthralling storytelling, Julius works his own conjuration on both John and the reader. Matthew A. Taylor suggests that "the agency of . . . resistance for Julius, as for Chesnutt, is a form of storytelling that stages power inequalities as a means of subtly redressing them in the teller's interests, thereby performatively disproving the charge of African Americans' nonintellectuality. . . . In this sense, conjure-as-rhetorical-performance does become a means to conjure oneself, for author and character alike" (118). Julius's speech hypnotizes his listeners, and the lessons he imparts throughout the course of the tales slowly alter his audience's perception of southern Black culture. Moreover, taking his time to tell his stories, Julius forces listeners to exist within his own dictation of time. As Jennifer Riddle Harding explains, "speaking is slower than sight-reading, and since the spellings are nonstandard approximations of the sounds of nonstandard speech, readers are forced to slow down as they sound out the words and 'hear' the speech of Julius. As a result, readers encounter the tale at a pace that is similar to the experience of listeners who are hearing rather than reading the story" (427). Chesnutt drew from the Uncle Remus figure popularized in Joel Chandler Harris's tales to both guile readers and satirize plantation storytelling. In "A Story of the War" (1880), for example, Uncle Remus complains of the new generation of "sun shine niggers," who are "too lazy ter wuk . . . en dey specks hones' fokes fer ter stan' up en s'port um" (206–7). Taylor details how Chesnutt subverts the plantation formula made famous by Harris: "Julius's tales . . . invoke the slave past as a way of reflecting on the lasting racism of Chesnutt's contemporary moment, including its at least partial embodiment in John (and his dismissive condescension toward Julius). Moreover, Chesnutt—in a direct repudiation of the marked one-dimensionality of Harris's Uncle Remus—endows his black characters with a capacity to frustrate those whites who, based on fallacious notions of their own superiority, would presume to exploit them" (118). Chesnutt employs many of the same literary conventions as Harris, but, as Taylor notes, Chesnutt's version calls into question the very stereotypes of African American life that were staples of plantation fiction, thereby challenging white notions of the South.

While Chesnutt lightheartedly satirizes the racism of white medicine and squatter rights in "A Deep Sleeper," he assumes a darker tone in "Mars Jeems's Nightmare" (1898), in which he foregrounds the harsh realities of slave labor. Featured third in the *Conjure* collection, the story begins with John expressing his disgust for Tom's poor work ethic. He hired the young man at Julius's request but quickly regrets the decision and terminates him. Tom's portrayal as the drowsy New Negro and the inner tale's sketch of Jeems as the "noo man" who suffers from a sleep-induced bewilderment can together be read as depicting the conditions of overwork and sleep deprivation that impeded and disoriented Black workers before and after slavery. Julius hopes his story will protect his grandson from what Brodhead characterizes as the "new cult of efficiency and productivity" that arose after Reconstruction (*Cultures* 202). As Henry B. Wonham explains, "Mars Jeems's transformation . . . provides a remarkably subtle commentary on Tom's uncertain predicament as a 'new negro' in the post-war plantation setting. Born in freedom and thus unfit to assume [a] servile role . . . , Jeems becomes the story's instructive representative of Tom's dilemma" (140). Upon concluding the tale, Julius tells John and Annie: "Dis yer tale goes ter show . . . dat w'ite folks w'at is so ha'd en stric', en doan make no 'lowance fer po' ign'ant niggers w'at ain' had no chanst ter l'arn, is li'ble ter hab bad dreams" (*Conjure* 101). Julius's closing comments correlate Jeems as the "noo man" with Tom and his postwar generation, who are neither enslaved nor truly free. Altogether, "Mars Jeems's Nightmare" illustrates the universal suffering of unrelenting labor, and the story warns against replicating the same environment on postwar plantations.

According to Julius, Mars Jeems prohibits nearly all social customs among his captives. Solomon, an enslaved man whose paramour is sent away, consults a conjure woman to alleviate Jeems's harsh practices. Her solution is a potion that will give Jeems a "monst'us bad dream" (*Conjure* 98), which causes the white enslaver to be transformed into an enslaved Black man with no recollection of his former self. After Solomon sneaks him the potion, Jeems goes off on business and leaves the running of the plantation to his hired overseer, Nick. Having transformed into an enslaved man, Jeems is brought to the plantation, where Nick beats him mercilessly, first for his failure to know his own name and later for "laziness en impidence" (96). After days of abuse and toil, Jeems is so exhausted that he eats the cure for his conjuration—Solomon's proffered sweet potato—in a state of somnambulism. Upon waking, Jeems shows a disgust for his own manufactured "cult of infinite productivity" (Brodhead, *Cultures* 200): he fires Nick, lessens labor time, and grants his captives limited social freedoms, such as marriage and celebratory gatherings. The moral of the story is that one's environment—not some innate, racial trait—forces the body into the condition Cartwright defines as *Dysæsthesia Æthiopis*. Julius's effort to rid John of his belief in the stereotypical lazy Black person represents Chesnutt's larger endeavor to refute popular medical and scientific claims of Black inferiority.

Rejecting theories of racial inheritance, Chesnutt attributes racial stereotypes to bodily responses to environmental factors. Shirley Moody-Turner details John's efforts to classify Tom according to a popular conception of Black manhood at the time: "John judges Tom on the basis of his unreliable impressions and draws a stereotype from the Lost Cause tradition to characterize Tom as lazy and shiftless" (143). Julius counters this assumption by portraying a white man who, disguised within an enslaved Black man's body, is swiftly punished for laziness. Wonham does well to articulate the emphasis Julius places on environmental factors: "Tom's shortcomings as a servant, Julius implies, have less to do with inherent laziness than with the effects of a major cultural transformation in African-American life, a transformation as disorienting as Mars Jeems's nightmare" (141). Yet, Jeems's experience as the "noo man" functions as more than just a metaphor for the confusion of cultural upheaval: it emphasizes the exhaustive bodily impact of exploitative labor. After the "noo man" is released from Ole Nick, Chesnutt emphasizes the somatic nature of Jeems's condition. He is so exhausted from his stint in slavery that Solomon feeds him a conjured sweet potato without his ever waking: "De nigger wuz layin' in a co'nder, 'sleep, en Solomon des slip' up ter 'im, en hilt dat sweet'n' 'tater 'fo' de nigger's nose, en he des nach'ly retch' up wid his han', en tuk de 'tater en eat it in his sleep, widout knowin' it" (*Conjure* 98). The "noo man" exhibits symptoms of *Dysæsthesia Æthiopis*, which, as Cartwright argued, is a racial characteristic. But as Chesnutt shows, the "noo man" is actually Mars Jeems, a white man whose body suffers from exhaustion after being enslaved on the plantation. Thus, Chesnutt demonstrates that it is the environment, rather than racial inheritance, that forces the "noo man" into a somnambulistic state.

This depiction of the somnambulist stands in stark contrast to the genius-somnambulist described in the previous chapter, in which Rowland

"A Monst'us Pow'ful Sleeper"   71

views Roderick as being able to perform great feats of art without having to put forth any conscious effort. Roderick, however, eventually embodies a figure more similar to the "noo man" somnambulist, for he comes to see the monotony of required labor as a physical ailment. This is more akin to Elam's 1869 somnambulism, which is brought on by "the mere mechanical repetitions of daily performances" (341–43). Like Jeems, who is able to return to his status as a white enslaver, Roderick can escape such work through his privileged whiteness, as exemplified by his escape to Baden and the other numerous times he slips away from Rowland's gaze. This is not the case for the enslaved men in Chesnutt's story like Solomon, who are forced to work mechanically day in and day out.

By imposing sleep deprivation on the enslaver in "Mars Jeems's Nightmare," Chesnutt reverses the sleep surveillance typical of antebellum plantations. When Solomon encounters his bewildered enslaver at the end of the tale, Jeems explains that he has had "a reg'lar, nach'ul nightmare" (*Conjure* 98). In his reading, Eric Sundquist notes that "nightmare and actual transformation are blurred" (372). Indeed, Julius's word choice implies that what Jeems undergoes is a typical night terror experienced by the sleep-deprived and enslaved. Earlier in the tale, for example, enslaved characters anguish in their sleep after hearing Jeems ask his overseer to run the plantation in his absence: "de way [Nick] . . . snap' de rawhide he useter kyar roun' wid 'im, made col' chills run up and down de backbone er dem niggers. . . . En dat night dey wuz mo'nin' en groanin' down in de qua'ters, fer de niggers all knowed w'at wuz comin'" (*Conjure* 95). Rather than find respite in rest, enslaved characters doze anxiously, possibly in fear of Nick's punishment for oversleep. This was a common, real-life occurrence as Frederick Douglass recalls in *My Bondage and My Freedom* (1855): "More slaves are whipped for oversleeping than for any other fault. Neither age nor sex finds any favor. The overseer stands at the quarter door, armed with stick and cowskin, ready to whip any who may be a few minutes behind time" (102). Solomon Northup's *Twelve Years a Slave* (1853) likewise attests to the dread brought on by fears of oversleep: "With a prayer that he may be on his feet and wide awake at the first sound of the horn, [the enslaved person] sinks to his slumbers nightly" (170). In "Mars Jeems's Nightmare," Julius is unclear as to whether the "mo'nin' en groanin'" in the slave quarters are expressed by those asleep, half awake, or wide eyed, that is, suffering from night terrors or deprived of sleep altogether in anticipation of the overseer's whip at dawn. What Chesnutt does make explicit are the pervading modes of oppression under slavery, forces that dictate every waking and sleeping moment.

In figure 8, a Voyant-generated term-link text visualization highlights associations between words in "Mars Jeems's Nightmare." The connections

FIGURE 8. Like figure 7, this Voyant-generated image populates words (in orange) that appear in proximity to specified words (in blue). These words are from "Mars Jeems's Nightmare."

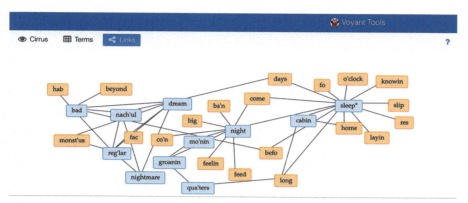

indicate the angst and fear that enslaved characters associate with nighttime rest. Rather than find a reprieve from a hard day's work, they face long hours filled with nightmares and sleepless dread of the day to come. The blue terms represent those included in my search, while the others represent the tool-generated words associated with them. Glimpsing this web of collocated terms helps visualize the story's attention to sleep-related fears and anxieties. For example, the line that connects *sleep** to another word in blue, particularly *night*, leads to acts of anguish, such as *mo'nin'* and *groanin'*. To conduct this search, I started with *sleep**, and related words were then generated in orange. From there, every term I clicked on turned blue and became a keyword, with collocates popping up in orange around it. I was thus able to manipulate the links to center on specific terms. If a user were to conduct a similar search, the visualization would likely be generated differently (unless they were to select the exact trail of terms as I did, thereby creating the same series of blue terms in connection with one another). This is why I find Voyant so fascinating: users can examine texts in new ways every time. Because of this variation, I found it pertinent to include screenshots (that is, static images) of what I encountered during my research, as I would be hard pressed to re-create the exact same visualization. This particular visualization was conducted in the midst of my work on this chapter, and, in the same way that my visualization for "A Deep Sleeper" helped inspire my reading of "Mars Jeems's Nightmare," this visualization enhanced my reading of another story, "Dave's Neckliss," as it focused my attention on sleep spaces and the experience of sleeping within those spaces for the enslaved.

In emphasizing the nighttime angst common in slave quarters, Chesnutt highlights the anxieties provoked by nightly surveillance. Although the nighttime often served as one of the only times enslaved people could engage in social activity, they were never able to do so without worrying about the watchful eyes of enslavers and overseers. Saidiya Hartman explains that the night could function as the "facilitation of collective identity," but that such "pleasure was ensnared in a web of domination, accumulation, abjection, resignation, and possibility . . . within the confines of surveillance and non-autonomy" (49–50). Chesnutt's depiction of "mo'nin' en groanin'" in the slave quarters emphasizes such uneasiness. One of Jeems's rules, as Julius explains at the start of his tale, is that "w'en night come [the enslaved] mus' sleep en res', so dey'd be ready ter git up soon in de mawnin' en go ter dey wuk fresh en strong" (*Conjure* 94). Historically, one aspect of an overseer's job was to conduct "random spotchecks of slaves' sleeping quarters" to ensure each person was asleep. These inspections, Reiss notes, "were seen [by the enslaved] as matters of life and death" (127). For enslavers and overseers, the dangers were more abstract: they feared that the enslaved might use the cover of night to engage in plots of rebellion or escape, or otherwise conduct business not profitable to the enslaver. Those held captive, on the other hand, faced immediate danger. In his 1845 memoir, Douglass describes being "awakened at the dawn of day by the most heart-rending shrieks of an own aunt of mine," who was discovered outside her sleeping quarters at night and mercilessly whipped by the overseer (*Narrative* 6).

The consequence of this nightly torture is dramatized allegorically in "The Gray Wolf's Ha'nt" (1899), the sixth tale in the *Conjure* collection. Julius recounts a story of vengeance in which a conjure man, Jube, terrorizes the enslaved Dan (who killed Jube's son in self-defense) through a spell in which he takes Dan out of bed night after night and rides him like a beast: "dis cunjuh man 'mence' by gwine up ter Dan's cabin eve'y night, en takin' Dan out in his sleep en ridin' 'im roun' de roads en fiel's ober de rough groun'." As a result Dan feels "ez ti'ed ez ef he had n' be'n ter sleep" (*Conjure* 84). Eventually, Jube tricks Dan into believing that his abuse derives from an evil witch, who by night assumes the form of a black cat. Jube then proposes that Dan be transformed into a wolf so that he may kill the witch. The drama climaxes in Jube's kidnapping Dan's wife, Mahaly, transforming her into a black cat, and leading Dan to mistakenly murder her out of a dire desperation for rest. Whereas Julius is specific in his detail of animal transformation at the tale's conclusion—Dan becomes lupine and Mahaly feline—he leaves the reader uncertain about what form Dan takes when he is ridden nightly by Jube. The story suggests that it is Dan's own body in a somnambulistic state that is routinely mistreated. "The Gray Wolf's Ha'nt" therefore provides a fantastical portrait of a common occurrence among the enslaved, in which individuals—worn down by constant abuse—awoke each morning in a state of perpetual sleeplessness.

Chesnutt brings such oppressive forces to light in his later writing. Take, for example, Sandy's observation to Tom Delamere in *The Marrow of Tradition* (1901): "Dere's somethin' wrong 'bout dese clo's er mine—I don' never seem ter be able ter keep 'em clean no mo'. Ef I b'lieved in dem ole-timey sayin's, I'd 'low dere wuz a witch come here eve'y night an' tuk 'em out an' wo' 'em, er tuk me out an' rid me in 'em" (161). In citing one of "dem ole-timey sayin's," Sandy recalls the days when the enslaved used superstition to reconcile trauma. Whether from anxiety over the next day's mistreatment or abuse during the night, captives felt as if their bodies were constantly worn away and possessed by others, even in moments of rest. Not unlike the malevolent tactics Jube uses to torture Dan, enslavers and their hired overseers moderated captives' sleep so that they had just enough energy to get through a day's work. Depending on plantation conditions, enslaved people were prescribed a specific window of time in which to rest. For most, however, this was their only time to meet the myriad needs they were denied during the day. According to Reiss, "controlling and interpreting sleep had important ramifications in a slaveholding society. Taking charge of the sleep-wake cycle was a way to break slaves, to make maximum profit, and to protect the white slaveholding class from retribution. Slaveholders had to strike a careful balance: they had to allow enough sleep for their captive workforce's labor to be profitable, yet not so much that they might be clear-eyed and energetic enough to escape" (134). This "careful balance" of intended sleeping hours stymied enslaved people's efforts to provide for their own needs. Douglass, for instance, often spent his nightly hours plotting his escape, despite being granted only a few hours' sleep. Recalling his worst years of slavery, Douglass portrays the experience of incessant exhaustion as akin to a "beast-like" state: "Sunday was my only leisure time. I spent this in a sort of beast-like stupor, between sleep and wake, under some large tree. At times I would rise up, a flash of energetic freedom would dart through my soul, accompanied with a faint beam of hope, that flickered for a moment, and then vanished" (*Narrative* 63). Douglass's description of being stuck "between sleep and wake" recalls Cartwright's definition of *Dysæsthesia Æthiopis*, in which the enslaved individual lives in a perpetual state of half-wakefulness. In his 1899 biography of Douglass, Chesnutt draws attention to Douglass's limited access to rest and cites his memory of his Sunday respite, the only time of the week he had to fill his belly and rest his body (*Frederick* 17). Chesnutt's studies of Douglass and other formerly enslaved writers may have inspired Henry's declaration in

Chesnutt's *The Colonel's Dream* (1905) that "environment controls the making of men. Some rise above it, the majority do not" (50). For Chesnutt, it is this rule that truly rendered enslaved people exhausted and listless.

Twinned deprivations of food and sleep are a common theme in the "Uncle Julius" tales, in which suffering from unmet bodily needs forces characters to choose between one or the other. Such decisions are painfully rendered in portraits of familial provision. Chesnutt first addresses this in "The Goophered Grapevine," when Julius tells John: "Befo' de wah, in slab'ry times, a nigger did n' mine goin' fi' er ten mile in a night, w'en dey wuz sump'n good ter eat at de yuther een'" (*Conjure* 7). Lack of sufficient food supplies led enslaved people to sacrifice sleep and commit thievery, particularly under the cover of night. Food theft propels the inner plot of "Dave's Neckliss," written in 1889 and rejected for publication in the *Conjure* collection. After "one dark night w'en somebody tuk a ham fum one er de smoke-'ouses," the story's protagonist is falsely accused of stealing the cured pork (*Conjure* 37). Despite having long proven to be both an obedient and productive worker, Dave is assumed guilty and forced to wear a ham chained around his neck for months. In the tale's conclusion, John reflects that "Dave's Neckliss" is unique to Julius's tales in that it enables one "to study, through the medium of his recollection, the simple but intensely human inner life of slavery" (33). Scholars have likewise read the story in such a way, arguing that Dave eventually believes he *is* a ham, thus illustrating how slavery degrades the individual psyche (see Carpio; Christophersen). In particular, Julius describes the ham's intrusion on Dave's sleeping habits as acutely traumatizing: "Ef he turn ober in his sleep, dat ham would be tuggin' at his neck. It wuz de las' thing he seed at night, en de fus' thing he seed in de mawnin'" (38). Contributing to Dave's mental collapse is his lack of sufficient sleep while tethered to the ham.

Even after Dave is separated from the remaining pork bits, "he allus tied [a lighterd knot or pinewood knot] roun' his neck w'en he went ter sleep. Fac', it 'peared lack Dave done gone clean out'n his mine" (*Conjure* 39). Paradoxically, Dave finds comfort in the night by simulating the very thing that originally disrupted his sleep. His mental collapse is marked by his dependency to achieve some semblance of rest on a replacement object meant to dehumanize him. His decline culminates in suicide: Dave hangs himself in the smokehouse over an open fire, as Julius says, "fer ter kyo" (42). Blansett argues that "'curing' in this passage melds Dave's identity with the ham by signifying both a means of preserving food and the pathologizing of African Americans by the scientific and medical communities during this time period" (89). Such an assertion is underscored in "A Victim of

Heredity, or Why the Darkey Loves Chicken," another rejected story written the same year as "Dave's Neckliss." The outer frame illustrates how hunger and desperation continued to plague southern Black people under Jim Crow. It begins with John's endeavor to "protect [his] property": "I therefore kept close watch one night, and caught a chicken-thief in the very act." In an act reminiscent of Dave's suicide, John locks his captive in the smokehouse for the night. Before settling into comfortable rest, John explains: "I made up my mind . . . that an example must be made of this miscreant" (*Conjure* 71). The next morning, John discovers Sam Jones to be "insignificant looking" and "very much frightened," charged with providing for "a large family and sick wife." Despite these facts John is emphatic that he must enforce the "social order," blaming Sam's thievery on a "trifling disposition" and inability to "let chickens alone" (72). Chesnutt's efforts to defy racial stereotypes are clearly evident in "A Victim of Heredity." After Julius arrives, John asks him: "Why is it that your people can't let chickens alone?" (72). Annie chastises her husband for making such an assumption about an entire race. As the more astute reader of Julius's stories, Annie learns from "Victim" a lesson "about the influence of heredity and environment" (79). Annie's response represents Chesnutt's efforts to prove that environmental factors are the reason for supposed racial differences. Chesnutt makes evident John's deployment of racial stereotypes to justify his mistreatment of Black community members. In doing so, Chesnutt unmasks pseudoscientific typologies of race that labeled African Americans as predominantly gluttonous and slothful. These stereotypes are even more grossly disturbing when understood as having developed out of sheer deprivation. From the sleepy slave to the incessantly hungry Black person, white society essentialized Blackness in ways that punished African Americans for merely requiring the necessities to sustain human life.

For enslaved women, racial stereotypes were often even more sinister, as they demanded that mothers and domestic caretakers embody an automaton-like endurance. In *Up from Slavery* (1901), Washington recounts the childhood memory of his "mother cooking a chicken late at night, and awakening her children for the purpose of feeding them" (4). Because enslaved women were expected to stay perpetually alert to their enslavers' needs—particularly in caring for white offspring—they were rarely granted time to spend with their own children. Chesnutt notes in his biographical account of Douglass that "all his impressions of [his mother] were derived from a few brief visits made to him at Colonel Lloyd's plantation, most of them at night. These fleeting visits of the mother were important events in the life of the child" (*Frederick* 7). Chesnutt's observation may have derived from Douglass's recollection in the *Narrative* that his mother "made her journeys to see me in the night, travelling the whole distance on foot, after the performance of her day's work. She was a field hand, and a whipping is the penalty of not being in the field at sunrise" (3). He recalls how his mother, Harriet, would walk twelve miles each way only to lie down with him for a few hours. This exhausting trek, in combination with her long working hours, may have contributed to her untimely death when Douglass was only seven. His mother's extreme sleep deprivation suggests the many trade-offs that were forced on enslaved women.

Douglass's mother put herself in terrible danger with her nightly treks, as round-the-clock surveillance was typical in the life of an enslaved woman. In *Incidents in the Life of a Slave Girl* (1861), Harriet Jacobs details a particularly ominous role women were expected to fill at night: "[The overseer] entered every cabin, to see that men and their wives had gone to bed together, lest the men, from over-fatigue, should fall asleep in the chimney corner, and remain there till the morning horn called them to their daily task. Women are considered of no value, unless they continually increase their owner's stock" (76). Women were forced to procreate with assigned partners, regardless of their own feelings about partnership and intimacy. Jacobs also recalls being an object of white lust and experiencing the sexual harassment of her enslaver, "whose restless, craving, vicious nature roved about day and night" (29). In addition to facing the dangers of enforced procreation and sexual predation, enslaved women were required to labor throughout the day, tend to their own babies outside working hours, and then care nightly for their enslavers. For instance, Jacobs recollects an aunt who was forced to sleep on the floor in the entryway of her mistress's bedroom and, consequently, suffered six premature births and died an early death: "Finally, toiling all day, and being deprived of rest at night, completely broke down her constitution, and Dr. Flint declared it was impossible she could ever become the mother of a living child" (217–18). In Sarah Hopkins Bradford's biography of Harriet Tubman (1886), she paints a similar picture: "When the labors, unremitted for a moment, of the long day were over . . . there was a cross baby to be rocked continuously, lest it should wake and disturb the mother's rest. The black child [Harriet] sat beside the cradle of the white child, so near the bed, that the lash of the whip would reach her if she ventured for a moment to forget her fatigues and sufferings in sleep" (19–20). Douglass provides an even more harrowing portrait of how fatal the descent into sleep could be for enslaved girls:

> The wife of Mr. Giles Hicks, . . . murdered my wife's cousin, a young girl between fifteen and sixteen years of age. . . . It was ascertained that the

offense for which this girl was thus hurried out of the world, was this: she had been set that night, and several preceding nights, to mind Mrs. Hicks's baby, and having fallen into a sound sleep, the baby cried, waking Mrs. Hicks, but not the slave-girl. Mrs. Hicks, becoming infuriated at the girl's tardiness, after calling several times, jumped from her bed and seized a piece of fire-wood from the fireplace; and then, as she lay fast asleep, she deliberately pounded in her skull and breast-bone, and thus ended her life. (*My Bondage* 125–26)

Not only were enslaved girls and women forced to spend long evenings with their infant charges after working all day, but they were also expected to stay awake throughout the night in anticipation of every cry. The dire consequences these women and children faced for giving in to the natural lull of nighttime sleep often involved violent punishments, including lashings and even death.

While enslaved women seem the most vulnerable in a system of sleep surveillance where the risks of sexual violence and sleep deprivation were especially high, Chesnutt also attributes to them an almost supernatural power through sleep. Throughout the "Uncle Julius" tales, Chesnutt depicts enslaved women as being particularly adept at interpreting dreams. Cindy in "A Deep Sleeper," for instance, contributes to the deception of Mars Dugal by claiming to have dreamed of Skundus's return from his long slumber. The next morning, when Skundus arrives "rubbin' his eyes ez ef he hadn' got waked up good yit" (*Conjure* 48), Dugal perceives this as proof of Cindy's prediction, evincing Chesnutt's historical understanding that enslaved women were often believed to be gifted seers. As Chesnutt notes in his essay "Superstitions and Folk-Lore of the South" (1901), many southerners believed in the power of the dreamworld. Chesnutt explains that a key source of his information about conjure superstition was Old Aunt Harriet, a local North Carolina woman. He describes her as "a dreamer of dreams and a seer of visions": "I was able now and then to draw a little upon her reserves of superstition" (*Conjure* 202). He recounts her story of having awakened from a dream with the cure for an ailment inflicted on her by a curse. Chesnutt is quick to show his ambivalence in believing the woman's story—"education . . . has thrown the ban of disrepute upon witchcraft and conjuration" (199)—yet by scrutinizing the environment that shaped slave culture, Chesnutt lends a form of veracity to enslaved women's connection to the dreamworld.

Rather than rely on sexist notions that associate women with the realm of fancy and men with the world of facts, Chesnutt depicts the dreamworld as a means for enslaved women to process the trauma they endured in their waking lives. At night, if enslaved women were somehow left alone to sleep, they often underwent even worse torture: night terrors that replayed the atrocities of daily life. Historian Jonathan White explains that "the horrors and realities of slavery made indelible marks on the minds of slaves, sometimes keeping them from sleeping, and other times infiltrating their dreams" (85). Tubman is one well-known historical figure whose powers of evasion and subversion were often drawn from sleep visions, and her prominence may have influenced Chesnutt's interest in enslaved women, trauma, and premonition. According to Earl Conrad, her twentieth-century biographer, Tubman suffered from narcolepsy, a condition caused by a head injury she endured at the hands of an overseer when she was a teenager (White 83). With her lifetime of lethargy inflicted on her by a violent, oppressive environment, Tubman was, therefore, a real-life "deep sleeper." In her 1886 biography of Tubman, Bradford describes "the turns of somnolency to which [Harriet] has always been subject" (82), and explains that her head injury "left her subject to a sort of stupor . . . coming upon her in the midst of conversation, or whatever she may be doing, and throwing her into a deep slumber, from which she will presently rouse herself, and go on with her conversation or work" (110–11). In *The Rising Son* (1874), William Wells Brown similarly describes Tubman as being known for "taking her seat, [and] at once drop[ping] off into a sound sleep" (537). Abrupt sleep for a narcoleptic can initiate REM sleep, the dream-inducing cycle of sleep, in a matter of minutes or even seconds, often causing hallucinations and vivid dreaming ("Narcolepsy"). White explains that "accounts of [Tubman's] dreams have appeared in newspapers, children's books, and adult nonfiction. . . . One fugitive slave in Canada said in 1860 that . . . 'de whites can't catch [Tubman], kase you see she's born wid de charm,'" the charm being her ability to render predictions from dreams (82). Although Chesnutt lacked the medical knowledge we now have for interpreting such symptoms, he was keenly aware of connections—both oppressive and empowering—between southern environmental factors and the effects of sleep deprivation on the enslaved. Tubman's sleep revelations, considered to be a "charm" that eluded "de whites," suggest that the interpretative power of vivid dreaming is not merely a result of sleep deprivation and post-traumatic stress disorder but also an avenue for processing trauma and subverting white southern oppression.[2]

In "Sis' Becky's Pickaninny" (1898), included as the fifth story in the *Conjure* collection, Chesnutt uses the dreamworld to articulate the trauma Becky undergoes after being separated from her son. Becky's anguish mirrors the melancholy that John's wife, Annie, experiences, possibly as a result of childlessness, in the outer frame of the tale. Dean McWilliams observes that in "Sis' Becky's Pickaninny" Annie is deeply stirred by the tale and is restored to health by it (89). Annie's neurasthenia is evident from the first lines of the *Conjure* collection: "The Goophered Grapevine" opens with John's recalling the purpose for their relocation from Ohio to North Carolina: "Some years ago my wife was in poor health, and our family doctor . . . advised a change of climate" (*Conjure* 3). At the start of "Sis' Becky's Pickaninny" Annie has relapsed into "a settled melancholy" so deep that "nothing seemed to rouse her" (*Conjure* 102). Her illness seems less physiological than psychological, although its actual source is unclear. The couple is childless, so perhaps loss or an unanswered wish to conceive accounts for Annie's condition. After witnessing her sorrowful countenance, Julius tells a story that represents Chesnutt's efforts to upend the racial boundaries that doctors such as George Miller Beard established between white neurasthenia and Black hysteria.

Julius's story commences after Becky's husband is sold away, and she consoles herself with the company of her son, Mose. Like Douglass's mother, Becky can only spend time with her son at night after long days working in the fields—that is, until Becky's enslaver, Kunnel Pen'leton, trades her for a horse. He offers Mose as a free addition to the deal, but the trader refuses, telling Pen'leton: "I'll keep dat 'oman so busy she'll fergit de baby; fer niggers is made ter wuk, en dey ain' got no time fer no sich foolis'ness ez babies" (*Conjure* 105). But Becky does not forget, and both she and Mose suffer and grow ill from the separation. Aunt Nancy, Mose's caretaker, consults the conjure woman Peggy, who transforms Mose into a hummingbird so that he may see his mother. Becky and her son are overjoyed by their visit, and that night Becky "dremp all dat night dat she wuz holdin' her pickaninny in her arms, en kissin' him, en nussin' him, des lack she useter do back on de ole plantation whar he wuz bawn. En fer th'ee er fo' days Sis' Becky went 'bout her wuk wid mo' sperrit dan she'd showed since she'd be'n down dere ter dis man's plantation" (107). Just like sustenance or sleep, time with Mose—in the real world or in her dreams—has a nourishing effect on Becky. However, Aunt Nancy eventually becomes too exhausted to carry Mose to and from Peggy's. This renewed absence pushes Becky into fits of panic after she dreams for three nights that Mose has died. Her agitation grows to such an extent that her new enslaver sends her back to Pen'leton's plantation, reuniting mother and son.

As with "A Deep Sleeper," the inner tale of "Sis Becky's Pickaninny" concludes with an enslaved person exhibiting stereotypes of Blackness only for Julius to slyly reveal the subversive power of such behavior. In this case, Becky's hysterical demeanor enables her return to Mose. In the outer tale, Annie listens to the story with "greater interest than she had manifested in any subject for several days," and when John calls it a "very ingenious fairy tale," Annie chastises him: "Why John! . . . The story . . . is true to nature, and might have happened half a hundred times, and no doubt did happen, in those horrid days before the war" (*Conjure* 110). Lorne Fienberg observes that "by according the tale a truth value, [Annie] suggests a new status for Uncle Julius as historian and chronicler of his culture. Even more perplexing is the apparent therapeutic value of the tale, which seems to set Annie instantly on the road to recovery from her illness" (171). Annie's "perplexing" comment that Becky's story is "true to nature" may represent Chesnutt's ironic allusion to a singular distinction between Becky's hysteria and Annie's neurasthenia: while the former is forced to deal with her personal trauma amid bodily exploitation and prolonged sleep deprivation, Annie is afforded the restorative rest she requires to work through her depression. Thus, Chesnutt's fiction suggests that it is not a Black individual's innate "nature" that makes her hysterical while her white counterpart is composedly neurasthenic; rather, it is their adverse environments.

Nowhere to Sleep in the "Sleepy South"

The contrast between Black sleeplessness and white restfulness in the southern space is a common theme in Chesnutt's works. The tales indicate that while many enslavers punished their captives for exhibiting symptoms of lethargy, white people routinely embraced and encouraged idleness among their own and indulged in or even celebrated the South's sleepy atmosphere. In the opening tale ("The Goophered Grapevine"), John and Annie "had already caught some of the native infection of restfulness," and, as the tales progress, John grows increasingly dormant (*Conjure* 5). Gleason frames John's transition as a "decline from energetic 'pioneer' . . . to leisured capitalist," linking his transformation to the prewar era ("Chesnutt's Piazza" 65). This connection to the past derives from John's idealization of the customs of antebellum southern gentry. John seemingly ignores the fact that slavery maintained such traditions, a system in which white people were entitled to endless rest while their Black counterparts labored at their command.

By playing on the formulaic plantation tale and its descendants in postwar regionalist fiction, Chesnutt confronts popular efforts to idealize the historical South as a respite from northern industry. Jennifer Fleissner articulates a specific local color convention that Chesnutt sought to challenge: "A narrator standing in for the wearied fin-de-siècle urbanite typically finds respite in visiting rural outposts that retain the slow pace and quirky specificities of a fast-fading way of life" ("Earth-Eating" 316). John's entrance into the "slow" South and his transformation into a sleepy southerner represent a cultural desire to return to the boundaries that once clearly delineated white people's entitlement to rest from Black people's enforced productivity. John comes to embody the southern, white, indolent male that is viewed with disgust by James's Roderick Hudson. When describing his artistic outlook, Roderick declares that "we stand like a race with shrunken muscles. . . . But I don't hesitate to proclaim it—I mean to lift them again!" (123). As the son of an enslaver whose laziness and excessive drinking led to his early demise, Roderick relies on the doctrine of industry to revitalize white masculine power. Roderick's views are beyond disturbing and reflect an unease at the cultural moment about white leisure as a threat to racial superiority. While James makes it unclear as to whether Roderick's views align with his own or instead represent the many misguided notions that lead to his downfall, Chesnutt's objective is much more apparent: he takes particular aim at sleepy white people, whose indolence was the direct result of Black industry and toil. According to Gleason, "the popular genre of plantation fiction . . . sought, through an equally purposeful recourse to the perceived ideals of the past, to fix its own definitions of the proper meanings of 'place' for black Americans in the Jim Crow era. Chesnutt wrote in part . . . to challenge their assumptions and expose their motives, often by literally and figuratively playing with their forms" ("Chesnutt's Piazza" 35). Moreover, Reiss explains that authors such as Harriet Beecher Stowe contributed to a popular depiction of "'the sleepy South' as a zone where black people did all the bone-wearying work and slaveholding whites lolled in indolent repose" (134). Chesnutt continues the efforts of Stowe and others who sought to expose the interconnections between southern white lethargic lifestyles and the exploitation of Black bodies.

In *The House behind the Cedars*, George Tryon, like John, embodies the fin de siècle urbanite. In the novel's twelfth chapter, Tryon and Dr. Green pay a visit to Judge Straight's office: "[The judge] was seated by the rear window, and had fallen into a gentle doze—the air of Patesville was conducive to slumber. A visitor from some bustling city might have rubbed his eyes, on any but a market-day, and imagined the whole town asleep—that the people were somnambulists and did not know it. The judge, an old hand, roused himself so skillfully, at the sound of approaching footsteps, that his visitors could not guess but that he had been wide awake" (110). The Judge, the narrator implies, is keen to avoid being caught asleep on the job. Interestingly, the inhabitants of Patesville (the same fictional town where John takes up his residence in the "Uncle Julius" tales) are depicted as unwitting "somnambulists." Chesnutt suggests here that white southerners like the judge subconsciously indulge in a lethargic lifestyle: white people in power embraced the idea of leisure while simultaneously carrying on as if they were constantly productive, alert, and on guard. Chesnutt counters such notions by making white people seem more anachronistic within an industrialized world than their modern Black counterparts. Moreover, Chesnutt emphasizes that CPT stereotypes, which derided "black people as lazy" (Popik) during the Progressive-Era efficiency movement (Popik), emerged out of a passive, white adherence to Taylorism that hypocritically demanded industry from nonwhite workers (see Rabinbach 239).

Chesnutt depicts John as a neo-antebellum planter whose romanticized interpretation of southern agrarianism involves overseeing production at his own leisure. Chesnutt counters such nostalgia in his other works by commonly featuring indolent white southerners who are constantly dozing. Oftentimes, such sleepers expect their Black servants or loved ones to watch over their resting selves. In *The Marrow of Tradition*, for example, Polly Ochiltree unwittingly drifts off to sleep, and despite her Black maid, Dinah, having shaken the old woman "vigorously," she exclaims, "sitting suddenly upright with a defiant assumption of wakefulness, 'why do you take so long to come when I call?'" (126). Refusing to acknowledge her descent into sleep, Polly pretends to have been awake, accusing Dinah of neglect. Polly's failure to admit to snoozing exemplifies how white people indulged in having Black servants watch over their resting bodies while hypocritically resenting them for any possible slip in hypervigilance.

Chesnutt disrupts white sleep in a postwar South to disabuse white northerners' of the romantic view of the region as all nostalgia, escape, and leisure, a place where one can sleep and be lazy while others do the work. With nearly every tale, Julius succeeds in violating John's rest. At the end of "Po' Sandy," John is "startled . . . out of an incipient doze" when Annie awakens him in the night (*Conjure* 22). Julius's tale centers on the enslaved Sandy, who suffers from exhaustion because he is constantly transported between his master's many plantations. Eventually, he asks his wife, Tenie, to conjure him, telling her: "I wisht I wuz a tree, er a stump, er a rock, er sump'n w'at could stay on de plantation fer a w'ile" (17). She grants his wish and turns him into a pine tree. Later, when the master's wife requests a new kitchen, Sandy the tree is chopped down and sawed into construction lumber to complete the build. Before hearing Sandy's story, Annie had plans to take over that same kitchen, but she ultimately decides against it. In digesting the meaning of Julius's tale, Annie is compelled to awaken her husband and share with him her new understanding. Upon rumination, Annie realizes that the story provides insight into capitalist consumption and the exploitation of Black labor. By appealing to Annie as the more sympathetic reader (see Gilligan), Julius forces his moral on John in so personal a way that it invades his precious sleep.

As the tales progress, John develops the daily routine of a plantation-owning white person, and by the last story, "Hot-Foot Hannibal" (1898), John is introduced as a trope of the sleepy southerner. Indulging in a midday nap on his piazza, he is rudely awakened by a loud argument between his sister-in-law and her southern fiancé. He takes offense and worries over this intrusion, revealing how inviolable John believes his sleep to be. John's midday nap recalls Mr. Covey, the plantation owner in Douglass's autobiography, who "would spend the most of his afternoons in bed" (*Narrative* 6). Chesnutt recalls Mr. Covey's "ministrations" in his biography of Douglass, which forced on the slave a "lack of sufficient time in which to eat or to sleep" (*Frederick* 17). John's napping reflects an entitlement to rest that enslavers practiced daily. Jacobs, too, articulates the sleep hypocrisy exhibited by white southerners. She remembers her aunt Nancy's enslaver, Mrs. Flint, who obsessed over Nancy's diligent attendance at her nightly repose: "Mrs. Flint . . . had ruined [Nancy's] health by years of incessant, unrequited toil, and broken rest" (221). One requirement was that Nancy sleep nearby on the floor. Upon Nancy's death, Mrs. Flint even requested that they be buried side by side so that Nancy might stand guard over her eternal slumber. Protecting the sleep of the mistress was so entrenched in the customs of antebellum slavery that even in wartime, as Washington recalls in *Up from Slavery*, enslaved men guarded over their sleeping mistresses: "Any one attempting to harm 'young Mistress' or 'old Mistress' during the night would have had to cross the dead body of the slave to do so" (13). White enslavers enacted surveillance over their captives every night while simultaneously expecting those same individuals to diligently watch over their sleep.

In the cultural moment in which Chesnutt was writing, there was widespread anxiety about the vulnerability of white sleep in a postslavery nation. In *Cedars*, just before visiting the judge, Tryon waits for Dr. Green in his office: "Finding the armchair wonderfully comfortable, and feeling the fatigue of his journey, he yielded to a drowsy impulse, leaned his head on the cushioned back of the chair, and fell asleep" (106). His nap is disturbed by a patient looking for Dr. Green. Tryon struggles to rouse himself: "Tryon was in that state of somnolence in which one may dream and yet be aware that one is dreaming. . . . The shock was sufficient to disturb Tryon's slumber, and he struggled slowly back to consciousness." When he learns the skin color of the caller, he feels "a momentary touch of annoyance that a negro woman should have intruded herself into his dream at its most interesting point" (107). Nestled in the doctor's cozy office, Tryon is taken aback by a Black individual's ability not only to interrupt but also to "shock" and "disturb" him while resting.

Chesnutt's caricatures lampoon tendencies by white authors to thematize the threat of Black invasion. For instance, *The Leopard's Spots* (1902), the first installment in Thomas Dixon's Ku Klux Klan trilogy, is replete with white characters who cannot sleep for fear of Black invasion and retribution. At one point, white South Carolinians gather to pray "for deliverance from the ruin that threatened the state under the dominion of . . . the negroes": "In many places they . . . held all-night watches and prayer meetings. . . . About ten o'clock in the morning, pale and haggard from a sleepless night of prayer and thought, the Preacher arose to address the people" (93–94). Henry James's canon also includes evidence of racist anxieties like those expressed in Dixon's work. For example, halfway through *The Bostonians* (1886) the protagonist, Basil Ransom, suggests to Miss Birdseye that she "ought to come down South. . . . In that languid air you would doze deliciously!" The old woman disagrees, retorting, "I have been down South . . . , and I can't say [the Negroes] let me sleep very much; they were always round after me! . . . I couldn't think of anything else" (215). These turn of the century white anxieties reflect lingering concerns held by enslavers long before the war. Nat Turner's slave rebellion, for example, serves as a historical impetus for nighttime anxiety among southern white people. In August 1831, Turner and other enslaved rebels used the cover of night to slaughter enslavers throughout Southampton County, Virginia. Fears of being murdered in their sleep led other enslavers to further restrict the liberties of both enslaved and free Black people in the aftermath of the massacre. In Charleston, for instance, wealthy landowners encircled their homes with chevaux-de-frise—wrought iron fences topped with spears—to prevent marauding Black people from murdering them in their sleep (Kytle and Roberts, prelude). Despite numerous precautions, the fear of Black violence on sleeping white bodies was ever present in the antebellum South. In a postwar setting, white southerners worried that Black communities—empowered by abolition—would use the cover of night and the vulnerability of sleep as opportunities to attack.

Another popular novel at the turn of the century, Albion Tourgee's *A Fool's Errand* (1879), reverses the anxieties expressed in Dixon's and James's works. It reveals how white supremacist violence prevented southern Black people from attaining rest. Tourgee's protagonist, Comfort Servosse, is a carpetbagger whose efforts to advance Black civil rights in North Carolina are constantly stymied by white supremacy. Like Annie in the "Uncle Julius" tales, Servosse relocates to the South to improve his symptoms of neurasthenia. After settling into a small community similar to Chesnutt's fictional

Patesville, Servosse uncovers the dark side of southern life during Reconstruction. Halfway through the novel, Servosse cites a newspaper account of the disappearance of John Walters, a Black politician, which read: "The niggers of Rockford are in tribulation, but the white people of the good old county will sleep easier" (185). Later, Servosse recounts the discovery that Walters was being held in the courthouse: "The colored people . . . were sure their lost leader was within—dying or dead, they knew not which. They called him by name, but knew he could not answer. None slept of the colored people: they waited, watched, and mourned" (192–93). In Tourgee's novel, white southerners can only rest easy when African Americans are plagued with fear. Whereas the white people in Dixon's and James's stories lose sleep over the fear of abstract Black aggression, those in *A Fool's Errand* "sleep easier" only after the murder of a community leader inflicts anxiety and sleeplessness on the Black community.

Toward the end of Dixon's *The Leopard's Spots*, the protagonist, Gaston, boards a sleeper car bound for Atlanta in search of his romantic interest, Sallie, described as "a daughter of the old fashioned South" (xi). Gaston consults the porter, whose speech is presented in the Black southern vernacular characteristic of plantation fiction. Gaston demands entry to Sallie's sleeper car to awaken her, but the porter refuses: "Lordy boss, I cain do dat. Hit ergin de rules" (295). The porter as protector of the sleeping southern belle, Dixon implies, is the proper role for post-Reconstruction southern Black people. In Chesnutt's tales, John similarly views the rail system as a post-Reconstruction means for redefining Black labor roles. "The Conjurer's Revenge," written in 1889 and featured as the fourth story in the *Conjure* collection, opens with John boasting of the new railroad that will enable him to ship his produce north. Julius, meanwhile, is weary of the impact expanding railways will have on Black workers and alludes to efforts to keep white sleep inviolable (on trains) as dependent on the sleep deprivation of Black porters. Through his characteristic orality with its underlying subtext, Julius schools John on the railroad's exploitation of Black labor. He implies that to generate enough shippable product, John will need to purchase an additional horse for plowing. When John replies that he would rather purchase a mule, Julius tells him: "I doan lack ter dribe a mule. I's alluz afeared I mought be imposin' on some human creetur; eve'y time I cuts a mule wid a hick'ry, 'pears ter me mos' lackly I's cuttin' some er my own relations, er somebody e'se w'at can't he'p deyse'ves" (*Conjure* 24). John evinces little understanding of the mule metaphor in Julius's tale, but, as one of the editors of the authoritative texts points out, "as symbols of agricultural life in the South, mules have been historically associated in US culture with enslaved African American laborers, often to racist ends" (24). Chesnutt associates the mule metaphor with the new railroad, a connection that suggests the mass employment of African American men as railroad porters at the turn of the century. Like mules forced to bear heavy loads, porters were required to cart around the possessions of white travelers. And on Pullman sleeper cars, porters also had to diligently protect the privacy of snoozing passengers.

More broadly, Chesnutt correlates plantation farming and railroad expansion with objectified Black labor to highlight the limited professional opportunities for Black southerners in the postwar period: railroad work or sharecropper tenancies. One represented (literal) mobility, the other (indentured) stasis, but neither greatly exceeded the exploitative conditions Black southerners endured during slavery. For porters, prolonged sleep deprivation was typical: they were granted no space for sleeping and were often forced to go days on end with little to no rest. According to Alan Derickson, "From its founding in 1867, [the] Pullman [Company] hired only African American porters for its sleeping cars" (87). Over the next forty years, Pullman continued to employ Black men with little to no protection under labor laws. Citing the 1907 Hours of Service Act, Derickson notes that legislation did not protect railroad porters "because neither Congress nor the Interstate Commerce Commission considered their work essential to the safety of the traveling public" (88). Derickson refers to a 1901 account from a Pullman conductor, who "estimated that [porters] got four or fewer hours sleep per night" and expressed admiration for a particular porter's "ability to keep wide awake when he is a living corpse from want of sleep" (90). Not only were Black porters required to function on little to no sleep, but they were also deprived of private sleeping quarters and were expected instead to "sleep in public places, mainly in the men's lounges and restrooms of the sleeping cars" (85). Despite working on trains composed of sleeper cars, Black service workers were relegated to taking brief snatches of rest in bustling shared spaces.

For Black workers who remained in the South, attaining one's own space to sleep was also a challenge. Whereas Pullman porters were expected to snooze in public spaces, Black southerners shared cramped quarters or had no home at all. They also found little respite in sleeping outdoors due to the vagrancy laws that escalated in the years after Reconstruction. In his reading of the "Uncle Julius" tales, Jeffrey Myers notes that "in the late nineteenth century, plantation owners, . . . of an increasingly industrialized South, benefitted from a convict-lease system, where inmates, often convicted of nothing more than 'vagrancy,' labored under essentially slave conditions" (7). Within Chesnutt's fiction, Peter's suffering in *The Colonel's Dream* most acutely exposes the effects of both railroad labor and vagrancy laws. Upon returning to his hometown in North Carolina, the novel's white protagonist, Henry, encounters Peter, a formerly enslaved man from his childhood plantation. Peter recounts his life since their separation, describing his work as a "railroad contractor . . . until overwork had laid him up" (28). Later, the old man is arrested for vagrancy and auctioned off as a convict laborer. Fortunately, Henry purchases Peter's labor in order to provide him with shelter and other provisions not afforded to the other poor souls sold off to landowning southern white people. Thus, railroad exploitation and vagrancy laws exemplify the many methods employed by white elites to force Black southerners into Brodhead's articulation of a "new cult of efficiency and productivity" (*Cultures* 202), which entailed the deprivation of personal restoration—particularly regarding time and space—for African Americans in the decades following Reconstruction.

Conclusion

At the outset of the twentieth century, the cultural phenomenon of adapting to less sleep became a sign of masculine strength in the urban North. As I mention in my introduction, Booker T. Washington joined Thomas Edison in emblematizing Derickson's "heroic wakefulness" (5). In the previous chapter, I suggest that Edison did not completely discount sleep. Instead, he advocated attaining rest only as necessary to carry out one's work: indulgence in "unproductive rest" was a threat to white masculinity (Derickson 5). Washington's particular doctrine of sleep discipline, on the other hand, sought to counter stereotypes of Black lethargy, which, as I have shown, only became more entrenched after slavery was abolished. Unlike Washington, Chesnutt subtly suggests that Black southerners should elevate their own bodily needs over the demands of the cultural and industrial clock. Like Solomon in "Mars Jeems's Nightmare" (who feeds a mystical sweet potato to the somnambulant sleeper), Chesnutt proffers conjuration to his readers so that they may awaken from his nightmarish tales of overwork, exhaustion, and internment with a newfound understanding of racial exploitation. Through Uncle Julius's storytelling, Chesnutt aims to conjure a white audience at large. His tales subvert the stereotypes propagated by nineteenth-century pseudoscience, as he argues against the "racial" characteristics attributed to African Americans, showing that these supposed traits instead evolved from the deprivation of enslaved Black people's most basic human needs, such as sleep, food, and familial connection. Moreover, Chesnutt shows the interconnections between these needs, with the enslaved forced to substitute one for the other. Thus, the conditions of antebellum slavery forced Black southerners into states of lethargy, starvation, and social isolation. While Chesnutt satirizes the racism of white medicine in "A Deep Sleeper," he also reveals the harsh realities of sleep deprivation and the cult of productivity in "Mars Jeems's Nightmare."

Chesnutt is attuned to what Michael Greaney calls the "geography of sleep" (6). This attentiveness is evident in the sleeper himself—such as Skundus, who could "sleep in de fiel'. . . . He could sleep in de sun er sleep in de shade. He could lean upon his hoe en' sleep. He went ter sleep walk'n' 'long de road oncet, . . . he oncet went ter sleep while he wuz in swimmin'" (*Conjure* 45)—as well as in the sleeping space, which in the enslaved quarters of "Mars Jeems's Nightmare" is filled with sounds of dreadful "mo'nin' en groanin'" (95). In addition to studying "how spaces are designed, adapted or even appropriated for sleep," Greaney explains that a "particular focus of scholarship in this field has been on the unspoken rules and informal systems that govern relations and interactions between sleepers and non-sleepers in any given society" (6). Chesnutt's enslaved and indentured characters are "non-sleepers" who are forced to adapt to meager sleep spaces and capitulate to sleep in undesirable or unsafe environments. With these renderings, Chesnutt imbues his tales with historical reality, a fact evident by the many testimonies in nineteenth-century slave narratives.

Writing in his journal in May 1880, Chesnutt explains: "The object of my writings would be not so much the elevation of the colored people as the elevation of the whites. . . . The Negro's part is to prepare himself for recognition and equality, and it is the province of literature to open the way for him to get it—to accustom the public mind to the idea; to lead people out, imperceptibly, unconsciously, step by step, to the desired state of feeling" (*Journals* 140). Andrews reads "A Deep Sleeper" as likewise imposing a lesson of patient understanding on the reader: "The proverbial laziness of the black man is a ploy by which to outlast the more impatient white man. . . . Only an acute reader (perhaps not even [Chesnutt's editor Walter Hines] Page himself) would detect these thematic undercurrents. On the surface, the general reader . . . would only find a story of a slave's improbable triumph over a rather dull-witted and credulous master" (33). The rejection of "A Deep Sleeper" for inclusion in the *Conjure* collection, Andrews implies, was a result of Page's impatient misreading of the tale and a reflection of Chesnutt's contemporary readership at large. As new readers of Chesnutt's tales, we must embrace the patience the stories impose on us, taking the time to thoroughly comprehend Julius's layered and complex storytelling. Only then can we begin to glimpse the suffering long endured by African Americans throughout the history of the US South, and the intensification of that suffering through medical and scientific stereotypes of Black embodiment.

CHAPTER 3

"A Great Blaze of Electric Light"

Illuminating Sleeplessness in Edith Wharton's
The House of Mirth

> She had not imagined that such a multiplication of
> wakefulness was possible: her whole past was reenacting
> itself at a hundred different points of consciousness.
> Where was the drug that could still this legion of
> insurgent nerves? The sense of exhaustion would have
> been sweet compared to this shrill beat of activities;
> but weariness had dropped from her as though some
> cruel stimulant had been forced into her veins.
> —Edith Wharton, *The House of Mirth*

In her 1898 home decor guidebook *The Decoration of Houses*, written in collaboration with architect Ogden Codman Jr., Edith Wharton scrutinizes the emergence of imitation "bric-à-brac" and domestic electricity (184). Lecturing on the "unhealthiness of sleeping in a room with stuff hangings," she maintains that "dust-collecting upholstery and knick-knacks" contradict the bedroom's purpose as a resting space (70, 165). She also critiques the artificially lit home, declaring that "nothing has done more to vulgarize interior decoration than [electric light], which . . . has taken from our drawing-rooms all air of privacy" (126). Such a vexation is reflected in *The House of Mirth* (1905) when Mrs. Peniston, upon being introduced to the reader, frets over a partially uncovered window. Because she has an electrically lit front room, she bemoans her maid's accidental exposure of artificial illumination through "the streak of light under one of the blinds" (84). An artificially lit home is even more embarrassing for Mrs. Peniston's niece and ward, the protagonist of the novel, Lily Bart: "Seated under the cheerless blaze of the drawing-room chandelier—Mrs. Peniston never lit the lamps unless there was 'company'—Lily seemed to watch her own figure retreating down vistas of neutral-tinted dulness" (80). All distinction of decorative expression is achromatized by the harsh glare of electricity, leaving Lily's future to be housed in a home of "neutral-tinted dulness." For Lily, Mrs. Peniston's reliance on electricity represents social inferiority. She finds it distressing to live amid the vulgarity of artificial light and is plagued by electricity's intrusion into her private life. The bedroom is where she most manifests such anxieties. Throughout the novel, Lily obsesses over the impossibility of attaining restful sleep in subpar sleeping quarters.

Wharton's aversion to festooned bedrooms and twenty-four-hour light fixtures illuminates her critique of society's devaluation of both sleep and its designated spaces. Thomas Edison, famous for his light bulb innovation, personifies the impact electric light had on American sleep practices. In 1895 he claimed that "people do not need several hours of continuous sleep, and that a few minutes, or an hour, of unconscious rest now and then is all that is required. . . . The habit of sleep was formed before the era of artificial light when people had no other way of spending hours in the darkness" (qtd. in Derickson 10). As mentioned in the introduction, Edison saw no need to sleep more than absolutely necessary, and he thought that retiring to the bedroom ran the risk of overindulgence. Instead, Edison encouraged professional and social activity throughout the day and night. He advocated for brief naps, either erect or seated, amid ongoing activity. Contrary to Wharton's appreciation of private sleep spaces, Edison's "manly wakefulness" deemphasized such a necessity (Derickson 5), promoting a myth that the mind—via sociocultural practices—could overpower the body's physiological dependence on routine rest.

In line with Victorian gendering of public and private spaces, Wharton's *The Decoration of Houses* provides a feminine antithesis to Edison's "manly wakefulness" in the workplace. Wharton correlates electric luminescence with arenas of municipality and transport, and its candlelit counterpart with the private and domestic: "In passageways and offices, electricity is of great service; but were it not that all 'modern improvements' are thought equally applicable to every condition of life, it would be difficult to account for the adoption of a mode of lighting which makes the salon look like a railway-station" (126). Wharton characterizes artificial light as a complement to the constant commotion of "passageways" and "rail-way station[s]," and aligns herself with Edison in relating electricity to industry. Unlike Edison, however, Wharton reveals in *The House of Mirth* the dangerous toll an electrifying and highly mobile lifestyle can have on the private interiors of the home and the intimate practice of sleep. Moreover, she anticipates concerns about what Michael Greaney defines as the "geography of sleep," which, "having been written off in some quarters as a non-subject, . . . [but] is now an emerging field of interest, . . . question[s] . . . how spaces are designed, adapted or even appropriated for sleep" (6).

In *The House of Mirth*, perpetual wakefulness does not result from or facilitate a healthy, productive lifestyle, nor is it something the body can endure for long. The novel critiques the Edisonian cult of wakefulness as defined by Alan Derickson by exploring how modern innovation and shifting socialities interrupt bodily rest, something best exemplified in the moments before Lily's death: "She felt so profoundly tired that she thought she must fall asleep at once; but as soon as she had lain down every nerve started once more into separate wakefulness. It was as though a great blaze of electric light had been turned on in her head, and her poor little anguished self shrank and cowered in it, without knowing where to take refuge" (250). This passage reveals the frayed nerves that result from Lily's destructive cultural surroundings. Despite the darkness of her bedroom, artificial brightness pervades Lily's headspace and prevents her enervated body from attaining the most basic human need: restful sleep.

Much Wharton scholarship reveals the author's reticence toward a society centered on technologically enhanced ways of living. Carol Baker Sapora, for instance, emphasizes the "conspicuousness" of artificial lighting in Wharton's domestic spaces, noting that electricity "first served only those who could afford the costly installation" (268). Sapora identifies these early home installments of electricity as a form of Thorstein Veblen's "conspicuous consumption." As detailed in chapter 1, Veblen's theory defined a turn of the century trend in which elites asserted upper-class status through overt displays of consumptive leisure and nonproductive social activity. Like Henry James's Roderick Hudson, Lily is only a liminal member of the leisure class. Just as Roderick depends on Rowland to maintain his class status, Lily relies on the generosity of her female patrons to keep herself afloat. Veblen's socioeconomic lens is employed specifically in *Mirth* studies to understand the effect that a milieu centered on "conspicuous consumption" has on the socially marginalized Lily. Wai-Chee Dimock, whose foundational study focuses on the inescapability of the marketplace, claims: "The fluidity of currencies in *The House of Mirth* . . . attests to the reduction of human experience to abstract equivalents for exchange" (784). Dimock argues that Lily's thematic deterioration reflects Wharton's condemnation of a society that would commodify both human bodies and social performances. Indeed, Lily's most coveted items for trade are her beauty and youthful energy. However, she comes to realize that her prized resources are fast-waning currency in a society newly shaped by technological innovation. Martha Banta, identifying electricity as one of Wharton's "vivid historical markers," observes that electric light "is a threat to . . . Lily Bart, whose 'last asset' is a waning physical beauty more kindly set off by 'candle-flames'" (62). Furthermore, Lori Merish notes that *Mirth*'s upper-class female characters succeed only through their display of feminine beauty and masculine wealth. Consequently, Lily's avoidance of marriage—her desire for an identity beyond the ornamental—imperils her social standing.

Another factor in Lily's decline can be found in her bloodline. Barbara Hochman explores the failings that result from what Wharton describes as Lily's "slowly accumulated past [which] lives in the blood" (229). Jennie A. Kassanoff—referring to Laura Otis's notion of "organic memory," in which "repeated patterns of sensations, whether of the recent or distant past, had left traces in the body"—focuses on Lily's declaration to her friend Gerty that she has inherited the traits of "some wicked pleasure-loving ancestress" (Otis 3; Kassanoff 60). Otis's concept partially underscores the significance of Lily's lengthy recollections of her lineage, specifically her parents' ineptitudes and failures, which she comes to see in herself. What is central to *Mirth* scholarship is Wharton's curiosity about the cultural, environmental, and inherited factors that shape and, in Lily's case, condemn an individual.

This chapter draws from analyses of Lily's many forms of indebtedness—economic, social, and biological—to focus particularly on her accrual of sleep debt. This latter deficit has not been a central focus within *Mirth* criticism, yet it inhibits Lily from fully repaying her social and financial debts (articulated by Dimock) or those of a biological nature (separately traced by Hochman and Kassanoff). Preserving her upper-class membership incessantly commands Lily's time and energy and deprives her of restful sleeping hours. Swayed by the American ethos of efficiency and productivity and the machinelike rhythms of modernity, Lily begins to consider sleep itself a weakness. Unlike her protagonist, however, Wharton clearly cares for sleep. Her detailed renderings of Lily's various sleep acts, some of which occur beyond Lily's consciousness, portray sleep as both biological impulse and physiological necessity. Discussing Lily's string of marital rejections, Donna M. Campbell notes Lily's "curiously maladaptive habit of procrastination and refusal," phrasing that also connotes Lily's treatment of sleep, for she constantly resists or ignores bodily fatigue ("Bitter" 249). Numerous critics, Campbell included, have commented on the significance of Carry Fisher's perceptive description of Lily: "She works like a slave preparing the ground and sowing her seed; but the day she ought to be reaping the harvest she over-sleeps herself or goes off on a picnic" (147–48; see Hochman;

94   CHAPTER 3

Gerard; Restuccia). The odd verb phrase "over-sleeps herself" is not simply a throwaway line in a moral parable for the Gilded Age, such as an updated "The Ant and the Grasshopper" or "The Tortoise and the Hare." Rather, Wharton's choice of reflexive verb emphasizes Carry Fisher's presumption that Lily's very act of sleeping is both a bodily indulgence and a social impediment. Therefore, I propose that the disruptive action of "over-sleep" reflects Wharton's deeper physiological and philosophical concerns about the consequences of modernity's cult of wakefulness. It is through Lily's sleep deprivation, which ultimately leads to her fatal overdose of chloral, that Wharton reveals her critique of a society that left no room for rest or regeneration.

Sleeplessness and Cultural Compulsion

Wharton's failure to singularly identify the traits that cause Lily's insomnia—whether they be genetically inherited or caused by her environment—echoes a similar gap in the period's debates over nature versus nurture. Prior to William Bateson's definition of "genetics" in 1909, turn of the century thinkers investigated inherited and environmental factors that rendered certain bodies ill-equipped for urban life. Laying the groundwork for what is now referred to as neurophysiology, medical studies began correlating the human body's bioelectric activity with external systems of electricity. The prominence of the War of Currents boosted debates over the safety of electrical grids and augmented public concern over electricity's interaction with fast-paced, urban lives.[1] Even with improvements in electrical safety at the start of the twentieth century, the medical community worried over the heterogeneous effects of electric light. Cultural historian Ernest Freeberg observes that "as Americans worked to realize all of electric light's possibilities, [they] saw that the light was . . . changing their relationship to the natural world, shaping the rhythm of their days and transforming their culture. . . . This new regime of intensified light energized some and exhausted others. Doctors warned that electricity's light disrupted sleep patterns" (7). Through Lily's private struggle with sleep and its phenomena, Wharton presents Lily's sleep dysfunction as idiosyncratic, something unique to her interactions within a technologically enmeshed society. Lily's secrecy in using chloral to escape her mind's "great blaze of electric light" is emblematic of her fear that sleep struggles equate to social oddity. Struggling to attain sleep was indeed a new concern in turn of the century society, as medical historian James Horne reflects: "Aids to better sleep abounded as did notions about what sleep was for" (208). Presentations of sleeplessness, which spurred medical classification and soporific dispensation, became a marker for those who failed to adapt to the modern world.

The period's codification of nervous disorders classified those "exhausted others" to whom sleep aids were prescribed. In his definition of neurasthenia, George Miller Beard observes that "one of the most constant symptoms . . . is wakefulness" and identifies sleep as "the best of all barometers of functional nervous disorder" (*Practical* 182). Beard confirms that neurasthenia "run[s] in families . . . [via] inheritance" but notes variations in neurasthenia's symptomatic sleep dysfunction: "Some neurasthenic patients can only sleep by night—never by day, however wearied. Others can sleep by day; often fall to sleep when they especially desire to keep awake, but at night toss in painful activity" (2, 45). Beard's inability to clearly delineate between nature and nurture recalls his theory of the degenerative artist-genius, discussed in chapter 1: although he suggests that neurasthenia is inherited, Beard cannot account for its varied effects on sufferers' sleep habits and implies that those factors could be environmental. Thus, Lily's neurasthenic disposition can be viewed as similar to Roderick Hudson's degenerative artistic genius, for both protagonists suffer from inherited deficiencies as well as sociocultural factors.

Despite the period's scientific shortcomings, Wharton was nonetheless influenced by turn of the century investigations into sleep, which preceded modern studies in sleep medicine. Lily's sleeplessness is symptomatic of the twenty-first-century concept of sleep debt, defined as the "cumulative build-up of sleep pressure, especially from inadequate recovery sleep over multiple days" (Van Dongen et al., 6). "Recovery sleep" specifically refers to the achievement of proficient sleeping hours per the body's natural rhythms. Modern sleep studies have concluded that adjusting to sleep debt is impossible, for the human body is ill-equipped to handle a prolonged sleep deficit, which can lead to serious health consequences, including death (Wells and Vaughn 235). Even now, sleep studies focus on the implications inherent in American culture's reorganization of time, which reflects values of industriousness and technological interaction over an adherence to biological sleep patterns. The American Academy of Sleep Medicine, for example, has dedicated much of its post-1990 sleep education efforts to understanding the impact technology has on American sleep cycles, as well as the effects that biological sleep rhythms have on the performance of night-shift laborers (*AASM*). Thus, Wharton's novel serves as a literary testament to contemporaneous investigations into sleeplessness, including those that remain central to medical research today.

Lily's accrual of sleep debt is evident by the novel's second chapter. After retiring from a late night of card playing, she is acutely aware of her precarity as an unwed twenty-nine-year-old woman. She is "conscious of having to pay her way" to attain Judy Trenor's hospitality, with "pay" referring more to her relinquishment of time than actual money (23). Although she does lose coins to cards, her primary duty to is to entertain fellow guests, and Lily attributes her visible signs of aging and her financial deficiency to this exhausting subjugation. Examining her reflection in the mirror, Lily "was frightened by two little lines near her mouth, faint flaws in the smooth curve of the cheek. 'Oh, I must stop worrying!' she exclaimed. 'Unless it's the electric light'" (25). Lily frets over electric light's exaggerating effects, fearing its negative impact on her image of marriageability.

She also worries about her risky financial choices, as she is dismayed by her reckless gambling. With only twenty dollars left, Lily "fancied that she must have been robbed" and only convinces herself otherwise by exhaustively recounting her finances: "Her head was throbbing with fatigue, and she had to go over the figures again and again" (24). In her younger years, Lily resisted gambling, understanding it to be dangerously addictive. However, after she began routinely playing, "the passion had grown in her . . . and the increasing exhilaration of the game drove her to risk higher stakes at each fresh venture" (24). On this night, Lily risks too much and plays terribly. According to a neuroscientific study of sleep debt, sleep deficits negatively affect visual cognition, causing "a marked decline in viewing-task performance [that] is proportional to individual vulnerability to sleep deprivation" (Motomura et al.). Another study found that sleep debt is a leading cause of reckless and addictive behavior and presents a range of symptoms, including "fatigue, irritability, concentration difficulties, disorientation, changes in mood, visual hallucinations, and paranoid thoughts" (Wells and Vaughn 235). In this scene, Lily presents many of these symptoms, such as paranoia, fatigue, and difficulty concentrating. Her economic anxieties match her mental paranoia and bodily fatigue, all of which combine to strain her financial calculations and complicate her social maneuvering. Although Wharton lacked a twenty-first-century lexicon for symptoms of sleep deprivation, the author uncannily captures the bodily repercussions of prolonged wakefulness in ways that precede later scientific discoveries.

Lily's internal conflict—between anxious worry and physical exhaustion—brings about concentration difficulties and paranoid thoughts. These symptoms of sleeplessness prevent her from falling into a restful sleep state. After she finally settles into bed, her cognitive descent into troubled sleep functions as a narrative device to inform the reader of her tumultuous past: "She remembered how her mother after they had lost their money used to say to her with a kind of fierce vindictiveness: 'But you'll get it all back . . . with your face'" (25). Lily's wrinkles—emphasized by electric light—are

"A Great Blaze of Electric Light"   97

detrimental to her mother's definition of success, which hinges on youthful attractiveness. The pressures forced on her by her mother are like those endured by Christina Light in *Roderick Hudson* (1875), who by the age of ten already felt like "a little wrinkled old woman" (227). Like Christina, Lily grows angsty when thinking of her mother, as it "roused a whole train of association, and she lay in the darkness reconstructing the past out of which her present had grown" (25). Despite the comfort of her Bellomont bedroom, Lily cannot calm her nerves for restful sleep. Instead, a "train of association" flickers through her anxious mind, recollecting her past and illuminating her present predicament.

The following day, Lily's "state of dependence" is reinforced when she awakens to an early morning summons from Judy, which prevents Lily from sleeping into the afternoon as do the other female guests (34). Lily's indebtedness to Judy highlights a particular aspect of leisure-class culture. According to Veblen, leisure takes on a specific definition within the context of female conspicuous consumption: "The leisure rendered by the wife . . . is, of course, not a simple manifestation of idleness or indolence. It almost invariably occurs disguised under some form of work or household duties or social amenities, which . . . serve little or no ulterior end beyond showing that she does not occupy herself with anything that is gainful or that is of substantial use" (81–82). At the start of the novel, Lily finds herself carrying out "social amenities" at Judy's command. In this way, Lily furthers Judy's leisurely status by performing the tasks Judy would typically do herself. After Lily "took a day off" to be with Selden, Judy takes "nearly an hour to admonish her friend," whose "gambling debt" has scared away the ideal suitor: wealthy bachelor Percy Gryce (60–61). The purpose of Judy's chastisement is to reproach Lily "for missing the opportunity to eclipse her rivals," but Lily senses from Judy's words her "mounting tide of indebtedness" (62).

In *The Ethnography of Manners*, Nancy Bentley observes that within the context of Gilded Age New York society, "Wharton revises and exhibits manners as the essential, sometimes disguised, rites of social cohesion and punishment rather than as inherent standards of propriety" (2). Lily's social subjugation results in her being forced to perform duties that no one else desires to do. One of those chores is to pick up Gus Trenor from the train station, a task previously delegated to Carry Fisher. Carry's divorcée status allows her to spend time with, and receive money from, married men. For the unwed Lily, however, it is taboo for her to engage in either activity. Despite the risk, Lily accepts Gus's offer to "make a handsome sum of money for her without endangering the small amount she possessed" (67). In her discussion of the naturalist trope of the "modern young woman,"

Jennifer Fleissner defines one of its conventions as "compulsive behavior," which condemns its character even more so than does determinism, for it "indicate[s] more of a participation, even an investment, in one's own reduction from agent to automaton" (*Women* 9, 39). Given the distinctly exhaustive nature of compulsive behavior, Fleissner articulates the ways in which Lily's sleep deprivation correlates with her cultural compulsions. Indeed, during her exchange with Gus, Lily exhibits symptoms of sleeplessness, specifically those that enhance one's inclination for risk and the avoidance of undesirable truths (Wells and Vaughn 235). Lily evinces her concession to recklessness the previous night when she delays reckoning with her gambling losses until after leaving the card table. She similarly ignores Gus's presumptive "lean[ing] a little nearer and rest[ing] his hand reassuringly on hers" to distance herself from the reality of the situation: "The haziness enveloping the transaction served as a veil for her embarrassment" (68). Yet, she is aware that new risks are now necessary given her advanced age and decreasing social status. At a younger age, as Lily recalls the previous night, she could bask in the splendid lives of her friends without having to partake in the production of such events. Now, however, with her having surpassed "marrying age," her increasing marginality forces her to take on a string of duties: "Now she was beginning to chafe at the obligations it imposed, to feel herself a mere pensioner on the splendor which had once seemed to belong to her" (23). Despite such self-awareness, Lily views her entanglement with Gus through a diffusely lit haze, thereby passively avoiding its scandalous insinuations. This dreamlike disassociation, which removes Lily's agency from the ordeal, accords with her symptoms of fatigued sleeplessness.

Lily's sleep debt intensifies alongside the sinister nature of her financial dealings with Gus, who eventually tricks her into a late-night house call. Upon discerning his motive, Lily rejects his request for a few minutes of her time. To her protestations, he viciously retorts: "I'll take 'em. And as many more as I want" (113). Gus's aggression, verging on attempted rape, suddenly ceases at the scene's conclusion, and the narrator presents Gus's savagery as the result of his own silent struggle with sleep deprivation: "The hand of inherited order, plucked back the bewildered mind which passion had jolted from its ruts. Trenor's eyes had the haggard look of the sleep-walker waked on a deathly ledge" (117). Such a figure recalls the naturalist inner brute who remains, if only temporarily, masked by civility. Furthermore, the juxtaposition of Gus's impulsive desire and "the hand of inherited order" parallels the oxymoronic sleepwalker, whose sleeping body resists rest and, instead, wanders around perilously. Although Darwinian instinct and social civility

"A Great Blaze of Electric Light"   99

are clearly at war within Gus, the text obscures what causes him to ultimately withdrawal from Lily. Hochman notes that this scene, reinforcing Lily's "slowly accumulated past that lives in the blood," links Gus's ancestry to "the norms of 'gentlemanly' behavior that . . . reassert their hold on Trenor when he is about to rape Lily" (229). What Hochman leaves open for interpretation is the catalyst for Gus's malicious behavior. It is difficult to discern whether he is motivated by affective response, instinctual impulse, or exhausted weakness. The scene's foreshadowing, however, is apparent. It reinforces how sleeplessness saps self-control. It also conjoins Fleissner's compulsive behavior—defined as an individual's exhaustive and futile strivings, such as Gus's pursuit of Lily—with that of the perilously meandering sleepwalker.

Later in the novel and upon leaving Selden's apartment for the last time, Lily embodies the image of a sleepwalker suddenly awakened to the physical experience of exhaustion. Unaware of the street's activity, she feels as if she were under sedation: "Lily walked on unconscious of her surroundings. She was still treading the buoyant ether which emanates from the high moments of life. But gradually it shrank from her and she felt the dull pavement beneath her feet. The sense of weariness returned with accumulated force, and for a moment she felt that she could walk no farther" (242). She takes shelter in Bryant Park, exhaustedly collapsing on a nearby bench: "She told herself she must not sit long. . . . But her will-power seemed to have spent itself." Unwilling to move, she asks herself: "What was there to go home to?" Sitting in the "glare of an electric street-lamp," Lily listens to the "roar of traffic in Forty-second Street." Oddly enough she senses more comfort for her tired body on the park bench than she expects to find in her "cheerless" boardinghouse bedroom, where the "silence of the night . . . may be more racking to tired nerves than the most discordant noises" (242). Lily's stimulated engagement with urbanity—its sounds of rapid transportation and buzzing electricity—provide her with a longed-for distraction and sense of rejuvenation. Aaron Worth claims that *Mirth* depicts the body as an "unmediated . . . communications network" and argues that Wharton blurs the boundaries between human nervous systems and external mechanical ones: "The movements of Lily's nerves, their 'throbbing,' 'tremors,' the messages sent and received by them . . . form a running motif . . . [that reveals] the danger of an anarchic network, whose center cannot hold, or can no longer govern" (100–101). Lily's biological and somatic drives for sleep conflict with her enmeshment in the "throbbing" and "tremors" of her modern, electrified environment. The park-bench scene suggests Lily's mental neglect of her exhausted body. Even after she emerges disoriented and exhausted from a sleepwalker-like trance, she would rather sit amid urban commotion than retire to her bedroom.

After Lily escapes Gus's late-night advances, the exhaustive aftereffects of trauma exacerbate her symptoms of sleeplessness and expose her bedtime anxieties. Cloistered in a cab, she closes her eyes and rests her head against the window. Yet, rather than find calmness in repose, Lily fancies that she is being chased by the furies of *Eumenides*. She hears the metallic thrashing of fury wings and—like Orestes, who in the night only "snatches an hour's repose"—believes the furies are "awake and the iron clang of their wings was in her brain" (117). Hochman speculates that the furies represent "the inescapability of Lily's tragic entanglements . . . [and] provide both the reader and Lily herself with a lens through which to focus Lily's experience" (228). In her dreamlike state, Lily imagines the furies as forces that aurally antagonize her mind and isolate her within "a place of darkness" (*House* 117). Her psychosomatic fantasies, or hallucinations, are symptomatic of sleep deprivation and are classified in modern medicine as parasomnia (see Pacheco). While Hochman notes that "Lily's own preoccupation with the furies is difficult to interpret" (229), I read these fear-ridden passages as Lily's lapsing in and out of a semi-dreaming state. As her adrenaline crashes, Lily exhibits the sensorial experiences of parasomnia's "hypnagogic reverie" (Goel et al.). This is a state of wakeful sleepiness that causes a range of olfactory hallucinations, something to which Lily testifies when she tells Gerty: "It must be awful to be sleepless—everything stands by the bed and stares" (131). Lily's personification of bedroom items exemplifies visual hypnagogia, which "occurs in the border between sleep and wakeful states, predominately before going to sleep. A person suffering from [this] has some breakdown in the boundaries between the dream state and wakefulness, with the former flowing through into the latter" (Gathercole 169). Lily's description may account for her conscious feeling of vulnerability to the undesired scrutiny of inanimate objects. In this situation, Lily's nervousness provokes her into a conscious surfacing during moments when she should be drifting into unconscious sleeping. Beard anticipates the notion of sleep paralysis— a disruption of REM sleep in which visual hypnagogia often occurs—when he observes that in "half-awakened moments at midnight, we are conscious of not having full possession of our powers to meet any attack or danger" (*Practical* 25).[2] By specifying that "the nervously exhausted man is always in this state" (25), Beard implies that a hypnagogic experience—outside normal midnight hours—is symptomatic of the sleep-deprived neurasthenic. Similarly, when Lily senses a threat in the "iron clang" of "fury wings," her body is snatching an unbidden moment of rest beyond her conscious awareness, which results in her experience of frightening parasomnia.

At the start of book 2, Lily again subjects herself to the whims of a wealthy couple, eventually renewing her sleep in a desperate effort to please her patrons. Having been invited by Bertha Dorset on a European cruise, Lily enjoys three months of waking late and indulging in the coastal luxuries of the Mediterranean seascape. Like Roderick, who flees to Baden to escape Rowland's controlling gaze and consequently sleeps as he likes, Lily achieves restorative rest during her respite from the "odious debt" she owes to Trenor and the increasing pressure to marry Sim Rosedale: "The accident of placing the Atlantic between herself and her obligations made them dwindle out of sight as if they had been milestones and she had travelled past them" (153). Yet despite having sailed away from her problems in New York, Lily faces imminent collision with a formidable Bertha Dorset. Dimock notes that "nowhere is the injustice of exchange more clearly demonstrated than on board the Sabrina. Lily's presence on the yacht is, as everyone recognizes, simply a business arrangement" (784). Lily's employment revolves around her ability to slyly divert the attention of Bertha's husband, George, while Bertha engages in an affair with the couple's other guest, Ned Silverton. In exchange, Lily is provided with her own lavish personal quarters on the yacht. As Bertha's charade becomes increasingly risky, Lily begins to lose sleep in her effort to remain perpetually attentive to both Bertha's and George's activities.

Lily succeeds in pulling her weight until Bertha's own prolonged wakefulness wreaks havoc on Lily's good fortune. After a social evening in Monaco, Bertha and Ned fail to return to the ship until morning, leaving George to speculate on Bertha's infidelity. Lily has no rejoinder to account for Bertha's "fatal lapse of hours" when she is confronted by the cuckolded husband (157). Lily, the reader learns, was asleep in bed. Rather than wait for Bertha at the train station on the night in question, she returned on her own. As the debacle unfolds, the narrative frames the Dorsets' actions—Bertha's imprudence and George's shame—as the storm that sinks Lily's ship. Try as she may, Lily cannot cultivate an excuse for Bertha. Instead, she tries to "guide and uplift" George with friendly encouragement (158). However, Lily's marginal status renders her a useless support system. She is left to suffer for Bertha's brashness: "If [George] clung to [Lily], it was not in order to be dragged up, but to feel some one floundering in the depths with him: he wanted her to suffer with him, not to help him suffer less" (158). After Bertha awakes in the early evening, Lily is dealt the final blow. According to Bertha, her nightlong absence was simply a result of Lily's burdensome behavior: "Having you so conspicuously on [George's] hands in the small hours . . . you're rather a big responsibility in such a scandalous place after midnight" (162). Bentley reads this scene as symbolic of the ways in which Lily is unable to compete with the forces of modernity. Bertha's reckless behavior betokens high-speed trains and rapid sailing ships: her married status secures her, while Lily remains a "body on the margins of the plans and power of the rich that . . . will take the force of the crash" (*Frantic* 156). Bertha uses her social power to punish Lily for sleeping as she pleases. Moreover, Bertha hypocritically identifies Lily's evening behavior as scandalous. Although Bertha is actually guilty of late-night escapades, Lily's embodiment of the cash-strapped, single woman makes her an easy scapegoat. Wielding gossip as her weapon, Bertha circulates the rumor that Lily is the "type" of woman to stay awake all hours of the night and partake in salacious behavior.

Lily's biological debt—her sleep deficit—is once more renewed. While dining among social elites and with a reporter present, Bertha announces that Lily may not return to the yacht. She easily blames her erroneous behavior on Lily since Bertha's "social credit," we later learn, "was based on an impregnable bank-account" (204). Tossed aside, Lily finds herself without a bed in the late Monaco evening. Selden anxiously tries to find her room and board, but Lily refuses to openly acknowledge the extent of her situation, joking that it is "too wet to sleep in the gardens" (170). The narrator highlights Lily's vulnerability here, as she is so near homelessness that she might be forced to sleep outside. Later, when her cousin Jack Stepney reluctantly takes her in, his condition that she not disturb his wife's sleep underscores the Victorian ideal of a woman's need for undisturbed sleep in the tranquil domestic space and emphasizes the impregnable sleep of characters more privileged than Lily.

Lost Time and Inherited Vulnerability

After Lily returns to New York, she experiences "long sleepless nights" as she yearns for the social security of women such as Stepney's wife (194). She vacillates between her suitors: an apologetic George Dorset and the opportunistic Sim Rosedale. Lily's destructive desire for marital wealth in book 1 occurs more ominously at the outset of book 2, leaving her once again to suffer from social disaster as she loses sleep over the prospect of poverty and social alienation. Despite her mental resistance to sleep, her exhausted body snatches bits of rest when it can, doing so beyond her awareness and warping her perception of time passing. According to Beard, "[neurasthenic] patients . . . generally sleep more than they believe; they say that they get no sleep, when they do perhaps lose themselves several hours. . . . It is impossible, as a rule, to convince such people that they sleep at all" (*Practical* 45). Beard's conclusion lends insight into Lily's fear of slippage from linear time.

For instance, during her flight from Gus, Lily rises above a tide of fitful sleep as she rests in the cab. She opens her eyes to an illuminated clock face, and the time frightens her: "Only half-past eleven—there were hours and hours left of the night! And she must spend them alone, shuddering sleepless on her bed" (117). Time suddenly seems minutely sensorial for Lily, who feels the "slow cold drip of the minutes on her head" (118). Lily's vivid imaginings and acute sensations throughout this passage match the myriad torturous, parasomnia-like symptoms enumerated in Beard's study: "troubled dreaming," "tossing and pitching about," "positive unrest," "different forms of morbid fear," "local chills," and "startings on falling to sleep" (106, 182). Wharton's evocation of a prolonged and shiver-inducing restlessness echoes Beard's terrifying manifestations of failed bedrest.

Lily's anxiety about time and sleep vacillates when she considers the possibility of attaining rest. In her exhaustive state, Lily feels plagued in her mind's eye by an electric "blaze" of light. Her visual renderings of external surroundings are warped and magnified. When Lily's cab passes bright streetlamps or blazing storefronts, these visions project nightmarish images in her sleep-deprived mind. Lily seeks comfort from Gerty and enters her friend's apartment "in a blaze of her misery . . . [and] blind to everything outside of it" (131). Hoping Gerty can alleviate her suffering, Lily attempts to articulate her frantic thoughts: "Can you imagine looking into your glass some morning and seeing a disfigurement—some hideous change that has come to you while you slept?" (131). Although Lily draws no explicit connection between "disfigurement" and aging here, previous consternation over her creasing face attests to such a concern; and, later in book 2, Lily confesses to Gerty: "I can see the lines coming in my face— the lines of worry and disappointment and failure! Every sleepless night leaves a new one—and how can I sleep, when I have such dreadful things to think about?" (207). Her fear of grotesque transformation during sleep is compounded by the despicable drabness of her room at Mrs. Peniston's. As Lily flees the Trenors' home, "She had a vision of herself lying on the black walnut bed—and the darkness would frighten her, and if she left the light burning the dreary details of the room would brand themselves forever on her brain. She had always hated her room at Mrs. Peniston's—its ugliness, its impersonality, the fact that nothing in it was really hers. To a torn heart uncomforted by human nearness a room may open almost human arms, and the being to whom no four walls mean more than any others, is, at such hours, expatriate everywhere" (118). Such incongruity anticipates the "double logic" that defines the human relationship to technology in the twenty-first century. As Lee Scrivner explains, "insomnia is . . . a fundamental paradox of being and willing, where, in willing to sleep, we express a will to be without will. This fundamental disconnect . . . mirrors technology's oft-cited 'double logic,' in which technologies enhance our lives and facilitate our wills, but also secretly subject us to new regimes of servitude" (11). Lily's fear of the darkness and her anxieties about the burning light provide a metaphorical framework for Scrivner's insomnia paradox, in which Lily refuses to acquiesce to sleep while simultaneously longing for it.

Having been made to feel utterly unsafe by Gus's advances, Lily realizes the precarity she faces in lacking a home space. Her sense of imminent danger is heightened by her need for sleep, a state that deprives her of vigilance over bodily safety or sexual chastity. Yet, she finds no solace in her room at Mrs. Peniston's, as it makes her feel so isolated that she imagines the room will brand itself forever on her brain. In this way, Lily's mind is a glass plate on which an image of dinginess and alienation is printed. The physicality of branding implies another possible physical transformation, in which Lily fears that if she remains in such a space, over time her aging face will reflect the drabness of the room itself. Together, Lily's aversions to bedrest become paradoxical, for although she resists the perturbations of parasomnia and slippage from linear time, she also fears the "dreadful things" that pervade her sleepless mind and the bodily deterioration that she anticipates from prolonged exhaustion.

In depicting a psychological slippage from time, Wharton echoes William James's experiments with psychical temporality. James's *The Principles of Psychology* (1890) probed the relationship between time and the human psyche and ascertained that "the life of the individual consciousness in time seems . . . to be an interrupted one" (198).[3] Specifically, James believed in sleep's potential to overtake a person unaware, so that, upon waking, one experiences an uncanny slippage of time. James posits the possibility that sleep's interruption of time "may exist where we do not suspect it, and even perhaps in an incessant and fine-grained form? This might happen, and yet the subject himself never know it. . . . We think we have had no nap, and it takes the clock to assure us that we are wrong" (200). By pinpointing microsleeps as potentially time warping, James's observation evinces the disruptive effect of Lily's own brief snatches of sleep on her perceived temporality. Gerty, for instance, is taken aback when Lily, after being expelled from the Gormers' circle, slips into a state of unconsciousness midway through animated chatter: "She leaned back for a moment, closing her eyes, and as she sat there, her pale lips slightly parted, and the lids dropped above her fagged brilliant gaze, Gerty had a startled perception of the change in her face—of the way in which an ashen daylight seemed suddenly to extinguish its artificial brightness. She looked up, and the vision vanished" (208). As Lily's physiological requirement for rest takes over, she loses consciousness. Her cultural compulsion to maintain an "artificial brightness" also slips, extinguishing from her face an internalized identification with electrified modernity.

Lily's microsleep occurs amid a dramatic monologue in which she recounts the social performances required of her to "live on the rich." After declaring that she "pays it by . . . always keeping herself fresh and exquisite and amusing," Lily dozes off. When she awakens, she mechanically resumes her speech, asking rhetorically: "It doesn't sound very amusing, does it?" (208). The irony of Lily's unconscious sleep act during her impassioned dialogue is overt, since she dozes off just as she is exposing the exhaustive nature of always "keeping herself fresh." Lily then glances at the clock and declares herself late to a meeting with Carry Fisher. Because Lily is unaware of her momentary descent into sleep, time vanishes from her perception, and, as Gerty observes, so too does her "artificial brightness" briefly dissipate. Lily relies on her "artificial brightness" as a power source for social eminence. Sleep, however, interrupts her automaton-like display as well as her regimented social schedule.

Lily's complicated perceptions of time and sleep are in part due to the conflicting worldviews she inherits from her parents. Bonnie Lynn Gerard suggests that Wharton presents in Lily a "'discontinuity' between 'what can be grasped'—materially, rationally—and 'what is felt to be meaningful' through some more elusive means of comprehension. Ironically, Lily imagines this discontinuity to be a matter of heredity and environment, as she reflects that she has inherited from her parents two opposing natures" (411). Lily's father presents to her a practical embodiment of routine and hard work, while her mother's elusiveness confounds her. Lily recalls that her mother's decisiveness served somehow to prolong her beauty, for she vividly remembers her mother's retention of a youthful appearance: "[Her mother] was as alert, determined and high in colour as if she had risen from an untroubled sleep" (27). Lily learned from her mother that sleeplessness is the antithesis of both beauty rest and self-assertion. However, Lily attributes her own self-perception, that of passivity and marginality, to her father:

> Ruling the turbulent element called home was the vigorous and determined figure of a mother still young enough to dance her ball-dresses to rags, while the hazy outline of a neutral-tinted father filled an intermediate space between butler and the man who came to wind the clocks. Even to the eyes of infancy, Mrs. Hudson Bart had appeared young; but Lily could not recall the time when her father had not been bald, slightly stooping,

with streaks of grey in his hair, and a tired walk. It was a shock to her to learn afterward that he was but two years older than her mother. (25–26)

Contrary to her mother's perpetual youthfulness, her father's appearance in Lily's memories is prematurely aged. Such a distinction is paralleled by the roles her parents play within her recollections of home. While her mother dominated the household, her father seemed no more privileged than a house servant.

Furthermore, her father's habitual movement, spatially and temporally, emphasizes his embodiment of a mechanical clock. In Lily's mind, her father's time was indebted to an obscure labor system with which he could not keep pace. This is like Henry James's depiction of Roderick Hudson— who shares his name with Lily's father—as a broken-down clock, unable to tick along steadily to Rowland's dictation of rhythmic production. Like Rowland, who grows increasingly disappointed in Roderick, Lily's mother, in her recollection, rejected her father following his financial and bodily ruin: "To his wife he no longer counted: he had become extinct when he ceased to fulfil his purpose" (28). As Lily's sense of social extinction grows, she associates her shortcomings with her father, perceiving herself as a continuation of his deficiencies. According to Fleissner, Lily internalizes her mother's final wish, whose "last adjuration to her daughter was to escape from dinginess if she could" (*Mirth* 31). Fleissner claims that it is "not only Lily's rootlessness but her own 'indefatigable' dancing and, indeed, her oscillatory movement through life [at] the bequest of Mrs. Hudson Bart . . . [that] Lily finds herself mimicking . . . in her own adulthood, where her financial and social dependence on others leads to . . . a genuine lack of decisiveness" (*Women* 197). Lily's vacillations merely alleviate certain debts while increasing others. Determined to escape her financial debt to Gus and her subsequent sleeplessness, she flees to Europe, only to fall into social ruin at the hands of Bertha Dorset. Upon returning to New York, Lily increases her sleep debt by keeping nighttime hours at the hotel with Mrs. Hatch. The focus of book 2, then, is to painstakingly detail Lily's ruination after failing to balance social demands with her biological need for sleep.

Lily's powerlessness in her bedroom—either to protect herself from the glare of surrounding objects or to provide herself with necessary rest— reflects the lack of agency her father exhibits in her childhood memories. At Gerty's, Lily's eyes "fell on the clock," and she exclaims, "How long the night is! And I know I shan't sleep tomorrow. Someone told me my father used to lie sleepless and think of horrors" (131). The clock is a reminder of her father, whose presence in her childhood was as remote and routine as "the man who came to wind the clocks." In contrast to Gerty's self-maintained clock, the timepiece of Lily's childhood was a grandfather clock that required routine upkeep by a hired hand. Lily identifies with her father's pendulum piece, which relied on weekly windings and necessitated her family's financial earnings. Once Hudson Bart became "extinct when he ceased to fulfil his purpose," Lily's stability of home collapsed, forcing her to rely on the hospitality of others. Thus, Lily sees herself as being wound by the routine provisions she is given by others in exchange for her time.

For Lily, time is slippery: it passes painfully slowly when she is anxious for sleep, while at other times, it passes too quickly for her to keep pace. Lily's precarious relationship to time, then, has a real effect on her bodily well-being and social stability. Fleissner argues that Lily's anxieties over aging, as well as her oscillations between life choices, encapsulate an important message in the novel: "The readings of *House of Mirth* that would scold Lily for attempting to stop time in its tracks with her 'hesitations' treat her physical body very much as the bearer of 'time-bound realities' . . . ; ending by giving Lily a baby, the novel almost seems in such interpretations to act on behalf of the 'biological clock'" (*Women* 200). However, Fleissner views other critics' condemnation of Lily's avoidance of her biological clock as a misreading. Instead, she argues that Wharton problematizes temporal treatments of womanhood: "Placed up against the older, more clearly linear notion of woman as 'lily' that blooms and fades, the clock figure holds the capacity to 'denaturalize the natural'" (200). Therefore, Lily—as a "clock figure"—constantly oscillates between ways to escape her debts. Each deficit is tied to the emerging demands of modernity, and together they represent tensions between the physical body and cultural constructions of linear time.

As Lily's social arrangements falter in their steadiness, Lily begins to anticipate a fate like her father's death by exhaustion. Lily's pendulous motion—from one deficit to another—forms a paradox of her own making. As she associates sleep with wasted time, she also drains herself of the energy she needs to persevere. Fleissner correlates Lily's "vacillating, terminally indecisive behavior" with the naturalist New Woman, who is "marked by neither the steep arc of decline nor that of triumph, but rather by an ongoing, nonlinear, repetitive motion—back and forth, around and around, on and on—that has the distinctive effect of seeming also like a stuckness in place" (*Women* 9). This connection, between Lily's compulsive behavior and an externally maintained timepiece, exposes the clash between her tenuous grip on temporality and her avid adherence to the cultural clock. Lily, the novel implies, is too fine a creature, too delicately made, to force herself to correspond to a mechanical clock. Lily's subjective richness is not a successful trait in the fin de siècle environment of Wharton's novel.

Biological Impulsion and Self-Extinction

Lily's scandalous encounters with Gus Trenor and George Dorset shatter her social prospects, leaving her desirous of immediate reprieve. As book 2 progresses, she seeks a reprieve from fatigue, anxiety, and financial destitution through the patronage of Mrs. Hatch and Mattie Gormer. Judy Trenor's meticulous schedule does little to prepare Lily for the frenzied, disordered experiences that Wharton associates with these new-money women, and all that Lily gains from them is fleeting relief. In joining Mrs. Hatch, Lily initially ignores the signs of social marginality, focusing instead on the somatic pleasures of waking well rested: "When Lily woke on the morning after her translation to the Emporium Hotel, her first feeling was one of purely physical satisfaction. . . . [There was] the luxury of lying once more in a soft-pillowed bed. . . . Introspection could come later; but for the moment she was not even troubled by the excesses of the upholstery or the restless convolutions of the furniture" (212). In time, however, the "restless convolutions" of a neurotic mind consume Lily, as she sees signs of social descent in her interactions and observations at the modern hotel. Upon meeting her hostess, "Lily found [Mrs. Hatch] seated in a blaze of electric light, impartially projected from various ornamental excrescences on a vast concavity of pink damask and gilding, from which she rose like a Venus from her shell" (212). Evoking Botticelli's *The Birth of Venus* (1485–86), Mrs. Hatch seems to be unnaturally birthed from electric light. She radiates with a conspicuous display of modern-age wealth and is staged complementarily to the hotel's electrified ambiance, which is to Lily "a world over-heated, over-upholstered, and over-fitted with mechanical appliances" (213). Lily associates electric light, and the hotel's other gaudy features, with the déclassé and nouveau riche.

Spatially, the hotel is far removed from traditional routine and seems to Lily a strange, new world. Rests and pauses do not exist within the "stifling inertia of the hotel routine." Lily's surroundings and the hotel inhabitants feel to her as surreal as a stage performance: "Somewhere behind them, in the background of their lives, there was doubtless a real past, peopled by human activities . . . yet they had no more real existence than the poet's shades in limbo" (213). Despite their fortitude, Lily perceives the hotel inhabitants as living a timeless, and therefore meaningless, existence (along the lines of Dante's *Inferno*). Lily observes that "night and day flowed into one another in a blur of confused and retarded engagements" (214). Lily's unsatisfied compulsion to maintain a strict schedule complicates her stay with a hostess who "seemed to float . . . outside the bounds of time and space.

No definite hours were kept; no fixed obligations existed" (214). Because she cannot perform "specific duties [that] would have simplified [her] position," Lily listlessly despairs over her new way of life: "Compared with the vast gilded void of Mrs. Hatch's existence, the life of Lily's former friends seemed packed with ordered activities" (215). She interprets her presence in Mrs. Hatch's milieu as "an odd sense of being behind the social tapestry, on the side where the threads were knotted and the loose ends hung. . . . These flashes of amusement were but brief reactions from the long disgust of her days" (215). Gerard understands this to be Lily's worldview resonating "with that of her mother, who 'died of a deep disgust,' leaving the reader with an uncanny sense of the circularity of the novel's naturalist trajectory" (417). Such a description also highlights Lily's paternal inheritance, as her clinging to the loose ends of the "social tapestry" recalls her father's similar precarity.

Lily experiences another fleeting moment of peaceful rest when she joins Mattie Gormer. Despite her reflection that "the Gormer milieu represented a social out-skirt which Lily had always fastidiously avoided," she initially finds pleasure in her stay: "The sudden escape . . . had produced a state of moral lassitude agreeable enough after the nervous tension and physical discomfort of the past weeks. For the moment, she must yield to the refreshment her senses craved—after that she would reconsider her situation, and take counsel with her dignity" (182, 184). Lily's temporary valuation of physical pleasure over practical concern unburdens her mind of worries, relieves her of cultural compulsion, and beckons her to rest easy. Nonetheless, her neuroses again take over when she comes to understand how little her current situation will be of long-term help to her: "The renewed habit of luxury—the daily waking to an assured absence of care and presence of material ease—gradually blunted her appreciation of these values, and left her more conscious of the void they could not fill" (185). That Lily routinely wakes to a sense of serenity implies that she has attained, albeit temporarily, a healthy rhythmicity of sleep. However, her cultural compulsion toward sociofinancial ascendancy reignites her sleeplessness, as she becomes "weary of being swept passively along a current of pleasure and business in which she had no share; weary of seeing other people pursue amusement and squander money, while she felt herself of no more account among them than an expensive toy in the hands of a spoiled child" (189). Lily likens her ineptitude to that of an "expensive toy," a powerless form of embodiment. In a way that resonates with the playthings in Frank Norris's story "The Puppets and the Puppy" (1897), Lily experiences a lack of agency over her body and subjectivity that prevents her from feeling the security, satisfaction, and pleasure that those around her take for granted.

Because Lily's social situations are always in flux, she constantly has to recenter and adapt. However, as her drives alter from self-conscious modes to afferent impulses, the novel itself lapses from a focus on Lily's social adaptation to an emphasis on her organic, environmental responses. Worth observes that "one of the text's most repeated motifs is that of the 'center,' particularly inasmuch as it is depicted as undergoing a process of renegotiation or replacement. The novel is full of threatened centers and the production of new nodal points throwing surrounding elements into new configurations" (101). When Lily is suffering from exhaustion, her somatic needs plunge her into a state of undesired sleep and compromise her ability to adapt within a given circumstance. As her situation grows stark, Lily reverts to baser impulses that appease her immediate needs and desires, rather than gratifying future social plans. Worth argues that the novel "imagine[s] the secret and immediate, if fitful and transitory, exchange of sympathetic energies patterned after electrical networks" (117). Such a parallel between the human body and an electrical network reflects Lily's desire to switch her body's alertness on and off: acting as if her bodily functions are that of an electric lamp, Lily seeks alertness through caffeine and sedation with the aid of a soporific.

Lily's tea drinking—as a means for avoiding rest—is overtly framed as a dangerous addiction. Hoping that Gerty will appease her craving, Lily identifies her social marginality as "what keeps me awake at night, and makes me so crazy for your strong tea" (208). Seeing Lily's "pale face" and eyes that "shone with a peculiar sleepless lustre," Gerty declares: "You look horribly tired, Lily; take your tea, and let me give you this cushion to lean against." Lily receives the tea but refuses the pillow: "Don't give me that! I don't want to lean back—I shall go to sleep if I do." Gerty encourages her friend to do just that, but Lily protests: "Talk to me—keep me awake! I don't sleep at night, and in the afternoon a dreadful drowsiness creeps over me" (207). Lily's "dreadful" sensation of fatigue correlates with the microsleep terrors that she experiences at the end of book 1. Lily tells Gerty about her prolonged resistance to nightly rest and begs for "another [tea], and stronger, please" (207). In her discussion of "Lily's downward spiral of drug use," Gerard remarks that "while tea itself seemed before to supply only an excuse for self-display, it now comes to be desired for its physical effects" (417). Lily wishes to put off sleep for another night so that she can avoid the "perfect horrors" she associates with bedrest (*Mirth* 207). With the vicious retort of "don't preach, please," Lily demands more tea: "Her voice had a dangerous edge, and Gerty noticed that her hand shook as she held it out to receive the second cup" (207). As Gerard implies, this scene shows Lily to be an addict

"A Great Blaze of Electric Light"   111

seeking relief. Lily's tea addiction, then, reveals the extent to which Lily's cultural compulsions will drive her toward perpetual wakefulness.

Mirroring the caffeine addiction that she develops as book 1 closes, Lily comes to rely on chloral hydrate to attain rest after she goes to work at a women's hat shop near the end of book 2. While her reliance on tea stems from cultural compulsion, her dependence on chloral hydrate derives from her biological impulse toward routine rest. At the millinery, Lily refuses to be a hat model. Her growing revelations throughout the novel—about aging and the social and financial burdens of fashion—lead her to conclude that she must learn to support herself via "profitable activity" as opposed to physical beauty (221). However, despite exhausting effort, manual industry proves too much for her, and she is ultimately laid off due to poor workmanship. Although many readers attribute Lily's failure to her upper-class rearing and "charming listless hands" (221; see Mullen; Duvall; Showalter), Lily's sleep deprivation more fully accounts for her deficiencies at the hat factory. While other female workers labor on despite their "fagged profiles . . . [and] the unwholesomeness of hot air and sedentary toil" (219), Lily's fatigued body wavers between conscious wakefulness and unconscious dozing. "Lily's head was so heavy with the weight of a sleepless night that the chatter of her companions had the incoherence of a dream. . . . On and on it flowed, a current of meaningless sounds" (223). Lily's physical reaction to incessant industry resembles the experience of the white enslaver who is transformed into the "noo man" in Charles Chesnutt's "Mars Jeems's Nightmare" (1899). The bodily strain that Jeems endures after descending from his position of privilege is, at it is to Lily, so exhausting that he is unable to perform the tasks demanded of him. After Lily's overseer reproaches her for poor handiwork, she reflects: "The forewoman was right: the sewing . . . was inexcusably bad. What made her so much more clumsy than usual? Was it . . . [an] actual physical disability? She felt tired and confused: it was an effort to put her thoughts together" (223). Lily's comprehension that she is, indeed, disabled by her sleeplessness is proof of her revelation that insomnia has caused her deterioration.

Lily reconciles her dread of parasomnia with her body's need for rest through the use of chloral. This reconciliation, however, poses a new threat when Lily learns from her druggist that even a slight overdose of chloral can be fatal. She initially expresses trepidation: "What she dreaded most of all was having to pass the chemist's . . . [but] her steps were irresistibly drawn toward the flaring plate-glass corner" (225). Like with her caffeine addiction, the language of this passage implies Lily's reliance on a material substance to appease her needs: "When at length she emerged safely from the shop she was almost dizzy with the intensity of her relief. The mere touch of the packet thrilled her tired nerves with the delicious promise of a night of sleep" (225). After purchasing the chloral hydrate, Lily stumbles into Rosedale, who is shocked by her gauntness. Through Rosedale's eyes, the reader is apprised of Lily's "ebbing vitality," as he notes "the dark pencil-ling of fatigue under her eyes, [and] the morbid blue-veined palour of the temples" (226). He invites her into a nearby café to have a cup of tea. As Lily struggles between the stimulants of her external environment and her need to replenish her body with sleep, she reacts to Rosedale's "injunction to take her tea strong" with the internal observation that "her craving for the keen stimulant was forever conflicting with that other craving for sleep" (226). Such a thought reinforces Lily's inner contradiction between cultural com-pulsion, her social reliance on strong tea, and biological impulse, her bodily dependence on chloral. Lily's oscillation between stimulant and sedative implies that she lacks the bodily capacity to moderate her own wakefulness and rest: she tries to manipulate herself with chemicals, but then the chemi-cals hurt her. As we see through Rosedale's eyes, Lily is made up of stuff too fine for the world she inhabits, and her frailty renders her body more vulnerable to the forces of restlessness and exhaustion.

Unlike the dark terror she feels for natural sleep, Lily finds artificially induced sleep to be "the only spot of light in the dark prospect" (242). Spe-cifically, she discovers that chloral remedies the sleep-wake disturbances that are symptomatic of her exhaustion. When her anxious mind suc-cumbs to undesired sleep, parasomnia summons "half-waking visions" that frighten her. However, this is not the case with chloral-induced sleep: "In the sleep which the phial procured . . . she sank into depths of dreamless annihilation" (230). To her dismay, she soon discovers that chloral's effects are merely ephemeral: "She was troubled by the thought that it was losing its power. . . . Of late the sleep it had brought her had been more broken and less profound; there had been nights when she was perpetually floating up through it to consciousness" (242). The chloral's inefficiency reinforces Lily's failure to realign her anxiety-ridden body with routine bedrest. In this moment, Wharton provides uncanny evidence of Lily's biological need for REM sleep, a term coined only after the author's lifetime. For the body to attain restorative rest, it must achieve a natural flow of sleep. Such a process includes time spent in the unconscious state of REM sleep, which, according to Horne, is harder to attain for one who is under stress and experiencing "fitful sleep" (153). The "dreamless annihilation" that Lily cherishes is char-acteristic of REM sleep, for the conscious mind cannot recall any memories of having dreamed during this state of deep sleep. Thus, in this moment,

"A Great Blaze of Electric Light"   113

Lily is devastated to discover that her one means of lulling her body into "dreamless annihilation," a characteristic of routine rest, is through a treatment with fast-waning potency.

The chart in figure 9 reveals the mildness of Lily's sleep struggles at the start of books 1 and 2, in contrast with her increasing obsession with her lack of sleep at the end of both books. As the novel's events become more acute for Lily, the narrative focuses more intensely on her relationship to rest. Variations on the word *sleep* reach a peak at the novel's end, when

FIGURE 9. Depicting Voyant's same "Trends" feature as figures 5 and 6, this graph charts the distribution of *sleep** throughout *The House of Mirth* (asterisk includes terms with the same root word).

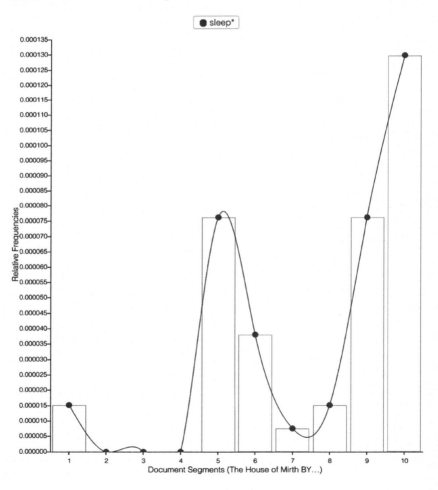

Lily's obsession with attaining rest leads to her overdose. The waxing and waning of the term follow a similar pattern to the visualization in figure 6, in which Roderick's sleep concerns peak at the start, middle, and end, with intervening drops. These two visualizations show how the plot structure of the two novels is quite similar. Sleep anxieties exist from the start but are kept at bay until Roderick's and Lily's social statuses become more precarious. This precarity reaches a peak at the midpoint of both texts, yet both characters manage a brief escape—Roderick to Baden and Lily to Europe—before returning to even more dire predicaments. The midpoint peak is mirrored in the novels' conclusions, in which both characters are propelled by exhaustion to a tragic end.

Just before her death, Lily's mind wanders through a paradoxically wakeful sleep state, in which dozing thoughts evoke a sense of mental escape: "An immense weariness once more possessed her. It was not the stealing sense of sleep, but a vivid wakeful fatigue, a wan lucidity of mind against which all the possibilities of the future were shadowed forth gigantically. She was appalled by the intense cleanness of the vision" (249). The passage's oxymoronic "vivid wakeful fatigue" and "wan lucidity of mind" imply a psychical severance of Lily's inner self from her physical body and its environment: "In the mysterious nocturnal separation from all outward signs of life, she felt herself more strangely confronted with her fate. . . . But the terrible silence and emptiness seemed to symbolize her future—she felt as though the house, the street, the world were all empty, and she alone left sentient in a lifeless universe" (250). Lily's suspicions of time and space as unfixed outside the physical demands of the cultural clock are verified by her mind's sensation of a "lifeless universe." According to Worth, "Lily's death, significantly, is attributed to the failure of her nervous system; specifically, it is this network's incapability of being centrally governed, the oppressive new autonomy of her nerves, which becomes intolerable" (101). Lily's incessant anxieties over her inability to adapt to modernity figuratively fry her system, as her very own neurophysiology becomes a match for mechanical networks. This electrified decentering climactically clashes with Lily's reliance on passive rest. Inevitably, her biological impulse overpowers cultural compulsion, as Lily's body meets a fatal end through her achievement of enduring, tranquil sleep.

Lily's death is implicitly deliberate. She is conscious of the danger, something the reader is reminded of twice over. Once in the chemist's shop and again just before her encounter with Nettie, Lily reminds herself of chloral's dangerous potential: "She remembered the chemist's warning against increasing the dose; and she had heard before of the capricious and incalculable action of the drug" (242). Despite Lily's knowledge of the drug's

"A Great Blaze of Electric Light" 115

potency, her dalliance with suicide has long been up for critical debate. Lois Tyson, for instance, reads Lily's suicide as a subconscious act, arguing that "although Lily doesn't commit suicide in the deliberate and premeditated way, . . . she deliberately refrains from considering the risk she is taking when she increases the dose" (8). Lily's conscious resistance to suicidal thoughts conflicts with her body's addiction to chloral's deep sleep. The reader is told that Lily "did not, in truth, consider the question very closely—the physical craving for sleep was her only sustained sensation. Her mind shrank from the glare of thought as instinctively as eyes contract in a blaze of light—darkness, darkness was what she must have at any cost. She raised herself in bed and swallowed the contents of the glass" (250). Her consumption of the chloral in its entirety, along with her previous vision of a "lifeless universe," evinces the desperation of suicidal behavior, as well as her most intense craving—for sleep—having been taken to the brink. Moreover, the narrator's comment that Lily disregards chloral's danger implies that Lily *chooses* not to consider a potential overdose.

My reading conflicts with many critical arguments about Lily's death. Dimock's foundational reading, for one, argues that Lily's final dose of chloral extends her addiction to risk-taking to a fatal conclusion. I argue instead that Lily's reckless consumption of chloral represents her desperate desire to achieve profound sleep, such as that typical of newborns like Nettie Struther's infant. As Lily lies dying, she imagines that she is carefully cradling the baby in her arms. In my reading of Lily's death, her choice is also not subconscious, as Tyson suggests. Rather, it represents her most lucid moment in the novel, in which both mind and body reject the potential for assuming an alternative identity or embodiment and, instead, seek oblivion through eternal sleep. Lily's identification with the baby symbolizes her desire for the organic force, beginning at infancy, that compels the human body to sleep (see Tillman). At her life's end, Lily reconciles herself with the natural force that she could never seem to channel, despite her efforts to remake her own physiology with teas and chemicals.

From a historical perspective, there is evidence to support Wharton's intention for Lily to die by suicide. In 2007, the *New York Times* reported the story of a newly recovered letter from Wharton to Dr. Francis Kinnicutt, who was treating her husband's mental illness at the time. Journalist Charles McGrath highlights the contents of the letter, which was written in December 1904, precisely as she was writing *The House of Mirth*:

> "A friend of mine has made up her mind to commit suicide . . . and has asked me to find out . . . the most painless and least unpleasant method of effacing herself." Only on the second page does Wharton reveal that her

"friend" is in fact a fictional character appearing in the pages of Scribner's, … "What soporific, or nerve-calming drug, would a nervous and worried young lady in the smart set be likely to take to, and what would be its effects if deliberately taken with the intent to kill herself? I mean, how would she feel and look toward the end?"

Wharton's request provides fascinating insight into her authorial considerations as she detailed the final moments of Lily's life. Moreover, she insinuates that Lily's "dread" of being drawn to the chemist's shop refers to her reticence toward suicide, as well as her inability to keep herself from pursuing it. In her moment of death, then, Lily does not accidentally overdose. She acts on a decision to extinguish her inner blaze of dissatisfaction and social isolation.

Figure 10 provides a Voyant-generated visualization of words found in proximity to *sleep* in *The House of Mirth*. As this was the first chapter I drafted for this project, the visualizations I produced were done well after I had conducted my close reading of the novel. As with figure 9, which charts the novel's plot in relation to Lily's sleep obsession, this collocates list confirms what I already suspected. The list of associated words emphasizes the negative perception Lily has of nightly rest throughout much of the novel, as the narrative associates sleep with terms including *deathly*, *disappointing*, *dreadful*, and *failure*. *Craving* is also a prevalent association and does well

FIGURE 10. Like figures 7 and 8, this Voyant visualization generates a collocation pattern. In this version, words that appear around *sleep** in *The House of Mirth* are listed in order of prevalence (asterisk includes terms with the same root word).

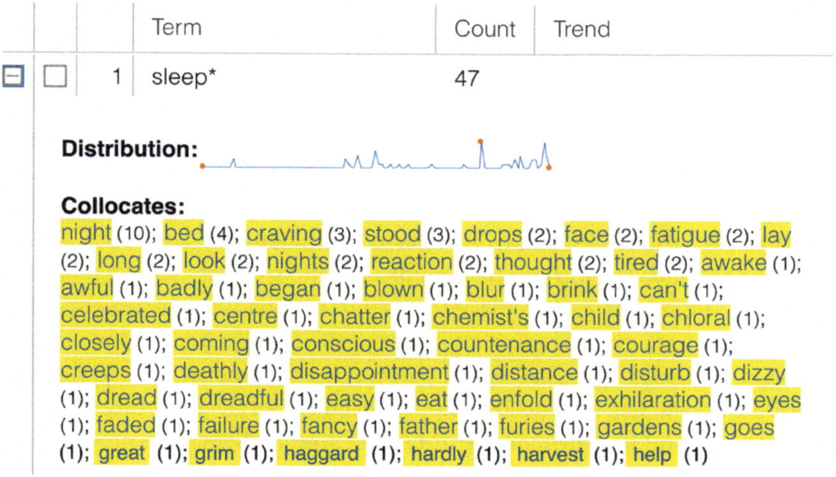

			Term	Count	Trend
⊟	☐	1	sleep*	47	

Distribution:

Collocates:
night (10); bed (4); craving (3); stood (3); drops (2); face (2); fatigue (2); lay (2); long (2); look (2); nights (2); reaction (2); thought (2); tired (2); awake (1); awful (1); badly (1); began (1); blown (1); blur (1); brink (1); can't (1); celebrated (1); centre (1); chatter (1); chemist's (1); child (1); chloral (1); closely (1); coming (1); conscious (1); countenance (1); courage (1); creeps (1); deathly (1); disappointment (1); distance (1); disturb (1); dizzy (1); dread (1); dreadful (1); easy (1); eat (1); enfold (1); exhilaration (1); eyes (1); faded (1); failure (1); fancy (1); father (1); furies (1); gardens (1); goes (1); great (1); grim (1); haggard (1); hardly (1); harvest (1); help (1)

"A Great Blaze of Electric Light" 117

to represent the myriad and contradictory cravings Lily has throughout the novel. That *night* occurs the most often—ten times—seems a red herring as we do most of our sleeping at night, but when considered within the context of my reading of the novel, it is a testament to Lily's struggles with social isolation, loneliness, itinerancy, and insomnia. Furthermore, the collocated terms reinforce my choices in highlighting key passages related to sleep debt throughout the novel, as many of the words in this visualization are present in the quotations featured on these pages. This panorama of terms thus encapsulates in one succinct image Wharton's articulation of Lily's obsession with sleep and sleeplessness.

Conclusion

Just as book 1 concludes with Lily's horrific epiphany that she is doomed by inherited sleeplessness, book 2 concludes with her (purposefully or otherwise) killing herself to overcome it. Such a thematic parallel spans Wharton's literary career, for, in her 1927 novel *Twilight Sleep*, sleeplessness is again illuminated. This time, it is sardonically rendered through Lita Wyant's flippant mistreatment of her goldfish, which suffer the fatal consequences of sleep deprivation. Echoing the architectural criticism Wharton penned three decades earlier, *Twilight Sleep* offers Nona Manford's critique of Lita's drawing room: "It looked, for all its studied effects . . . the things the modern decorator lies awake over, more like the waiting-room of a glorified railway station than the setting of an established way of life" (31). Wharton's remark in *The Decoration of Houses* that "it would be difficult to account for the adoption of a mode of lighting which makes the salon look like a railway-station" merges with the restless decorator of *Twilight Sleep*, who forgoes sleep in pursuit of perfecting the modernized home and neglects the accommodation of bodily repose (*Decoration* 126).

Twilight Sleep satirizes a decorator's preference for spaces that emphasize and electrify the display of wealth and that ignore the comfort of their inhabitants. Nona observes: "The only life in the room was contributed by the agitations of the exotic goldfish in a huge spherical aquarium; and they too were but transients, since Lita insisted on having the aquarium illuminated night and day with electric bulbs, and the sleepless fish were always dying off and having to be replaced" (31). Lita's flippant mistreatment of her provisional pets evinces Lily's suffering at the hands of her patrons, who value her only for her constantly conspicuous ornamentation. In the revelation that she has irrevocably slipped from society's sight, Lily observes that "society did not turn away from her, it simply drifted by, preoccupied and inattentive, letting her feel . . . how completely she had been the creature of its favour" (204). Lily's conclusion reinforces her powerlessness, as well as her milieu's glib disregard for her welfare. Like the goldfish in Lita's tank, Lily depends for her livelihood on diligent exposure within the spaces of her benefactors, and her biological need for routine rest disrupts her participation in a never-ending cycle of social performance. In depriving Lily of cultural surroundings that accommodate rest and regeneration, Wharton exposes *The House of Mirth* to be a prime space of the Gilded Age, one reserved for whirling shows of electric light and high-speed social survival. Only those with the power to play their part may dwell within it, while those of Lily's marginality are snatched from the fishbowl only to be replaced by another.

CHAPTER 4

"Rest and Power"

The Social Currency of Sleep in
Charlotte Perkins Gilman's *Forerunner*

> We have a certain storage of nerve force, with which
> we can drive ourselves, but in all ordinary and habitual
> actions we do not spend that power. . . . For the conscious
> mind to compel the body to do what it has no inherited
> desire or acquired habit of doing, is a direct expense. . . .
> It is precisely this storage battery of nerve force called
> the will which gives us our high pre-eminence as a race
> and gives some of us pre-eminence over others.
> —Charlotte Perkins Gilman, *Our Brains and What Ails Them*

Whereas themes of insomnia and clinical neurasthenia are still left to be uncovered in Edith Wharton's fiction, scholars have long traced the themes of anxiety and restlessness in the works of Charlotte Perkins Gilman. Fifty years after the 1973 reprint and recovery of Gilman's 1892 short story "The Yellow Wall-Paper," feminist and literary scholars continue to explore Gilman's interest in the psychosomatic repercussions of domestic oppression amid the freneticism of modernity. Akin to Lily Bart's compulsive vacillations and fear that her brain might be scarred by bedroom dinginess, Gilman's narrator in "The Yellow Wall-Paper" believes that domestic confinement has deteriorated her mind, yet she still impulsively strives, as Jennifer Fleissner notes, to "master a fundamentally unmasterable environment" (*Women* 75), or, as Lee Scrivner puts it, "the unnamed protagonist . . . is a particular kind of brain-working insomniac. . . . Her mind, in attempting to trace this wallpaper tracery, becomes a kind of simulacrum of her surroundings and their complex, confused, superfluous, and interminable designs" (101). Like Lily, Gilman's character displays a paradoxical wakefulness. Scrivner explains that "[the narrator] does not want to write—telling us, through her writing, that she does not even feel able to write—yet she keeps writing. She is tired and wants to take a nap, yet she continues to demonstrate the typical insomniac paradox of a perpetuation of mental hyperactivity in exhaustion" (102). Scrivner describes the exhaustive loop that entraps these New Woman figures. The desire to process and express one's relationship to modernity, to understand the modes of oppression that flow through the mind and body like currents, deprives them of rest even as they long for sleep. Between 1909 and 1916, Gilman continued to explore the "woman question" in her self-published journal the *Forerunner* and imagined a means for white, middle-class women to escape the "unmasterable environment" of the home through the cultivation of their physical body and mental capacity.

For Gilman, the New Woman role was available almost exclusively to white, middle-class women, a group essential to her own identity. Gail Bederman attests to Gilman's feminism as a project to uplift primarily white bourgeois women: "Gilman always assumed that civilization's advancement occurred as individual races ascended the evolutionary ladder, and that the most advanced races—those closest to evolutionary perfection—were white" (122). Believing that women deteriorated under domestication, Gilman sought methods for removing the strain of domesticity on middle-class white women. Bederman provides extensive evidence for Gilman's theoretical assertion that the menial tasks of daily life, which she viewed as atavistic, should be relegated to minoritized Americans (121–69). Using the *Forerunner* as one of many platforms from which to answer the woman question, Gilman posed a solution based on a racial divide, which omitted certain bodies from the New Woman trajectory through the relegation of domestic labor to non-Anglo women.

"Her Housekeeper" (1910), a story I later discuss, is a prime example of such a divide. Mrs. Leland, a widowed mother and actress, requires that her African American maid, Alice, stand guard outside her bedroom to protect her sleep. Despite her pronounced emphasis on the importance of rest, Mrs. Leland assumes that Alice "did not seem to care where she slept, or if she slept at all" (*Forerunner*, vol. 1, no. 3, p. 2). Mrs. Leland is a fine representation of Gilman's literary approach to the New Woman, and a conflation of what Nancy Bentley describes as the "polarized figures of womanhood: the illusion of power in the stage performer's audacious movements and the unique self-understanding of the reflective woman's consciousness" (*Frantic* 139). Lily Bart represents the former of these two types: she longs to exude and maintain social power, but she is never able to achieve self-understanding. As I discuss in the previous chapter, Bentley describes Lily as a "body on the margins" (156). Mrs. Leland, on other hand, attains a fulfilling and autonomous life, both professionally and personally. She places herself as the center of her circle, yet this position is only manageable, so it seems, through her reliance on Alice.

Even in stories not overtly racist, such as "Turned" (1911), Gilman maintains, as Catherine Golden notes, a "xenophobic attitude" (158). In this tale, the white, middle-class female protagonist, Marion, promises to take care of her domestic servant, Gerta, who has been impregnated by Marion's husband. The story begins with a description of the women after Gerta has broken the news to her mistress, and the parallel imagery emphasizes their unequal sleeping conditions: "Mrs. Marroner lay sobbing on the wide, soft bed. . . . Gerta Petersen lay sobbing on the narrow, hard bed" (*Forerunner*, vol. 2, no. 9, p. 227). The contrasting beds are within the same home. While Gerta, as a live-in maid, is granted only a "poorly finished chamber" in the attic of Marion's home, Marion sleeps in the comfort of her "richly furnished chamber" (227). Golden describes these antithetical bedrooms as representative of Marion's home as "a place of social and ethnic segregation, reflecting Gilman's nativist tendency, evident in much of white America at the time Gilman wrote the story" (155). Compared to Mrs. Leland and the peripheral Alice, Marion puts herself on more equal footing with Gerta by the end of the story: she leaves her philandering husband and accepts Gerta and the child as her responsibilities. However, as Golden explains, this results merely in Marion's condescending reeducation and acculturation of Gerta (158). Together, "Her Housekeeper" and "Turned" emphasize the greater importance of sleeping conditions for the white, middle-class protagonists and the devaluation of rest for their ethnic, working-class counterparts.

In this chapter, I build on critical arguments about Gilman's racialized delegation of labor to elucidate the *Forerunner*'s depiction of sleep as a form of social power and, more specifically, a tool for social currency (see Mattis; Nadkarni; Newman; Scharnhorst; Seitler; Weinbaum). Gilman defines sleep's function as social currency on two levels. First, it serves as a tool for social empowerment, for it has a biologically empowering effect on the individual body, which enables a person to carry out their daily contributions to society through labor. Second, and simultaneously, it can serve as a tool for social oppression: those in power (often accrued by sleep itself) can extract time-consuming and sleep-depriving labor from subjugated others (and so, she claims, perpetual exhaustion is damning to white, middle-class women who suffer from social oppression). Gilman largely situates her concerns about sleep deprivation in the home, where wives and mothers forfeit necessary rest to carry out domestic tasks. Throughout the *Forerunner*, Gilman tells stories of women who overcome exhaustion and outsmart their male counterparts so that they may contribute to society outside the home. In each volume, she uses the metaphor of "waking up" in various contexts to articulate women's realization of sexual oppression.

In a volume 1 "Comment and Review" (1910), Gilman criticizes a popular woman's periodical for romanticizing the Sleeping Beauty myth. She observes sarcastically, "the Sleeping Beauty is a most happy instance of woman's right attitude toward love and marriage—she is to remain starkly unconscious, using absolutely no discretion; and cheerfully marry the first man that kisses her! In the fairy story he was a noble prince—but the average sleeping beauty of to-day is often waked up by the wrong man!" (vol. 1, no. 5, p. 23). Here, Gilman articulates the ways in which young women are socialized to be metaphorical sleepwalkers, constructed to rely on men to decide their life choices for them. Her cure for this cultural symptom of female lethargy is a social awakening that, ironically, takes the form of "power in repose," a key phrase in the *Forerunner*. She argues that women can achieve greater social power in repose through the self-disciplined habit of maintaining protected, regulated, and consistent sleeping hours. Moreover, Gilman's Sleeping Beauty comment identifies another paradox that underscores her theories of sleep and social power. Following her excoriation of the Sleeping Beauty myth, Gilman references Edward Lear's 1846 limerick "There Was an Old Man of Jamaica" to illustrate the ills of a contemporary Sleeping Beauty, noting that "sometimes she is married first, and wakes up afterward; like the lady in Lear's limerick":

> There was an old man of Jamaica,
> Who suddenly married a Quaker.
> But she cried out, 'O Lack!
> I have married a Black!'
> Which grieved that old man of Jamaica. (23)

In a troubling turn, Gilman warns that the oblivion of the common female condition will lead to social devolution, restricting middle-class white women to the limited social powers relegated to racialized others. Adhering to a nativist ideology, Gilman's theories of social evolution require not only a sexed competition, but a racialized one as well. Rather than see social evolution as a path toward social equality, Gilman views her preferred race—the white female populace—as fighting to excel in an ongoing competition with both white men and racial and ethnic others. For Gilman, like a number of her contemporary suffragists, white women needed to wake up to the fact that they were being subjugated in ways akin to the oppression of immigrant and nonwhite others (see Allen; Carter-Sanborn; Davis, "His"; Ganobcsik-Williams; Hudak; Lanser; Mattis; Nadkarni; Newman; Scharnhorst; Seitler; Weinbaum). Through her social evolutionary lens, white women as sleepwalkers served as a metaphor for atavistic degeneration.

The *Forerunner* combines theories of social evolution, sociology, and medicine to use "waking up" as a metaphor for the advancement of a white female social consciousness and portrays disciplined sleep as a restorative act for white women struggling in their pursuit of public service. Gilman also engages a capitalist lexicon and treats routine rest as a practice that is earned rather than required. While she argues for the importance of restorative rest, she claims that it should only serve those who contribute to society with what she describes in *Our Brains and What Ails Them* (1912) as "brain power" (*Forerunner*, vol. 3, no. 3, p. 79). Because the body serves as an "elaborate machine for the transmission of force," she identifies the physical act of resting as a mechanical instrument that, if utilized properly, has the potential to serve society's greater good. This reflects Roderick Hudson's philosophy in chapter 1 that sleep is only purposeful when it provides rest and a "reverie" to inspire his work. Yet, unlike Henry James, Gilman lays a much stronger theoretical foundation for rest and brainpower in her fiction. She invests in what Scrivner describes as the "nineteenth-century mental physiology [of the] . . . brain-worker": "Whereas brain-work referred to mental activity in general, a brain-worker was one who engaged in mental rather than manual labor, . . . urban-dwelling, educated, and dependent, for their livelihood, upon their interaction with the cutting-edge technologies of the day" (82). The social power of brain work and "power in repose"—a tool utilized by the utopian society of Gilman's novel *Moving the Mountain* (1911)—is a central tenet to Gilman's promotion of women's industry and the advancement of the white female social body. Paradoxically, Gilman speaks of people in *Moving the Mountain* as having "waken[ed] to the fact that they could do things with their brains" through the practice of principled rest (*Forerunner*, vol. 2, no. 8, p. 219). Thus, proper sleep requires its own form of "waking up" via education, disciplined brainpower, and physical effort (see Paravantes).

Throughout the trajectory of the *Forerunner*, Gilman details the social evolutionary value of brainpower and establishes hierarchies of labor forms that require more or less repose for renewed energy. In her essay "Rest and Power" (1915), Gilman specifies that only certain types of labor require such principles, while other forms of work demand very little brainpower. The completion of routine household tasks, for instance, result from the "process [of transferring] . . . habit . . . [to] unconscious action," and thus

124   CHAPTER 4

require little self-discipline or cultivated brainpower (vol. 6, no. 10, p. 271). This lends insight into Gilman's use of evolutionary discourse in *Our Brains and What Ails Them* to theorize that "humanity, as it progresses in social complexity, develops an increasing brain power, which is of necessity, possessed by individuals; and which of necessity differs in individuals, both in kind and in degree" (*Forerunner*, vol. 3, no. 3, p. 79). While Gilman's theories of brainpower and purposeful repose are clearly intended to empower white working women, they are also imbued with problematic doctrines of her day: subtending Gilman's utopian feminism are pro-eugenic and nativistic stances on women's progress. For Gilman, white women's best route to freedom outside the home depends on the labor of nonwhite and immigrant women. She argues that in order for women to achieve professional success, they must relegate the drudgery of domesticity to others. This is both similar to and distinct from the oppression Lily endures in *The House of Mirth* (1905). Lily's dependence on patronage, in which a young woman on the social margins still retains privilege through social connections as well as racial and familial status, is specific to the leisure class. Yet, the woman patrons who exploit Lily benefit from her labor, much as the female entrepreneurs benefit from others' labor in Gilman's writing. Gilman, meanwhile, envisions a complex, socio-industrial system of domestic labor delineated by race and ethnicity. The women drafted into Gilman's imagined workforce, in many of her stories, are of Black and immigrant descent and lack the social privilege of their higher-classed white overseers. As Gilman attests in her autobiography, she maintained only a precarious grip on middle-class status (*Living*). Throughout much of her life, she struggled to make ends meet and suffered from the exhaustion symptomatic of her role as a working-class, single mother. Thus, Gilman's class identity was mostly aspirational, and, as her dream of Herland exemplifies, Gilman longed for a truly democratic society. At the same time, however, her vision of a feminist utopia relied on the same capitalist and racialized exploitation that buoyed the very turn of the century patriarchy that she incessantly criticized. Therefore, this chapter explores Gilman's valuations of class, ethnic, and racial positions of privilege to reveal her systematic prescription of restorative rest, if only to those she deemed better equipped to carry out national progress.

Gilman's Lessons on Sleep Discipline

Gilman's approach to sleep is emblematic of Frederick Winslow Taylor's efficiency science, which, as Kellen H. Graham observes, "reached its greatest heights" as Gilman began her work on the *Forerunner*. Graham asserts that "scientific management was at the heart of [the] efficiency movement," a practice that can also account for Gilman's approach to the regulation of sleep as well as her efforts to enhance its rejuvenating effect (190). She merges her Taylorist approach to bodily restoration with her investment in sleep discipline, countering views espoused by Thomas Edison in an effort to embrace the importance of what she believed to be productive rest. Whereas "manly wakefulness" was in vogue among popular women's publications—reports in *Ladies' Home Journal* and *Godey's Lady's Book* praised Edison's ability to sleep less than "four hours a day" (Derickson 6)—the *Forerunner* does not evince a belief in the power of the "physiological reformer," as Edison is described in an 1894 issue of the *National Druggist*, which deprecatingly refers to Edison as "an advocate of the uselessness of sleep, and the consequent waste of time and energy spent in that state" ("Mr. Thomas" 167). Gilman likewise uses medical knowledge to counter tidbits of social advice in popular women's publications that she deems harmful to female advancement. Among the ideas she critiques is the cultural myth of "manly wakefulness": while she presents the body as a conditioned machine, she maintains a belief in sleep's value in both daily life and social evolution. She also aligns her work with Wharton's *The Decoration of Houses* (1898) by making explicit her belief in the sanctity of the sleep space. That said, as I will later explain, Gilman's valuations of sleep contradictorily depend on the context: when she discusses industrialized forms of labor (particularly with regard to hired domestic servants), her appreciation for industrial efficiency trumps for her the value of restorative rest. Conversely, when Gilman addresses the stresses of professional pursuits for white women, efficient sleep habits are a foremost concern.

The debate over sleep's role in modern life is best summarized through the twofold interpretations provoked by the title of Annie Payson Call's 1891 sleep discipline guidebook *Power through Repose*. On the one hand, Americans sought to *power through* sleep by resisting it altogether, as in Edison's case, while on the other, they pursued individual and social power *through sleep* by cultivating principles for proper repose. Call intended to do the latter in *Power through Repose*, and her conception of sleep precedes Gilman's discussion of "rest and power" in the *Forerunner*. For Call, repose—as an act of tranquil, restorative rest—is powerful when one has the freedom and self-discipline to decide when, where, and how to achieve it, either through enduring sleep throughout the night or through intermittent naps during the day. Reflecting a Taylorist reverence for mechanical efficiency, Call refers to the body as "the machine," asking her readers: "How can we expect repose of mind when we have not even repose of muscle? When the

most external of the machine is not at our command, surely the spirit that animates the whole cannot find its highest plane of action. . . . How can we . . . hope to realize the great repose behind every action, when we have not even learned the repose in rest?" (76). Call unites ideals of efficiency with an allegiance to animism, arguing that humans cannot reach a higher level of spiritual being without achieving adequate sleep habits.

Gilman applies a similar concept in her discussion of the social spirit in the *Forerunner*. Writing in 1911, she observes, "A living creature is a mechanism which carries within itself stored energy. It has a certain amount, in small bills and silver as it were, for everyday use" (vol. 2, no. 3, p. 65). This stored energy is exerted in daily activities, yet the amount of energy one has to expend, Gilman implies, depends on how much energy one has saved up. To save energy, an individual must attain proper rest, but that person can only do so as one's social situation permits. Here she departs somewhat from Call, who writes: "The locomotive engine only utilizes nineteen per cent of the amount of fuel it burns, and inventors are hard at work in all directions to make an engine that will burn only the fuel needed to run it. Here is a much more valuable machine—the human engine—burning perhaps eighty-one per cent more than is needed to accomplish its ends, not through the mistake of its Divine Maker, but through the stupid, shortsighted thoughtlessness of the engineer" (110). Whereas Call assumes that each engineer of a "human engine" should be blamed for excessively burning fuel, Gilman questions who actually maintains power over the energy that a body stores and expends in a given day. By comparing bodily acts of rest and expended energy to the exchange of currency, Gilman implies that rest is meted out to those according to their class and social means. For example, an employer determines a laborer's working hours and, thus, the amount of time the worker may reserve for daily rest. The amount of sleep a worker achieves each night represents a renewed amount of expendable energy that is then traded for wages. In the *Forerunner*, Gilman explores possibilities for white women to seize control over the social currency of sleep (as stored energy) within the context of the domestic economy. Harvesting and directing the energy of others is a concept earlier explored by James in *Roderick Hudson* (1875), as I note in chapter 1. Roderick is depicted as a trotting horse that, due to the sculptor's careless expenditure of energy, threatens to "stumble and balk" (129). James's metaphorical portrait of Roderick as a failed worker transitions from a stumbling horse to a broken-down clock, revealing the transition society underwent in viewing human workers as less animalistic and more mechanistic as the century progressed. Gilman explores the mechanical worker much more minutely—taking the standpoint of a social reformer, rather than simply a literary observer—to capitalize on domestic labor for the benefit of white, female progress.

Unlike Wharton, Gilman sees little individuality in sleep practices. Whereas Lily Bart's idiosyncrasies imply that sleep is different for everyone, Gilman accepts the standard belief (popularly espoused in Benjamin Franklin's mid-eighteenth-century *Poor Richard's Almanack*) that the amount of rest each person requires is universal (approximately eight hours of sleep within a twenty-four-hour period). The *Forerunner* notes this several times. Taking a scientific managerial approach to tracking one's productive hours within a given day is an important step in Gilman's notion of self-discipline. In the 1913 novella *Won Over*, Stella estimates the number of hours per day that she should dedicate to fulfilling work, considering that "few of us sleep more than eight hours" (*Forerunner*, vol. 4, no. 2, p. 43). A similar calculation occurs in the short story "Fulfilment" (1914). The story features a long discussion between two sisters, Irma and Elsie, about how the latter spends her time. Irma is disturbed by Elsie's "pass[ing] her life occupying rocking-chairs, merely eating and sleeping in the necessary intervals between one sitting and the next." She insists on counting out the hours of Elsie's daily activities, taking "eight out for sleep," and encourages her sister to use her hours more productively (*Forerunner*, vol. 5, no. 3, p. 57). When Elsie counters that "no two families are alike" in daily habits or sleep schedules, Irma disagrees (59). She explains that through social contribution (in Irma's case, working as a governess and serving as a foster mother), conscientious work not only provides uniformity to one's daily life but also betters society. According to Irma, Elsie's useless kinetic energy (rocking back and forth in her chair) could be redirected into helping humanity, if only she could break away from the domestic space. In short, if energy is currency, Elsie is squandering money rather than reinvesting it in the greater good.

Gilman believed that white, middle-class women wasted their energy when tethered to the home space. By working in isolation, women limited themselves to the poor stores of energy maintained by their individual bodies. In the 1916 *Forerunner* essay "Studies in Social Pathology," Gilman writes, "We do not consider individuals as creating force. Our own supply of energy, stored in the brain cells, is soon exhausted" (vol. 7, no. 5, p. 120). The "social spirit," on the other hand, "is what gives a member of society more power than an isolated individual. . . . It is stored in our great books, great pictures, great statues; every noble human work is at once an expression of social energy and a permanent transmitter of that energy to others" (121). Because middle-class white women are alienated from social structures that could provide a reprieve from domestic drudgery, they are not able to capitalize on the "noble human work" available to them.

128   CHAPTER 4

Throughout the *Forerunner*, Gilman ties sleep to self-improvement. Writing in 1909, she presents the cultivation of individual energy as the key to social progress for women. In the short story "Three Thanksgivings," the widowed Mrs. Morrison establishes the Rest and Improvement Club and offers up her home as a woman's club and a space for collective rest (vol. 1, no. 1, p. 9). By the end of the story, Mrs. Morrison's organization holds five hundred members, allowing her to continue life unwed and dedicated to social service. Gilman's essay "Improved Methods of Habit Culture" (1910) illustrates the types of lessons Mrs. Morrison and her colleagues might have discussed during their meetings for the Rest and Improvement Club. It details methods of scientific management and mental willpower to regulate one's sleeping hours. Gilman writes, "Suppose you have to get up at five, and have no alarm clock nor anyone to waken you. You 'make up your mind,' hard, that you must wake up at five; you rouse yourself from coming sleep with the renewed intense determination to wake up at five; your last waking thought is 'I must wake up at five!'—and you do wake up at five. You set an alarm inside—and it worked" (vol. 1, no. 9, p. 8). Routine rest, limited to the right amount of hours, allows a person to store up the proper amount of energy to persevere throughout the coming day. Gilman advises her reader: "Don't waste nerve force on foolish and unnecessary things—physical or moral; but invest it, carefully, without losing an ounce, in the gradual and easy acquisition of whatever new habits You, as the Conscious Master, desire to develop in your organism" (9). What Gilman adds to Call's emphasis on the individual mastery of one's machine—to ascertain the best method for effectively recharging it from day to day—is the importance that such efforts have for social evolution. Gilman argues that efficiently rested bodies enable the running of an increasingly efficient social engine.

The waste of nerve force is a serious concern for Gilman, whose story "The Yellow Wall-Paper" best depicts the white female neurasthenia she writes about in the *Forerunner*. Writing about this story, Jane F. Thrailkill argues that the narrator's "psychophysical elements of perpetual effort" do little to propel her beyond domestic confinement (119). Thrailkill notes that for Gilman, "the distinctive contours of the nineteenth-century household were literally sickening," in that "one's environment physically shaped one's state of mind" (130). Fleissner describes the narrator's symbiotic connection to the interiority of her bedroom as "the loop that has entrapped her" (*Women* 75). The story is well known for critiquing Silas Weir Mitchell's acclaimed "bedroom treatment" (or forced rest), but few scholars have taken a closer look at Gilman's appreciation of administered sleep, which surfaces in many of her publications and which she associates with disciplined practice. In this way, Gilman echoes Call's observation that "even the rest-cures, the most simple and harmless of the nerve restorers, serve a mistaken end. Patients go with nerves tired and worn out with misuse,—commonly called over-work. Through rest, Nature, with the warm, motherly help she is ever ready to bring us, restores the worn body to a normal state; but its owner has not learned to work the machine any better, . . . and most occupants of rest-cures find themselves driven back more than once for another 'rest'" (12). But rather than reject rest cures outright, Gilman hopes to avoid them by providing her readers with practices of sleep discipline that can enable them to achieve routine rest, so that they need not depend on recurring bouts of treatment. In "Rest and Power," for example, Gilman explains that "it takes some power to rest. Exhaustion is not rest" (vol. 6, no. 10, p. 271). She encourages readers to avoid nerve-destroying exhaustion altogether, which they can do by disciplining their bodies into habits of routine, restorative rest.

The 1915 *Forerunner* story "Dr. Clair's Place" exemplifies the suffering caused by prolonged exhaustion and issues Gilman's corrective on the ideal rest cure. For Octavia Welch, this condition can only be cured by suicide. She is on her way to do just that when a doctor offers her an escape from urban demands through medical rehabilitation. The story's narrator, a "graduate patient" of Dr. Clair, tells Octavia of this physician who "is profoundly interested in neurasthenia—melancholia—all that kind of thing" and asks her listener whether she might do one last good deed by lending her suicidal self to scientific experimentation (vol. 6, no. 6, p. 141–42). Octavia accepts the offer and is transported to Dr. Clair's "psycho-sanatorium" in the southern California mountains. Octavia's care centers on a "bedroom and balcony treatment," in which she attains a monthlong period of uninterrupted rest that results in renewed strength and happiness (145). Dr. Clair is reminiscent of Dr. Mary Prance in James's *The Bostonians* (1886), who is known for her attentiveness and good patient care. Like Dr. Clair, Dr. Prance includes rest as a key treatment in her practice, as Miss Birdseye tells Ransom: "She is trying to make me sleep; that's her principal occupation" (215). Despite this emphasis on rest among literary figurations of the New Woman doctor, some Gilman scholars have read "Dr. Clair's Place" as a mere antithesis of Mitchell's rest cure in "The Yellow Wall-Paper" (see, e.g., Tuttle). Such a tendency inadvertently causes readings of the 1915 story to overlook the importance of sleep in Dr. Clair's methods. After her treatment is complete, Octavia recalls: "I slept better than I had for years, and more than I knew at the time, for when restless misery came up they promptly put me to sleep and kept me there. . . . [Dr. Clair] made my body as strong as it might be, and rebuilt my worn-out nerves with sleep—sleep—sleep" (145).

As the trifold repetition of the word *sleep* suggests, Octavia learns—through bed rest—the value of habitual sleep, and she achieves bodily restoration as a result.

As "Dr. Clair's Place" shows, Gilman had a profound appreciation for restorative rest. Thus, "The Yellow Wall-Paper" is not a rejection of the rest cure; it is a warning against alienating an individual from her own relationship to restorative rest (a *misuse* of bedroom treatment). Dana Seitler refers to Gilman's well-known work as a "degeneration" story that, like Wharton's *The House of Mirth*, exposes the evolutionary deterioration of women if they remain oppressed, both mentally and physically, by a patriarchal system (82). Seitler then defines another popular fictional work by Gilman, *The Crux* (1911, serialized in the *Forerunner*'s second volume), as a "regeneration novel" in which going west frees and revives the oppressed female protagonist: "Female characters 'go west' to find themselves and regain their health, sanity, and bodies in open outdoor space, places where they engage in rigorous activity as opposed to 'rest'" (Seitler 81). However, this is only partly true for Gilman's novella, for the protagonist in *The Crux*, Vivian, actually enriches herself through both physical exercise and restorative rest: "[Vivian] tramped the hills with the girls; picked heaping pails of wild berries, learned to cook in primitive fashion, *slept as she had never slept in her life*, from dark to dawn, grew brown and hungry and cheerful" (vol. 2, no. 11, p. 297, added emphasis). Vivian's interactions with the natural world seem to train her body to sleep according to the Earth's diurnal rhythms ("from dark to dawn"). Her newfound freedom is thus, in part, manifested through her rejuvenating sleep practices. Vivian's restoration is like what James's Roderick experiences when he escapes to the Swiss countryside to indulge in "sleeping as you sleep" and returning to his natural, internal sleep rhythms (*Roderick* 135).

A "natural" means of sleeping, as portrayed in the 1912 *Forerunner* sketch "Morning Devotions," has profound powers in restoring individuals and unifying the social collective. This sketch begins with the lines, "Early sleep, because daylight was beloved, and darkness also, for rest and growth; long quiet hours of sleep, sound, dreamless, perfect. Then—the dawn" (vol. 3, no. 9, p. 251). Sleep is described as a precious blessing, offered by nature, to aid humanity in its social development: "The darkness was welcomed with soft acceptance, tired eyes closing; weary limbs relaxing; blessed sleep affectionately received; but the returning light brought consciousness, and consciousness, to humanity, was joy" (251). Whereas sleep deprivation leads to depression, diurnal sleep restores individuals and brings them "joy." Gilman seems to be describing the sleep practices of a future social utopia (like the one she envisions in the 1915 novel *Herland*, serialized in the *Forerunner*, vol. 6), in which a more enlightened society communes with the natural world to better rejuvenate their bodies through nighttime sleep: "As the east turned from gray to rose, . . . so stirred the myriad sleepers, smiling, as they woke to life again, in the new days. Clear of conscience and rested utterly; in pure health and vigor" (251). In these "new days," awakening at dawn unifies "the myriad sleepers," so that they are "held in one harmony by that long wave of rolling light, [and] soft music rose . . . of glad hope and new-born power" (251). This "waking world"—an unspecified human collective that, per the implicit class cues in these lines, obviously does not include factory workers (who would not experience sleep as such)—represents a new dawn in social evolution, in which social harmony can be achieved through shared sleeping practices (251).

Figure 11 provides a Voyant-generated webbing of words associated with *sleep*. The *Forerunner* texts used to generate this graphic are limited to the full-length selections featured on the digital companion website (thirty total), among them "Morning Devotions" and "Dr. Clair's Place" (see Huber, "Selections"). While I hope many observations can be drawn from the visualization in figure 11, it is most pertinent here to note the contrasting word associations between sleep and bodily rejuvenation (*refreshed, delicious, heavenly, power*, and *peace*) and sleep and bodily depletion (*cry, consciousness, noises, nerves, anesthetic*, and *exhausted*). Reading "Morning Devotions" and "Dr. Clair's Place" together highlights both the power of routine sleep habits and the danger of estranging oneself from sleep, and the Voyant graphic helps better visualize this juxtaposition. Figure 11 also provides a window into my analytic preoccupations with the *Forerunner*, in that while sleep is a persistent topic throughout Gilman's work, it represents myriad and often contradictory things depending on the context. For Gilman, sleep was a literal act of restoration and recuperation, a habit that must be practiced and fine tuned for maximum work output, and an instrument for empowering one's brain to discover and achieve new human and social feats. On the other hand, it could be a metaphor for social ignorance and decrepitude or even a fantastical means of time travel. This range is illustrated in the Voyant visualization, and the close readings I provide here reveal how such contexts shift according to the race and class of Gilman's female characters.

Through the lens of "Morning Devotions," *The Crux*'s Vivian can be interpreted as exemplifying the power of routine, natural sleep. Octavia in "Dr. Clair's Place," on the other hand, is representative of women who grow so estranged from sleep that they can only be saved by (the right kind of)

132   CHAPTER 4

FIGURE 11. This is another variation on visualizing collocation patterns. For this Voyant image, I used the "Centralize" feature of the "Links" visualization to see words connected to *sleep** in selections from the *Forerunner* (asterisk includes terms with the same root word).

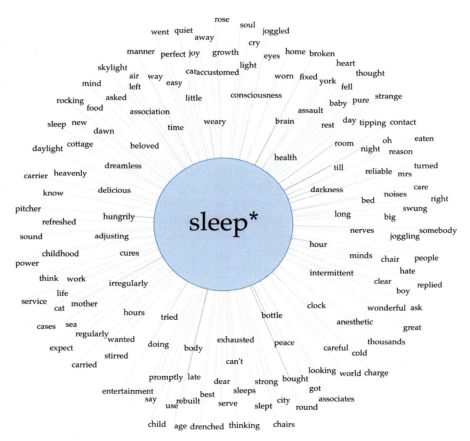

medical intervention. Conscious awareness of the social oppression one endures is both vital *and* dangerous knowledge, according to Gilman. The trauma of "waking up" to one's social oppression, as Octavia does, can be so painful that it tempts women to seek a deadly means of escape. Lily Bart's suicide is one example in fin de siècle literature in which a woman, aware of her social determinism, chooses death over oppression. The death of Edna Pontellier, Kate Chopin's heroine in *The Awakening* (1899), is another. If Lily or Edna would have had access to Dr. Clair's treatment, would they still have committed suicide? Like Lily, Edna "awakens" to a newfound understanding

"Rest and Power"   133

of patriarchal oppression and eventually kills herself. Unlike Gilman, Wharton and Chopin do not envision a possibility for their protagonists to be nursed back to health through an emphasis on rest. Gilman, meanwhile, resists such fatalism in her fiction. Instead, she imagines how white women can be saved from such a fate through the ingenuity of burgeoning female professionalism. The 1915 short story "Mrs. Merrill's Duties" exemplifies an important agenda in Gilman's *Forerunner*: to educate women on the importance of natural, rather than artificially induced, sleep. It tells the story of a woman who invents "a safe and simple sedative, something which induced natural sleep, with no ill results" (vol. 6, no. 3, p. 60). While the sedative is a work of invention, Gilman implies that Mrs. Merrill's purpose—to create a sedative with "no ill results"—renders it a natural substance, as opposed to an artificial one. Elsewhere in the *Forerunner*, Gilman expresses concern over the drugging of young women by sexual predators. Two 1914 stories— "His Mother" and "With a Difference"—address this issue. The former is about a young man whose mother catches him in his room with a young woman, whom he has drugged and intends to sexually assault (vol. 5, no. 7). The latter tells the story of a girl whose family is devastated after discovering she has been drugged and raped by a male acquaintance (vol. 5, no. 2). In "Mrs. Merrill's Duties," Gilman crafts a story in which women are provided with their own power to initiate sleep. This fictional discovery, in turn, represents Gilman's hope for a cure to what she viewed both literally and metaphorically as the improper—and, at times, dangerous—drugging of white women.

Mrs. Merrill's sedative represents Gilman's notion of a healthy means of sleep-induced drugging. Yet elsewhere in the *Forerunner*, Gilman mixes metaphorical and literal treatments of sleep and arousal to express her concerns over improper sedation. In the 1916 article "Studies in Social Pathology," she compares the "general condition of our present society" to "that of a man drugged, faintly conscious, at times, trying to move heavy limbs, with a dragging nightmare effort from which he continually sinks back to unconsciousness" (vol. 7, no. 5, p. 119). Interestingly, Gilman refers to men as improperly drugging themselves to sleep, while women, she implies, are more naturally attuned to achieving routine rest (or more likely to inventing and using "natural" methods for inducing sleep). In a 1912 sketch, "Improving on Nature," Mother Nature dozes for an extended period and awakens to find that Man has forced women to be "small and weak and foolish and timid and inefficient." The sketch ends as Mother Nature "began to pay attention to business again, rather regretting her nap" (vol. 3, no. 7, pp. 174, 176). As with her Sleeping Beauty metaphor, Gilman argues in this sketch that the archetypal American woman has allowed herself to rest easy in her naive trust of men. Men, meanwhile, constantly cheat the system, even when it comes to natural sleep. In the 1909 poem "His Crutches," Gilman writes, "Why should the Stronger Sex require, / To hold him to his tasks, / Two medicines of varied fire? / The Weaker Vessel asks. / Hobbling between the rosy cup / And dry narcotic brown,—/ One daily drug to stir him up / And one to soothe him down" (vol. 1, no. 2, p. 18). Gilman argues that between caffeine and soporific consumption, both the neurasthenic and brutish members of the "stronger sex" weaken themselves by resisting natural waking and sleeping states. She sees this as an opportunity for women to seize greater social power. She sketches a similar comparison in the 1915 "World Rousers," stating, "This is not the natural sleep of health which holds us. We are drugged, drugged these ages past, our brains dulled and clouded, our nerves relaxed, our muscles weak, our eyes unable to open. It is like trying to rescue one poisoned with laudanum; the patient must be kept walking, walking—must be made to move" (vol. 6, no. 5, p. 131). She uses soporifics as an analogy here to show that women, following their Mother Nature and Sleeping Beauty inclinations, have inadvertently drugged themselves into passivity.

Women, then, must wake from their half-asleep submission and seize social power. Gilman's 1910 parable "While the King Slept" features a woman who usurps patriarchal power by doing what the men are too tired to do. In the story, a king is presented with a series of problems within the kingdom, but he refuses to act, complaining: "I am tired of looking at these things, and tired of hearing about them" (vol. 1, no. 11, p. 17). Wearied by his empire's countless problems, the king falls into a prolonged slumber. His queen, meanwhile, takes his place, alleviates every issue, and doubles the kingdom's prosperity. This story, when read alongside the later "Improving on Nature," suggests that only one sex can be fully awake and in power, while the other is forced into a somnambulant state of submission. As the title "Improving on Nature" suggests, it is time for women to wake from their long naps and improve humankind. To work toward this vision, Gilman argues that middle-class women should harness the powers of natural sleep to advance their social standing among men.

This is just what happens in the 1911 serialized novel *Moving the Mountain*. The tale is told in the first person by John Robertson, a scholar of ancient languages. During a trip through the Himalayas, John suffers a fall and loses his memory. He is shaken from his thirty-year stupor only after his sister, Nellie, recognizes him while visiting Tibet. Upon returning to his native United States, John is shocked by the nation's immense social and technological changes. During the thirty years that the amnesiac John meandered a foreign land, the women of his homeland "woke up. . . . And being awake, they . . . saw their duty and they did it" (vol. 2, no. 4, p. 109). In hearing of the great changes that took place in his absence, John reflects that "it was as if I had slept, and, in my sleep, they had stolen my world" (vol. 2, no. 2, p. 51). Such an observation evinces the influence on Gilman's work of Edward Bellamy's 1888 utopian novel *Looking Backward: From 2000 to 1887* as well as H. G. Wells's 1899 novel *The Sleeper Awakes*. In both earlier tales, the narrators are given improper doses of a sleep aid to treat their insomnia. As a result, they sleep for a vast amount of time and wake to a future completely unknown to them. During the time that passes between John's accident and his "awakening," he functions like one of these drugged, sleeping protagonists—or, better, a sleepwalker. Rather than be drugged into prolonged sleep, he is like the people that Gilman describes in "World Rousers," who walk around and live life like somnambulists, their brains asleep while their bodies continue to function. Modern men, as Gilman imagines them, suffer from mismanagement and poor understanding of sleep, a weakness that could very well enable women to wake up and dismantle the patriarchy.

Women's Social Awakening

Gilman's goal with the *Forerunner* was to wake women up. She boasts in a 1911 "Comment and Review" of a letter from a subscriber that reads: "I should like to thank you for the great part your writings are taking in the awakening of our sex" (vol. 2, no. 1, 30). Her poems particularly voice this agenda. The 1910 poem "In How Little Time" associates an inner awakening with "Power in the hand and brain for what needs making" (vol. 1, no. 12, p. 9). Later, the 1913 poem "A March for Women" calls on *Forerunner* readers to "Wake! Wake! Wake to the work before you! / Rise! Rise! Rise to the toil to-day! / Brain and body, heart and soul, / Strain to win the splendid goal!" (vol. 4, no. 10, p. 258). This "splendid goal" is for white, middle-class women to achieve greater social power. Gilman emphasizes the importance of women's awakening and uses her poetry to compel readers to awareness and social action. Her novels, meanwhile, provide a practical account of what she hopes to achieve through such an awakening. *Moving the Mountain*, for instance, portrays a stratified society working collectively under the science of efficiency. In the novella, Gilman depicts how labor energy can be channeled within a socialist system, so that, just like with collective wealth, society at large can benefit from a collective expenditure of energy. As John's brother-in-law Frank explains, the nation's advancements in efficiency have resulted from the social body's strategic use of collective energy: "The business of the universe about us consists in the Transmission of Energy. . . . We ourselves, the human animals, were specially adapted for high efficiency in storing and transmitting this energy; and so were able to enter into a combination still more efficient; that is, into social relations. Humanity, man in social relation, is the best expression of the Energy that we know" (vol. 2, no. 11, p. 303). Such a system requires that each individual understand their position in the social strata and then habituate themselves to a lifestyle that facilitates efficiency in their given professional area. As Frank puts it, "Because of its special faculty of consciousness, this human engine can feel, see, think, about the power within it; and can use it more fully and wisely. All it has to learn is the *right* expression of its degree of life-force, of Social Energy" (303, added emphasis). The way in which life force is both channeled and expressed is decided by the committees that Gilman peppers throughout *Moving the Mountain*. These committees—it is implied that they are made up of local leaders, such as Nellie—decide what individuals do, how much rest they have access to, and how they spend their time throughout the day.

Thus, in Gilman's utopia, not every individual gets to freely choose their expression of social energy, or their amount of energy expended per day. Like Bellamy's socialist utopia, Gilman's society thrives on increased mechanical and human efficiency. When John is first introduced to the new world, he reflects: "Was that old dream of Bellamy's stalking abroad? Were young men portioned out to menial service, willy-nilly?" (vol. 2, no. 2, p. 52). Gilman purposely places John in the role of skeptic so that his myopic assumptions about a socialist society can be disproved at every turn. Yet, it is also possible that Gilman implies, through John, that *Moving the Mountain* represents an improvement on Bellamy's vision of socialist industry. In Bellamy's novel, the narrator, Julian, is told by his guide, Doctor Leete, that "while the obligation of service in some form is not to be evaded, voluntary election, subject only to necessary regulation, is depended on to determine the particular sort of service every man is to render" (91). Gilman's belief that such a process represents a "willy-nilly" order is evinced in passages detailing how laborers are assigned work. Specifically, the Commission on Human Efficiency, which had applied the "dawning notions of 'scientific management' . . . in the first decade of the new century," ensures that every person is reared within an ideal environment and is prescribed the appropriate social position (vol. 2, no. 6, p. 164). This process then prepares an individual for assignment to a particular form of labor, with guidance from the Social Service Union (166). The Commission on Human Efficiency, as its name implies, dictates an individual's working and resting hours, ensuring that a person's labor time is efficiently maximized for society's benefit.

For immigrants, an obscure yet clearly rigorous training is required, which Nellie refers to as "Compulsory Socialization." Gilman references Lester Frank Ward's concept of the "reintegration of the peoples" in Nellie's concession that although immigration is a "sociological process not possible to stop," it is "possible to assist and to guide [immigrants] to great advantage" (vol. 2, no. 3, p. 79; see also Davis, "His"). The exchange between Nellie and John that follows is quite disturbing. John reflects distastefully that "our family were pure English stock, and rightly proud of their descent." Nellie seems to read John's mind, for she "laughed appreciatively," replying, "Well, whether you like it or not, our people saw their place and power at last and rose to it. We refuse no one. We have discovered as many ways of utilizing human waste as we used to have for the waste products of coal tar" (79). Nellie does not clarify whether she is identifying with John's "pure English stock" when she speaks of "our people." She may, instead, be referring to socialist revolutionaries, but her subsequent comment about "utilizing human waste" as if it were "coal tar" is extremely disconcerting. In all, Gilman draws connections between a rise in power—for a particular subset of Americans—and the use of immigrant bodies as an energy source for the (white) social collective. *Moving the Mountain*, then, illustrates institutionalizing the power of repose for an upper strata of citizens, while enforcing efficiency in the communal recharging of human machines, specifically for those whose very bodies are considered "human waste."

The "Compulsory Socialization" forced on immigrants in *Moving the Mountain* could not be more different from the path to citizenship depicted in Gilman's second utopian novel, *Herland*, which appeared in the *Forerunner* four years later. Together, the utopian societies in these two novels establish a dichotomy between extracting energy from non-natives and cultivating rest in the bodies of birthright citizens. *Herland* is presented from the viewpoint of Van Jennings, who, along with two male friends, discovers an all-female society that has survived for two thousand years without men, reproducing via parthenogenesis. Van, fascinated by every subsequent discovery, provides an anthropological account of Herlander society. Unlike the inhabitants of Nellie's world, these women are not forced to adhere to a "melting pot" mentality and thus do not have to cope with the challenges of immigrant "human waste." As many scholars have observed, Van quickly declares "that these people were of Aryan stock" (vol. 6, no. 5, p. 125; see Davis, "His" 84; Hausman 499; Hudak 457; Nadkarni 43; Weinbaum 284). He also notes that the Herlanders lack any "hopeless substratum of paupers

138   CHAPTER 4

and degenerates" (vol. 6, no. 6, p. 153), revealing how the all-woman nation focuses its collective energy on cultivating new generations of Herlanders. While still babies, citizens are educated through the very act of sleep. Van witnesses the "natural sleep in which these heavenly babies passed their first years. They never knew they were being educated. They did not dream that . . . they were laying the foundation for that close beautiful group feeling into which they grew so firmly with the years. This was education for citizenship" (vol. 6, no. 9, p. 243). Collective rest is described as the foundation for instituting the flow of social energy, "that close beautiful group feeling." The mere practice of "natural sleep" contributes to the "education for citizenship" in *Herland* and constitutes one Herlander strategy for cultivating in their youngest citizens a means for accruing and sharing social power.

In Gilman's utopian visions, the antithesis of white women's attainment of social power is the "human waste" that inhibits social progress. Gilman's concerns about the latter are a recurring motif in the *Forerunner*. In *Moving the Mountain*, for instance, Nellie nonchalantly informs John that "we killed many hopeless degenerates, insane, idiots, and real perverts, after trying our best powers of cure" (vol. 2, no. 11, p. 307). Gilman's belief in eugenics, not uncommon at the time among public intellectuals, is a dark component to the author's life that Gilman scholars, especially since the mid-1990s, have worked hard to reconcile with her feminist ideals. Gilman biographer Cynthia Davis demonstrates how Gilman's support for eugenics cannot be separated from her racism. In discussing Gilman's flight from New York City to New England in 1922, Davis cites a letter in which Gilman wrote of her hope "to escape, forever, the hideous city—and its Jews"; as Davis notes, "the patrician New Yorker Madison Grant had predicted in 1916 that Americans of the 'old stock' would be 'literally driven off the streets of New York City by swarms of Polish Jews,' and Charlotte's reflections on her exodus suggest Grant's bigotry matched his foresight" (*Charlotte* 350). Davis is referring here to Grant's pseudo-anthropological study *The Passing of the Great Race*, which deplored the adulteration of Nordic and Anglo-Saxon bloodlines in the United States. As a work of scientific racism, *Passing* circulated racist propaganda through the guise of ethnographic observation. Like Gilman's personal letters, the *Forerunner* also evinces Gilman's disgust for the diversity of urban spaces, which she increasingly interpreted as a danger to Anglo-Saxon purity. Her solution to this issue, as she presents it in the *Forerunner*, is to seek out a means for white women to accrue social power through the exploitation of ethnic bodies.

Gilman's distaste for what she describes in her 1922 letter as the "nerve wearing noise—the dirt—the ugliness, the steaming masses" of New York

City is expressed in the *Forerunner* (qtd. in Davis, *Charlotte* 350). The 1910 story "When I Was a Witch" is a pro-eugenic fantasy in which the narrator alters and even eradicates populations (albeit in animal form) to improve the city. If *Herland* is, as Jennifer Hudak says, an indication of "what the world would look like if Gilman were offered the opportunity to 'play God'" (476), then "When I Was a Witch" is a dark magic prelude to Gilman's later novel. The story begins with the narrator's retreat to the roof of her New York City apartment at the stroke of midnight on Halloween. Suffering from heat and frayed nerves, she ruminates over the boisterousness of the city. Her sleep is constantly interrupted by shrieking street cats. On this night, she reacts violently, wishing "that every cat in the city was comfortably dead!" (vol. 1, no. 7, p. 2). She is surprised to find that all suddenly falls quiet and she can sleep with ease. The next day, after wishing that all dogs would "die at once," she discovers that this desire has also been granted (3). It may seem a stretch to argue that domesticated animals serve as a stand-in for the culturally diverse groups of New Yorkers that drove Gilman to flee the city. Yet, Gilman explicitly identifies one animal metaphor that stands in for a particular subset of humanity: the mistreatment of horses in the story parallels the patriarchal oppression of wives and mothers. Such an analogy echoes Charles Chesnutt's "The Conjurer's Revenge" (1889), in which Julius says that driving a mule feels like imposing on a human creature. Both Chesnutt's and Gilman's narrators evoke sympathy from their readers through the metaphor of the mistreated laborer as abused animal. While Chesnutt uses this device to highlight the violent exploitation of Black workers, Gilman co-opts it to dramatize the subjugation of white women in the domestic space. At the end of Gilman's story, the narrator observes that "the way women dress and behave . . . 'twas like seeing . . . real horses only used as rocking-horses" (6). According to Sari Edelstein's reading of the story, "Like urban pets, women are supposedly in the right place in the home, limited in 'the use of their limbs,' but [Gilman] denaturalizes the notion of house pets just as she destabilizes the association of women with domestic work" (137). However, I read the story not as an attempt to liken middle-class white women to domesticated pets, but as an attempt to elevate them to an equivalency with horses. The narrator wishes the dogs and cats dead, but for horses her wish is that cruel owners suffer the pain and poor conditions inflicted on their equine counterparts. This results in a "'new wave of humane feeling' [that] soon raised the status of horses in our city" (vol. 1, no. 7, p. 3). Why is it that the narrator chooses to euthanize the cats and dogs while elevating the status of horses? Meanwhile, a "starved black cat . . . [that] stole from behind a chimney and mewed dolefully," approaching the narrator like a beggar, represents those types of "human waste" that are likewise exterminated in *Moving the Mountain* (1).

In "When I Was a Witch," Gilman categorizes horses as a contributor to the social good, dogs as a source of misdirected human energy (their owners spend their days fretting over them), and cats, who never stop begging and mewing, as a mere drain on humanity's collective energy. This typology also applies to human groups, as Gilman observes in "Studies in Social Pathology": "One of the simplest processes of social replenishment is that which goes on unconsciously between individuals. We all know the difference between people who tire us, people who rest us, and people who strengthen and exhilarate us" (vol. 7, no. 5, p. 121). She argues that women should not allow domesticity to wall them off from society. Instead, they must foster communal relationships with those who can help them muster strength and social autonomy. Just a few pages later, in an article entitled "The Sanctity of Human Life," Gilman goes a step further by highlighting the dangers of allowing "hideous degeneracy" to go unchecked (vol. 7, no. 5, p. 128). Asha Nadkarni, noting this 1916 essay's criticism of the "feeble-minded and defective," argues that "Gilman's unflinching use of such rhetoric suggests her eugenic concerns outweigh her feminist ones (or, more accurately, they are one and the same)" (40). Because Gilman had no power to wish away "human waste" as the narrator does in "When I Was a Witch," she educated her ideal readers—white middle-class women—on how to capitalize on and cultivate the energy reserves of those with less social power.

Contrary to her impulse to flee New York, Gilman argues in her essay "Studies in Social Pathology" that the only way for women to advance in society is to immerse themselves in the diversified, modern world. She discourages her readers from remaining "shut apart from one another by conditions of economics, of education, of religion, of race, of mere prejudice and tradition" (vol. 7, no. 5, p. 122). This is a positive sentiment, but as Lisa Ganobcsik-Williams points out in her discussion of Gilman's 1908 article "A Suggestion on the Negro Problem," Gilman's focus on white social advancement was a constant undercurrent in her written work: "Gilman saw [the] gulf between blacks and whites as wasteful, because it prevented them from joining in a united effort for social progress. Although she hoped for racial unity, she assumed that it would be on white terms, that blacks naturally would and should want to 'progress' to white ways of living" (20). Thus, ethnic and nonwhite Americans could only serve productively in society if they cohered to white cultural ideals. Ganobcsik-Williams explains that "[Gilman] rationalized her underlying ethnic and racial elitism into an evolutionary story through which white Americans had progressed to the highest standard—or, at least, possessed the best potential for reaching this standard" (24). Gilman found it imperative that white women, who in her mind were the most socially advanced subset of American women, accrue greater social power by capitalizing on labor provided by immigrant and Black women.

Gilman's racist logic is, in large part, due to her adherence to the social evolutionary beliefs of her day. Gilman argues in the *Forerunner* that women must "wake up" to their own social potential. Waking up represents another step in social evolution for white women and implies that nonwhite women suffer from an atavism that renders them only partially awake. Gilman predicts, as exemplified by the androgynous women of *Herland*, that sexual differences among white people will decrease as society advances. As Louise Michele Newman explains, Gilman believed that "for civilized (white) peoples, sexual difference needed to be expunged because it interfered with the further development of industrial efficiency and individual and social morality and modern civilization. For primitive people, however, sexual difference needed to be injected into the society to help accelerate 'racial inferiors' along the path of social evolution" (137). Ethnic women, whom Gilman viewed as primitive, embodied a femininity and domesticity that was a requirement for their survival. She used this framework to construct her conception of modern domestic labor, in which non-Anglo women bear the burden of maintaining the home space while "advanced" white women pursue a feminist agenda in the public sphere.

Gilman never speaks explicitly of this hierarchy in the *Forerunner*. Instead, she reframes racialized exploitation as an avenue for "female professionalism." Ann Mattis underscores an important contradiction in Gilman's 1903 nonfiction book *The Home, Its Work and Influence*, in which Gilman finds it detestable that "strangers by birth, by class, by race, by education—as utterly alien as it is possible to conceive—these we introduce into our homes—in our very bed chambers" (42; qtd. in Mattis 290). At the same time as Gilman expresses this nativism, Mattis points out, she "refers to all women as the 'handmaids of the world' in order to establish a collective notion of women's oppression in the domestic sphere." Mattis explains this paradox as Gilman's attempt to redefine the "maid/mistress relationship" as an advancement in "American feminism . . . by [which] bourgeois women . . . [could] carve out a space for female professionalism" (290). Mattis's study unwittingly addresses a sleep-related concern in Gilman's work, in which resting spaces and sleeping hours for maids must be kept separate from "our very bed chambers," complicating efforts to keep them close at hand to ensure labor proficiency.

The 1910 story "Her Housekeeper" exemplifies the maid-mistress paradox and provides a frightening solution to the quagmire of sleep-in maids: simply assume that they need not sleep at all. The story centers on Mrs. Leland, a stage actress and widowed mother who lives in a New York City boardinghouse with her son and her maid, Alice. For Mrs. Leland, the two most important stress-relieving elements of her quarters are a top-floor bedroom and "a colored lady, named Alice, who did not seem to care where she slept, or if she slept at all." Mrs. Leland boasts of her restful sleeping space, as well as its protector, Alice, who "sits on the stairs and keeps everybody away" (vol. 1, no. 3, p. 2). Ironically, Mrs. Leland values Alice for protecting her much-needed sleep, yet she cannot conceive of Alice herself as having the same biological need for restorative rest. This scenario is disturbingly like one I detail in chapter 2, in which Harriet Jacobs reflects in *Incidents in the Life of a Slave Girl* (1861) that her aunt Nancy was expected to sleep on the floor next to her mistress's bed. This round-the-clock attentiveness and "broken rest" was ruinous to Nancy's health (221). Although Gilman never illustrates the impact of sleep deprivation on Alice as Jacobs does in her description of her aunt, she does elaborate on the bodily well-being that Mrs. Leland gains from keeping Alice awake during her resting time: "Possibly it was owing to the stillness and the air and the sleep till near lunchtime that Mrs. Leland kept her engaging youth, her vivid uncertain beauty" (2). Despite her dependency on Alice, Mrs. Leland has little regard for Alice's bodily needs. Instead, she harbors the racist assumption that Alice need not sleep at all. Thus, for Mrs. Leland, the path to New Woman status is only achieved through her possession of another's time and energy so that she may eschew traditional female duties.

In reading "Her Housekeeper" alongside *What Diantha Did* (1909–10, Gilman's first *Forerunner* novella), it is apparent that Mrs. Leland encourages the practice of a maid's "sleeping in." Like Alice, who must sleep outside her mistress's chambers, the servants in *What Diantha Did* are kept at a safe distance from their sleeping employers. In the chapter entitled "Sleeping In," Diantha (owner of a housecleaning business) and her colleagues, standing outside the maids' chambers, engage in a lengthy discussion about how to manage them at night. They discuss the dangers of "communicating doors" and Mrs. Weatherstone proposes that they should all be "permanently locked" (vol. 1, no. 9, 15). Controlling and keeping watch over one's domestic staff, then, is crucial to Gilman's modernization of industrialized housekeeping.

Another important aspect of improving domestic labor is to ensure that hired women do as Alice does and help energize their mistresses. In the

1911 tale "Making a Change," Gilman illustrates the dangers for ambitious white women who do not have access to the trained housemaids that businesses like Diantha's provide. The story also voices Gilman's concern over sleep deprivation's effect on a white, middle-class woman struggling under the burden of domesticity. After giving birth, Julia Gordins suffers from being "kept awake nearly all night, and for many nights," as "she spent her days in unremitting devotion to [her baby's] needs, and to the care for her neat flat; and her nights had long since ceased to refresh her" (vol. 2, no. 2, p. 311). Whereas Alice in "Her Housekeeper" supposedly needs no sleep at all, for Julia, sleep deprivation is so acute that Gilman compares it to "a form of torture" (311). Julia is described as having a mind "too exhausted to serve her properly," and she goes about her motherly tasks "mechanically," thinking only of "Sleep—Sleep—Sleep" (312). When she does catch a bit of respite, she is disturbed by her maid, Greta, who, with "heavy heels and hands," is constantly making noise (313). Despite her exhaustion, Julia can still perform her duties technically and efficiently while suffering from sleep deprivation. Prior to the *Forerunner*, Gilman expressed her concern over the perpetual, mechanical performance of household tasks in her 1893 story "Through This." Denise Knight considers Jane's activity in "Through This" as an inversion of the sleep deprivation experienced by the Jane of "The Yellow Wall-Paper," who increasingly exhausts herself by obsessively reading the wallpaper in her bedroom. Like the Jane in "Through This," described by Knight as having "subconscious signs of resentment toward her role as wife and mother" (291), Julia of "Making a Change" grows so frustrated with her domestic confinement that she attempts suicide. Yet, unlike with the disturbing psychotic break at the end of "The Yellow Wall-Paper," Julia is saved by her mother-in-law, who takes over care of the baby and encourages Julia to return to her musical career. She also makes sure to rid their home of the energy-sapping maid, "Greta the hammer-footed," and replaces her with "an amazing French matron" (314). Mrs. Gordins pays the new woman higher wages and is pleased with the many talents she exhibits, such as a refined cooking style and better meal planning. Julia vastly improves under this new regime, and "Making a Change" correlates efficient (ideally Anglo) domestic help with a working woman's access to restorative rest and professional opportunities.

However, as Graham explains, finding "an amazing French matron" to serve as one's housemaid was not an easy task at the turn of the century: "historians of the period have noted that generally only the most 'disadvantaged' women took jobs as domestic servants. . . . The inferior nature of the work, as well as the low social position granted to domestics meant that 'the well-schooled, well-trained young woman' Gilman had in mind often sought other kinds of work altogether" (195). In *What Diantha Did*, Gilman merges the woman question and the servant question by placing the domestic burden on those women whom she deems feminized by their primitive state. She poses the servant question as a way to solve the "'woman problem,' [which] as Gilman redefined it, was that Anglo-Protestant women had been 'denied time, place and opportunity' to develop those 'race' characteristics that were . . . now mistakenly referred to as 'male'" (Newman 138). Julia Gordins is a prime example of such a woman being denied these liberties. Perpetual housework exhausts her so much that she has no time to focus on her career as a music teacher. Moreover, her time is consumed by managing both her son and her poorly performing maid. Only once she is freed from those obligations, and is able to rest herself effectively each night, is she able to pursue her career.

As "Her Housekeeper" and "Making a Change" illustrate, restorative rest is considered by Gilman to be more important for her white, middle-class heroines. The sleep of domestic workers is secondary to the needs of the mistress, who must have access to her maid's services around the clock. *What Diantha Did* offers her best example of a large-scale system of "social replenishment" for white, bourgeois women. Diantha's goal, as she explains to the members of the Orchardina Home and Culture Club, is to reform the "inordinately wasteful" "domestic economy" (vol. 1, no. 7, p. 14). Graham argues that Diantha premises her business strategy for preventing waste on the "principles of scientific management" (199). Accordingly, the novel begins with an example of such waste, as it highlights the ineptitude of Diantha's family maid, Sukey. In the opening scene, Diantha's mother and sisters complain of Sukey's inability to plan ahead, and Diantha's father reflects that Sukey and her husband, the family's only hired help, "did the work of the place, so far as it was done" (vol. 1, no. 1, p. 16). As African American servants, Sukey and John represent a population that, from Gilman's perspective, must be utilized efficiently in order for white people to advance society. Seitler summarizes Gilman's view on appropriating Black labor in "A Suggestion on the Negro Problem": "Her 'proposed organization' was to place them in an 'industrial army' until such point as they evolved to as high a level as whites" (68). Gilman seems to have the same objective in mind in *What Diantha Did*: Diantha organizes an industrial domestic army of immigrant and Black women that will take up arms in defense of white female professionals.

Diantha eventually works her way up to running a "House Worker's Union," in which she houses maids together in a more industrialized version of the "sleeping in" tradition (vol. 1, no. 10, p. 16). Diantha collects thirty women to train, house, and send out to middle- and upper-class white clientele. Thus, Gilman separates these servants from the intimate sleeping spaces of their overseers. Gilman establishes a clear hierarchy regarding domestic labor: Diantha, as a professional housekeeper, and her clients, as employers of her services, are far superior to Diantha's employees. Graham explains that "most of the women employed by Diantha fit the typical profile of the lowly domestic servant": Irish, Danish, and African American women that Gilman reduces "to ethnic and racial caricatures" (195). In the passages describing the women Diantha hires, Gilman measures their "mediocrity": "Laundress after laundress she studied personally and tested professionally, finding a general level of mediocrity, till finally she hit upon a melancholy Dane—a big rawboned red-faced woman" (vol. 1, no. 10, p. 13). She finds Mrs. Thorald significant for the free labor that her mentally disabled husband will also provide. She follows the same reasoning when she hires a Black woman, Julianna, to assume kitchen duties, offering to board Julianna's son, Hector. Diantha acts as if taking on these male extensions of her new hires derives from charity, but even the child is expected to serve as a bellboy and kitchen aide. Diantha's workers are then expected to sleep under her roof and live according to her schedule. As Gary Scharnhorst deftly puts it, "Sponsored by a maternalistic capitalist, Gilman's middle-class, entrepreneurial white heroine . . . hires employees who are exclusively lower-class ethnic and racial types. . . . In effect, that is, Gilman envisions a scheme that merely transferred the drudgery of the traditional home to other shoulders, to those of dull-witted brutes and lower-class women, particularly women of color" (71). Although Diantha focuses on reforming domestic labor practices, she merely establishes a more rigid hierarchy that subjugates ethnic women—and exploits their bodily energy—in an effort to enhance white women's social power.

This is most evident in Gilman's minimal attention to the housemaids' point of view throughout the story. Like Alice in "Her Housekeeper," who never speaks in the story, the employed laborers in *What Diantha Did* are constantly pushed to the margins. As Graham observes, "the domestic servants stand very much on the periphery of the text—they are invoked by Diantha, but are seldom allowed to speak for themselves" (196). Moreover, Diantha keeps constant surveillance over their working hours, including resting and bedtime. Gilman provides extensive detail for how Diantha micromanages their schedules:

> For all her employees she demanded a ten-hour day, she worked fourteen; rising at six and not getting to bed till eleven, when her charges were all safely in their rooms for the night.

They were all up at five-thirty or thereabouts, breakfasting at six, and the girls off in time to reach their various places by seven. Their day was from 7 A. M. to 8.30 P. M., with half an hour out, from 11.30 to twelve, for their lunch; and three hours, between 2.20 and 5.30, for their own time, including their tea. Then they worked again from 5.30 to 8.30, on the dinner and the dishes, and then they came home to a pleasant nine o'clock supper, and had an hour to dance or rest before the 10.30 bell for bed time. (vol. 1, no. 11, p. 7)

Furthermore, Diantha speculates about the required sleeping hours for her servants without any input from them. She is described throughout the story as having unusual energy, yet she assumes that since she requires only seven hours of sleep per night, her employees need no more than that. Through constant management, she ensures that her hires are in bed by 10:30 at night and awake by 5:30 in the morning. There is no room for negotiation, as Laura R. Fisher explains: "race and class delimit which characters are permitted to explain themselves. . . . Domestic workers . . . perform the menial work that Diantha assigns them, and the racial and class stratification of US society changes not one iota; it is merely made more efficient" (507). Gilman remains oblivious to the possibility that Diantha's employees may require a sleep schedule different from the one that her protagonist follows. If Gilman borrows Call's argument that power through repose can only be achieved by resting whenever one feels compelled to sleep, then she ultimately classifies Diantha's workers as women with too little social power to rest as they see fit.

Gilman's conception of working hours for domestic labor changes according to race and class status throughout the *Forerunner*. When she advocates for the rights of a farmer's wife in the 1915 essay "The Power of the Farm Wife," she is adamant that such women be granted an "eight-hour law" to save them from exploitation (vol. 6, no. 12, p. 316). The ideal of the eight-hour working day was entrenched in American culture after Congress passed the eight-hour law for government employees in 1868. Later events, such as the Haymarket Square riot of 1886 and the International Socialist Conference's establishment of May Day in 1889, reinforced the idea that eight-hour days represented working-class autonomy and greater personal freedom. As scholars have observed, Gilman's feminism oscillated between socialist utopias and racist, capitalist exploitation (see Mattis 283–84; Nadkarni 34; Newman 134; Scharnhorst 67–68; Seitler 63; Weinbaum 271–72). While Gilman sought for rural (white) women to receive recompense for and a reprieve from domestic labor, she also appreciated Taylorism (more than the fairness of eight-hour days) when it came to the exploitation of laborers within a system of white, female, petit bourgeois entrepreneurialism. Thus, Diantha's conception of industrialized domesticity deprives her employees of any freedom over when their bodies can rest, as Mattis notes: "Unlike the middle-class wives who are granted privacy and flexibility by domestic service, domestic workers are kept under constant surveillance, with an hour to dance with 'special friends and cousins' before curfew. This social dimension of the text reflects the hierarchies of race and class underlying the structure of Diantha's reforms" (296–97). While Gilman asks in "The Power of the Farm Wife," "How about an 'eight-hour law' for all women who are mothers?" (316), her protagonist Diantha expects the Black kitchen maid, Julianna, to adhere to a strict twenty-four-hour schedule while simultaneously caring for her son. Such contradictions, prevalent throughout Gilman's writing, reveal a racist and classist mentality that shaped the author's conception of whose work deserved more or less rest.

Diantha believes that she has the power to channel the energy and time of her employees so that their labor may be more profitable. Graham explains that "for Diantha, mastering the clock allows her to control the lives of her workers, and it ensures their most effective, efficient production" (200). In doing so, she quantifies and measures her employees' every daily moment, viewing resting time as calculated loss. Gilman depicts the workers in Diantha's employ as if they are somnambulists, workers half asleep and only equipped to perform menial tasks. Graham hints at this possibility when he explains that "Taylor's version of scientific management rested on the principle that average workers could not grasp the science underlying their work and would have to rely on a manager to explain, model, and oversee their tasks. . . . This resulted in a 'radical separation between thinking and doing' which served to reinforce firmly established binaries between mental and manual labor" (200). Similar to the ways in which the white ruling class viewed enslaved people as perpetually half asleep during the antebellum period, Gilman presents nonwhite and ethnic women as sleepwalkers, individuals she believes must be constantly directed and controlled. From her perspective, while white women have the brainpower and social will to wake up from their Sleeping Beauty trances, "primitive" women remain trapped in a state of "half slumber."

Conclusion

In the poem "Two Callings," featured in the *Forerunner* in 1911, Gilman uses a somnambulist analogy to articulate her theory that women of different ethnic and racial origins have fallen behind Anglo-Saxon women in social evolutionary advancement. The poem begins when the sleeping speaker is awakened by mysterious callings. One derives from the safety of the home space, in which "warm Comfort . . . / Soft couches, cushions" nearly lull her back to sleep. The other is "Duty," which the speaker describes as "Allegiance in an idleness abhorred." Gilman implies that the speaker has exceeded her necessary amount of sleep, which in excess becomes "idleness." The speaker is only able to "shrink—half rise" to the true call of "Duty" because she remains "the squaw—the slave—the harem beauty—/ . . . the handmaid of the world" (vol. 2, no. 4, p. 104). While Mattis reads this "image of the napping woman . . . [as] distinctly . . . leisure-class," she argues that "still in a state of half slumber, the woman is presented with a false sense of duty that reduces her to . . . three female types [that] identify her with a racially marked past" (286). While I agree that the image of the speaker calls to mind a lady of leisure, I argue that is not some false sense of domestic duty but rather the perpetual "state of half slumber" that likens the speaker to the enumerated racialized figures. Gilman believes that white women of the middle and upper class can overcome this state of slumber if they separate themselves from their ethnic counterparts. Thus, "Two Callings" provides crucial insight into Gilman's bifurcation of white and non-white women through both metaphorical and literal treatments of rest and sleep in the *Forerunner*. Mattis explains that "by drawing parallels among these various women's domestic functions, Gilman evokes metaphorically how white, middle-class America and the specter of degraded, racialized, and backwards femininity converge dangerously at the cultural intersection of domestic labor" (287). I add that to mediate this dangerous convergence, Gilman sought to capitalize on immigrant and Black women laborers as an energy source, a resource that when tapped could enable white middle-class women to escape domestic drudgery.

Gilman presents ethnic domestic workers as akin to Charles Elam's somnambulistic laborers, who—as I describe in the first two chapters—repeat in their sleep the simple, mechanical tasks that they perform during the day. Julia, in "Making a Change," for example, can still "mechanically" carry out her daily household tasks while suffering from prolonged sleeplessness and subsequent depression. Yet, it is only after she is liberated from domestic drudgery that she can rest effectively and expend brainpower in providing music lessons. In *What Diantha Did*, women are hired based on their ability to mechanically perform the tasks Diantha assigns them. According to Graham, Gilman thinks "of her workers primarily as labor units and judg[es] their value based on their ability to keep her system running," and the "dis-individuating process" of depriving servants of agency makes them "appear to be more machine-like than human" (200). Moreover, Gilman attributes a certain type of domestic work to particular racial and ethnic identities. Mrs. Thorald, a Dane, has the "big" bones for washing laundry. For kitchen duties, Diantha chooses a Black woman, Julianna, and she subsequently measures Julianna and her son according to the large amount of foodstuffs they produce per day. Diantha is particularly impressed after the duo manages to put together "some six or eight hundred sandwiches" (vo. 1, no. 11, p. 8). Diantha's managerial practices resemble the immigrant training in *Moving the Mountain*, which Nellie likens to fattening and improving cattle. Even the bigoted narrator is disgusted by Nellie's comment and replies, "You can't sell people." Nellie's response—"No, but you can profit by their labor"—sheds light on the problematic practices in *What Diantha Did*. Like Nellie's declaration that "we have a standard of citizenship now—an idea of what people ought to be and how to make them so" (vol. 2, no. 3, p. 80), Diantha believes that she understands her employees' needs better than they do. She manages them with clockwork diligence as if they were a machine, directing their energy in ways that benefit the white women who have employed them.

The *Forerunner* provides a most expansive and thorough literary account of what Michael Greaney describes as detailing "the human significance of sleep [by] attend[ing] to its representational history, and . . . offer[ing] a remarkably rich and largely untapped archive of the ways in which the practices of modern sleep have been imagined, fantasized and reinvented" (3). Gilman encapsulates her aims in publishing the *Forerunner* in the 1916 essay "A Summary of Purpose." She explains that an individual's agency is dependent on their social connection to others: "That the individual may and should use the splendid powers given by the social organization, to develop body and mind to their highest capacity and should live, not only in the personal safety and comfort a highly developed society should assure to all its members, but in the boundless range of full consciousness; having our full history in mind, and looking forward to the glorious possibilities which are in our hands to achieve" (vol. 7, no. 11, p. 286). Belying her impressive endeavor to redefine and repurpose sleep, as well as her use of the collective, possessive pronoun in her conclusion to the *Forerunner*, Gilman enforces an implied social order, one in which cultural presumptions about mental capacity and social development dictate the role an individual is expected to assume. "Rest and Power" best exemplifies this shadowed proclamation, in which Gilman sees the power of sleep as a tool for helping the women of her race and class excel in the contests of social evolution, for, as its closing lines read, "We shall have power to rest. And we shall rest in full power" (vol. 6, no. 11, p. 272).

Conclusion

> A server is woken at hour four-thirty by stimulin in the air-
> flow, then yellow-up in our dorm room. . . . At hour five
> we man our tellers around the Hub, ready for the elevator
> to bring the new day's first consumers. For the following
> nineteen hours we greet diners, input orders, tray food, vend
> drinks, upstock condiments, wipe tables, and bin garbage.
> . . . Then we imbibe one Soapsac [to induce sleep] in the
> dorm room. That is the blueprint of every unvarying day.
> —David Mitchell, *Cloud Atlas*

> The Nap Ministry is a commitment to an ideal that may
> seem unattainable. This makes it revolutionary because
> it creates space to imagine and hope. Both are the keys
> to our liberation. We can begin to use rest as a path to
> cultivate our imagination. When we stop to investigate
> and examine all the tools we have within us to interrupt
> the dominant systems, the portal opens. We will have
> to pause to listen and hold space for slow inquiry. A
> rest practice will be a lifelong journey of curiosity. I
> am curious about the following: What does a rested
> future look or feel like? How can we collaborate to
> create a world where there is a space to rest for all?
> —Tricia Hersey, *Rest Is Resistance*

In the preceding chapters, I probe the connections between sleep phenomena, cultural compulsion, and social agency to uncover a turn of the
century literary attentiveness to the constraints that modernity imposes on
restorative rest. I argue that authors Henry James, Charles Chesnutt, Edith
Wharton, and Charlotte Perkins Gilman saw value in exploring the social
power that underscores a good night's rest. Their texts reveal how the sleep
schedule of a marginalized individual can be dictated by a range of forces,

from social and labor practices to cultural dismissals of—and pseudoscientific assumptions about—sleep. Moreover, these narratives depict how manipulations of sleep in the modern era became important components of a consumer capitalist society. Each story evinces numerous connections between adequate rest and socioeconomic mobility. In James's *Roderick Hudson* (1875), for instance, we witness a sculptor failing to generate profit from his artistry because he cannot master routine rest. In other chapters, we see characters who profit from sleep diagnoses and treatments. In Chesnutt's "Uncle Julius" tales (1887–1900), antebellum doctors are employed to evaluate an enslaved narcoleptic; in Wharton's *The House of Mirth* (1905), we accompany Lily to the chemist's shop, where she forfeits her last coins for soporifics; and in Gilman's *Forerunner* (1909–16), we see women scientists, such as Mrs. Merrill and Dr. Clair, achieve wealth and notoriety through their successes in sleep medicine. We also observe how socially privileged characters wring from their hirelings longer waking hours in the hopes of enhancing worker productivity. Examples abound: Rowland propels Roderick toward artistic creation at all hours of the day; John requires Uncle Julius's services around the clock; Lily's hostesses force her to stay awake late into the night and arise early in the morning to meet their whims; and Gilman's New Woman characters, such as Mrs. Leland and Diantha Bell, thrive off the service of maids whom they expect to exist on little-to-no sleep. These portrayals represent an important turning point in US cultural history, where the ethos of American industrial wakefulness enabled certain individuals to benefit from the twenty-four-hour labor of marginalized others. Moreover, the psychosomatic havoc that sleep deprivation wreaks on these stories' characters challenges turn of the century assumptions about the working body's ability to conquer sleep. Figures 12–15 visualize my research findings across these texts. The Voyant-generated word clouds highlight the most frequently used words within a provided text or corpus, revealing that *work* and *time*, which I have encircled through edits made to the visualizations, are prevalent across all the texts. This pattern reveals that social pressures for minimal rest and on-demand labor in a modern, time-obsessed society are a clear through line in the texts.

Concerns about work, time, and bodily efficiency have only worsened since their emergence at the turn of the century. Alan Derickson explains that "the drive to configure working time in physiologically unnatural ways threatens to derange the sleep of a growing share of American workers. The sleep deficits associated with extreme and demanding jobs point to a deep disparity, a sort of sleep divide, in American society, that separates a perpetually drowsy segment of the workforce from the well-rested majority" (143). Michael Greaney similarly discusses "the politics of sleep," which he

FIGURE 12. Voyant's "Cirrus" tool uses the word cluster template to illustrate word prevalence by increasing the scale of more commonly occurring words. In this figure and the ones that follow, I used an image editor during the research process to circle terms I found particularly enlightening. Here, I have encircled the following in *Roderick Hudson*: *restless*, *work*, and *time*. Compare to figures 13, 14, and 15.

FIGURE 13. Voyant's "Cirrus" visualization highlights the prevalence of *wuk*, *wukkin*, *time*, and *sleep* in the "Uncle Julius" tales. Compare to figures 12, 14, and 15.

describes as "anxieties about globalization, the spread of digital technology and the emergence of a '24/7' society," and which promotes "[transparently uneven] relationship[s] between those who sleep and those who wake" (6). This "sleep divide" is evident in the distinctions the authors draw between characters of obvious privilege and those whose social precarity render them vulnerable to externally dictated schedules.

FIGURE 14. Voyant's "Cirrus" visualization highlights the prevalence of *work* and *time* in *The House of Mirth*. Hovering over a particular word reveals the number of times that word appears in a text. In this figure, *sleep* (with no variation on the word) is shown to appear forty-three times. Compare to figures 12, 13, and 15.

Yet, as my chosen texts suggest, sleep troubles and anxieties are not exclusive to marginalized characters. Even those with greater social agency are portrayed as, at the very least, perturbed by disrupted sleep and conditions of sleeplessness. Endeavors to control sleep affect not only those whose bodies are regulated by more socially powerful overlords but also the overlords themselves, who inadvertently exhaust themselves through efforts to better control their inferiors and further increase their own efficiency. Benjamin Reiss explains that in today's society, sleep disruptions continue to pose a threat to all strata of social classes: "Our society is undergoing two sleep crises: a psychological struggle, in which those who live in relative states of comfort try to wrestle their sleep into submission, and a more existential struggle experienced by those who are expected to sleep by the rules of others yet are denied the time, space, and security to do so. What links these two sets of struggles is the growing economization of sleep, a process begun in the industrial revolution and accelerating today" (7). The authors I discuss document the emergence of these two cultural sleep crises described by Reiss. In James's novel, Rowland is kept awake in the late hours and increasingly loses sleep in his attempts to subdue Roderick's impulsive behavior. In *The House of Mirth*, Wharton portrays Gus Trenor as having the "haggard look of the sleep-walker" amid his near assault on Lily (117).

FIGURE 15. Voyant's "Cirrus" visualization highlights the prevalence of *work*, *time*, *sleep*, and *tired* in selected *Forerunner* texts (the digital companion site, sleepfictions.org, lists the *Forerunner* texts used to generate this visualization). Compare to figures 12, 13, and 14.

In Chesnutt's short stories, a frustrated John is startled awake by the cries of his wife and sister-in-law. For Gilman, sleep deprivation is especially acute for the middle-class white women of her narratives, such as stay-at-home mother Julia Gordins in "Making a Change" (1911), who is driven by exhaustion to attempt suicide. While there remain significant imbalances, each narrative reveals the ways in which modern life increased sleep concerns across both sides of the sleep divide.

As a result, these works of American literature provide insights into complexities of sleep that were yet to be fully understood in scientific terms. In fact, many sleep discoveries that pepper twentieth-century sleep science are reflected in these preceding literary texts. James's image of Roderick Hudson as a run-down clock predicts twenty-first-century discussions of the impact that long-term sleep deprivation has on the body's circadian rhythm: its internal, biological clock. In 1939, when Nathaniel Kleitman (commonly considered the father of modern US sleep medicine) published his study *Sleep and Wakefulness*, American readers could finally learn about scientific connections between the human body and diurnal sleep-wake phases; and only in 2017 did science definitively prove the existence of a "biological clock" that regulates a "molecular cycle" in each living cell of the human body (Nicholls 19–21).

While humans share a common diurnal biology, every person's relationship to sleep is different. Wharton's Lily Bart, plagued by sleeplessness, is, like Roderick, depicted as a deteriorating clock. What Wharton adds to this portrayal is a focus on familial inheritance: Wharton suggests that Lily's father likewise suffered from prolonged wakefulness, passing on his vulnerabilities to sleep deprivation. Interestingly, though, Wharton gives little proof that Lily's inheritance is genetic. Instead, she focuses on how her protagonist's anxieties, which Lily recalls as similarly plaguing her father prior to his death, are the result of the sociofinancial precarity that she inherited from her parents and are exacerbated by her status as an aging single woman in a social circle that values women for their youth and marriageability. Thus, Wharton suggests that environmental sleep detriments are inextricable from inherited factors, in which sleep disturbances plague generations of family members. Troublingly, Wharton leaves the genetic-versus-environmental nature of inheritance open to interpretation, hinting at an inheritable white fragility that is also implied in James's treatment of Roderick. Both authors render white fragility through white supremacist undertones, suggesting that modern multiculturality is a threat to an intellectually superior Anglo purity.

Chesnutt, meanwhile, asserts in no uncertain terms that inherited sleep issues are most certainly environmental. Julius's grandson, Tom, for instance, is a descendant of the "Seben Sleepers," whom Chesnutt tacitly suggests are men whose characteristic sleepiness was a direct result of the racial oppression they endured in slavery (*Conjure* 44). Julius provides no direct information about these ancestors, except for specifying that Skundus, the titular character of "A Deep Sleeper" (1893), was one of the "Seben." Chesnutt's reference to the "seven sleepers" can be traced back to the oral mythology of third-century Ephesus. In one rendering of the tale, seven Christian men fall asleep in a cave where they seek refuge from religious persecution, and centuries pass before they awaken from their slumber (Horst 93). The myth resurfaces in nineteenth-century transatlantic literature. Mark Twain, for instance, in his 1869 travel book *The Innocents Abroad,* parodies the tale in a segment titled "The Legend of the Seven Sleepers" (336–39). By comically blaming the men's long sleep on their imbibing "curious liquors," Twain plays on the phrase's common usage in the US South, in which a "seben sleeper" refers to an individual who sleeps through the morning and other inappropriate times of the day due to poor social habits (Shackelford and Weinberg 86). Chesnutt's correlation between the seven sleepers myth, Skundus's monthlong disappearance, and Tom's symptomatic sleepiness may parallel his symbolic connection between Dave's ham neckless and white Christian claims that African Americans were the descendants of the biblical Noah's cursed son, Ham (Swift and Mamoser 3). Altogether, these attempts represent Chesnutt's aim to trace the mythological origins of racial stereotypes in his effort to dispel pseudoscientific claims that lethargy was a common genetic marker among African Americans.

For Chesnutt, environmental factors are the cause of sleepiness. In Henry Nicholls's study *Sleepyhead,* he notes that less than 5 percent of narcolepsy cases are genetically transmitted (141). This means that an overwhelming majority of narcoleptics, like Harriet Tubman, developed narcolepsy and other sleep abnormalities—including advanced sleep phase disorder and delayed sleep-wake phase disorder—from factors involving either cerebral trauma or a suppressed autoimmune system (Nicholls 23, 107). Just as a knock on the head forced Tubman to endure an adulthood racked by narcolepsy, social, cultural, and environmental forces combine in Chesnutt's tales to bring about sleep disturbances that prevent his characters from sleeping easy.

Of all the texts discussed in this study, I am still amazed at the complexity of sleep imagery in *The House of Mirth.* Each time I revisit its pages, I find new evidence that I missed in previous readings. A passage that last struck me was Wharton's portrait of Lily undergoing sleep paralysis. Nicholls describes the long tradition of writers and authors who use their art to express this frightening experience. He cites Henry Fuseli's 1781 painting *The Nightmare* as a popular depiction, which he describes as "a woman lying on her back, muscles limp, with a demonic imp crouching on her chest" (189). In his cultural history of sleep paralysis, Nicholls notes one common sensation to be an immense pressure on one's chest (176–97, esp. 194). Perhaps influenced by Fuseli's painting, Wharton captures this in her

Conclusion   157

description of Lily in a night of tortured sleep: "Through the long hours of silence the dark spirit of fatigue and loneliness crouched upon her breast, leaving her so drained of bodily strength that her morning thoughts swam in a haze of weakness" (231). Nicholls explains that "the sense of pressure, trouble breathing and pain" that result from sleep paralysis cause its victims to awaken feeling more exhausted than before falling asleep (194). In the last two decades of the twentieth century, Japanese researchers found that disruptions of REM sleep increased the likelihood of an attack, meaning that insomniacs, who suffer from disrupted sleep, were particularly vulnerable to sleep paralysis (Nicholls 182–83). Given the abundant evidence provided in chapter 3, Lily's diagnosis of insomnia is glaringly apparent. Lily's many instances of hallucinations are typical of sleep paralysis, but the fears they induce in her suggest a history of sleep paralysis as marked by superstition. According to Nicholls, "although doctors have been talking about sleep paralysis and hypnagogic hallucinations for at least 150 years, these phenomena have remained at the margins of mainstream neuroscience.... For most of human history, these frightening experiences have been understood by recourse to the supernatural, variously interpreted as ghosts, demons, vampires, and witches" (184). Despite the mystery of sleep paralysis at the turn of the century, Wharton was remarkable in her ability to portray the psychosomatic symptoms of sleep paralysis and to attribute such phenomena to Lily's insomniac condition. Her correlation between sleep-related terrors and the incessant pace of modernity reflects US literature's larger effort to counter cultural beliefs in "heroic wakefulness" (Derickson 5).

An important fact about sleep that underlies each text is that while heredity may play a role in sleep troubles, it is primarily an individual's environment that dictates how and when one sleeps. Meir Kryger confirms this in his sleep study when he notes that while "recent research suggests that some [sleep-related] problems are the result of genetic changes in the system that controls the circadian clock," most sleep phase issues involve biological clocks that are merely "out of sync with the demands of [individuals'] work or other schedules" (93). Thus, the search for successful methods of sleep adjustment is widespread in US culture. Among my selected authors, Gilman is the most focused on sleep's role in evolutionary development, and she draws important connections between sleep culture and social evolution, forecasting vital concerns about class dynamics in the twenty-first century. If we view my analysis in chapter 4 through the lens of Reiss's sleep divide, Gilman anticipates two important components of sleep in modern US culture. First, she illustrates middle- and upper-class efforts to totally control sleep, to find ways to turn it on and off as people had just begun to do with their electric light bulbs. She reveals this in her fictional sketches of women such as Mrs. Merrill and Dr. Clair who invent "natural" and "safe" methods for medically inducing sleep, and in her nonfiction writing when she draws on self-help books by writers like Annie Payson Call to school her readers on improved sleep habits. Second, she uses her fiction to illustrate how entrepreneurs such as Diantha Bell and New Woman figures like Mrs. Leland achieve success by capitalizing on the labor of sleep-deprived minoritized domestic workers. Last, she suggests in her utopian novels that the future of social evolution requires scientific ingenuity, discoveries that can increase the productivity of exploited human labor, as evinced in the Commission on Human Efficiency in *Moving the Mountain* (1911).

Gilman's premonitions are so not different from the fictional fabricants in David Mitchell's 2004 sci-fi novel *Cloud Atlas*. In a dystopian subplot set in Korea in the far future, genomicists discover how to manufacture humanoid fabricants, which are genetically modified to stay awake longer in service of social elites. While "purebloods are entitled to 'rests,'" Sonmi 451, a restaurant worker, explains, "for fabricants, 'rests' would be an act of time theft. Until curfew at hour zero, every minute must be devoted to the service and enrichment of [the employer]" (186). Both fabricants and purebloods (biological humans) continue to divide their time in this future world into twenty-four-hour cycles and maintain a diurnal sleep schedule. Fabricants, however, are genetically modified to sleep only four of those hours. The "time theft" mentioned by Sonmi 451 calls to mind the principles of scientific management that Diantha uses in her employment of domestic workers in the *Forerunner*. As described in chapter 4, Gilman's heroine of *What Diantha Did* (1909–10) methodically directs every moment of her workers' twenty-four-hour cycles to particular tasks, including an allotment for personal and sleeping time. This resonance teaches us that "time theft," while blatantly terrible in *Cloud Atlas*, was similarly insidious within the women's rights movement at the start of the twentieth century. As Katherine A. Fama observes in her discussion of *What Diantha Did*, the ethnic and Black working women of Gilman's fiction "inherit only the labor middle-class white women refuse to perform" (120). This reflects a real-life hypocrisy during Gilman's lifetime and after, in which white middle-class women championed new opportunities in the public sector only by relegating round-the-clock domestic work to less privileged female workers. Like the narrator who liberates herself from the confinement that other women suffer inside Gilman's yellow wallpaper, white middle-class women escaped domesticity oftentimes only by entrapping more vulnerable women within the unregulated hours of domestic work.

Conclusion   159

Presently, scientists across the globe are researching possibilities for meeting goals similar to those Diantha had in mind. Contemporary developments in wakefulness-prolonging drugs, for example, are marketed toward night-shift laborers and extended-shift workers, such as truck drivers. These same drugs translate across the sleep divide into a means for getting ahead in the twenty-four-hour business world. Whereas marginalized laborers curtail sleep at the expense of their bodily health to secure profit for capitalists, privileged Americans—from college students to Silicon Valley executives—imbibe neurological and nervous system stimulants to reduce time "wasted" on sleep in an effort to excel in academic and corporate settings.

At the same time, those pesky circadian rhythms that prevent humans from fully capitalizing on round-the-clock electric lighting continue to inspire investigations into the essentiality of sleep. Recent popular sleep books, including Kryger's *The Mystery of Sleep* (2017) and Nicholls's *Sleepyhead* (2018), draw on science to make the case for sleep hygiene by stressing the importance of qualitative and quantitative sleep measures, which include sleeping routinely, consistently, and adequately, so that over time one feels reliably rested, within spaces primed for restorative rest. Sleep hygiene advocates express concern over the inundation of "light pollution" via increasingly pervasive forms of artificial lighting: televisions, smart phones, tablets, and laptops (Nicholls 44). These new technologies interfere with the body's natural regulation of sleep cycles and can lead to sleep disruption and, over time, long-term sleep deprivation. Sleep education and hygiene, then, are key to helping Americans achieve restorative rest each night.

Meanwhile, bestseller lists are rife with self-help books such as James B. Maas's *Power Sleep* (2012) and his coauthored *Sleep for Success* (2010) and *Sleep to Win!* (2013), along with Terry Cralle and colleagues' *Sleeping Your Way to the Top* (2016), Arianna Huffington's *The Sleep Revolution* (2016), and Chris Winter's *The Sleep Solution* (2017). While some of these texts emphasize sleep efficiency, others reflect the turn of the century leisure class ethic. In the latter sense, the display of scientific- and technologically enhanced sleep routines has been reported by the *New York Times* to be in vogue among wealthy Americans. In the 2017 article "Sleep Is the New Status Symbol," Penelope Green describes the plethora of consumer sleep products marketed toward upper-class American urbanites, from weighted blankets, pillows with thermo-sensitive technology, and sleep-inducing headbands to online sleep coaches and "Deep Rest" meditation classes in Manhattan. She notes that some twenty-first-century figures of American industry have now begun to counter "the familiar paradigm of success [as] the narrative of the short sleeper." Amazon's Jeff Bezos, one of the world's richest entrepreneurs, reportedly stated "that his eight hours of sleep each night were good for his stockholders" (Green). Subsequently, pricey sleep-enhancing technology, primed sleep spaces, and undisturbed resting hours are increasingly becoming symbols of American elitism and social success.

Popular periodicals and activist organizations have begun to draw attention to the sleep divide that underscores the elitism of fashionable rest and racial sleep disparities. The *Atlantic*, for instance, has in recent years published articles that cite sleep studies and other research initiatives to provide scientific evidence for a sleep disparity between wealthy, white Americans and their Black, working-class, and displaced counterparts. Brian Resnick cites numerous sleep studies in a 2015 article in the *Atlantic* to support his claim that "African Americans . . . were five times more likely to get short sleep, defined as less than six hours a night," compared to white sleep study participants. Resnick lists discrimination-related stress, inadequate sleeping environments, low income, and poor health as potential contributors to the sleep disparity. Those who cannot afford private sleeping quarters and the steady, daily routine necessary for normal sleep face health risks and social stigma. In another *Atlantic* article, published in 2014, Hanna Brooks Olsen reports on the dangers of sleep deprivation among America's homeless population: "For individuals without permanent housing, sleep is difficult to come by. When there's no way to secure your personal belongings, it's dangerous and frightening to be as vulnerable as we are when we're in a truly restful sleep." Moreover, the looming threat of arrest further prevents dispossessed persons from sleeping easy. Olsen reports that nearly half of America's major cities "make it a crime to sleep in public spaces." In response to racial sleep inequities, Black-led organizations are utilizing the power of rest to fight systemic and institutional racism. A prime example of this is the Nap Ministry, an organization founded in 2016 by artist and theologian Tricia Hersey that promotes collective napping experiences, leads immersive workshops, and provides rest education coaching. Hersey's 2022 manifesto, *Rest Is Resistance*, proclaims that "rest is a form of resistance because it disrupts and pushes back against capitalism and white supremacy" (7). *Rest Is Resistance* defies the falsehoods peddled by whitewashed and classed self-help books that render sleep a vehicle for cultural success. Hersey disentangles rest from any productivity to which it might lead, and instead redefines rest as a tool for resisting "the brainwashing and socialization of grind culture" and, more profoundly, as a "healing portal to our deepest selves" (129, 7). This latter definition casts sleep as an action with the potential to exist outside and beyond social and cultural constructs: "We are resting *not* to do more and to come back stronger and more productive for a capitalist system" (152, emphasis added).

In contrast to the fictional dystopia of *Cloud Atlas*, Hersey's manifesto offers a glimpse into a more hopeful future:

> The concept of filling up your cup first, so you can have enough in it to pour to others feels off balance. It reeks of the capitalist language that is now a part of our daily mantras. Language like "I will sleep when I am dead," "Rise and grind," "While they sleep, I grind," "If it doesn't make money, it doesn't make sense," "Wake up to hustle," and many more. The cup metaphor also is most often geared toward women, who, because of patriarchy and sexism, carry the burden of labor. Marginalized women, specifically Black and Latina women, make up the largest group of laborers in a capitalist system. Our labor historically has been used to make the lives of white women less hectic and more relaxed. So when I hear and see this "filling your cup" language repeated on memes on social media and in the larger wellness community, I realize that our view of rest is still burdened with the lies of grind culture. I propose that the cups all be broken into little pieces, and we replace pouring with resting and connecting with our bodies in a way that is centered on experimentation and repair. I don't want to pour anymore. It is time to begin the dismantling of the cult of busyness one person at a time. One heart at a time. One body at a time. (62–63)

As technological and scientific advancements propel us through the twenty-first century, the frightening future imagined in *Cloud Atlas* is one of many scenarios in which sleep supremacy—the ability for more powerful individuals to claim sleep for themselves and to capitalize on the sleep of others—may evolve in the decades to come. The push for prolonged wakefulness among the working class and an increasing class gulf in which more and more disadvantaged Americans sleep in improper environments and for shorter intervals of time will combine to further expand the sleep divide. Thus, scholars and greater society alike must follow the lead of sleep-awareness organizations like the Nap Ministry to resist ongoing sleep disparities. This is an undertaking that requires not only looking forward but glancing back: we must all reflect on the premonitions made in the literary texts that emerged at the advent of modernity so that we can better foresee the dangerous possibilities that await an ever-wakeful world.

Notes

Introduction. From Mystery to Medicine

1. For a history of sleep and literature beyond the United States, see Michael Greaney's *Sleep and the Novel*, which situates sleep in "the formal realm of western literary narrative" and "include[s] sleep and dreams in classical antiquity and biblical narrative; the Sleeping Beauties and Rip Van Winkles of fairy tale and folklore; the fatally vulnerable sleeping monarchs of Shakespeare's tragedies; the night terrors, somnambulists and unsleeping monsters of the Gothic; the visionary slumbers of Romantic poetry; and the bedridden aesthetes of Proustian modernism" (7–8).

2. Several Hawthorne scholars have observed the influence that Aylmer's dreams have on his decision to remove Georgiana's birthmark (see Herndon 539; Rucker 454; Browner 47).

3. This consensus can be summarized accordingly: blood flow decreased as the body fatigued and digested food matter; during a sleep state, one's blood would accumulate and congeal in either the body or the brain as the body cooled (for a hematological history of sleep science, see Scrivner 106–15; Horne 208–9).

4. Benjamin Reiss, in *Wild Nights*, charts a history of somnambulism as a wide cultural phenomenon that swept through medical, legal, and literary narratives during the eighteenth and nineteenth centuries (91–118).

5. Wolf-Meyer elaborates on "Edison's views on sleep [as] pervasive and particularly American" (2).

6. Nathaniel Wallace's *Scanning the Hypnoglyph* serves somewhat as a foil to my argument. Wallace argues that sleep in early twentieth-century literature was associated with stability and equilibrium, and he reads sleep in art and literature of the era as a mode of stopping "temporal progression" (18).

7. Here, Southworth adapts a quotation from Isaiah 1:5: "the whole head is sick, and the whole heart faint" (KJV). This convention of the literary melodramas emphasize

Traverse's role as a messiah figure. More interestingly, Southworth appropriates the quotation, which in the Old Testament describes the physical toll of revolting against God, to better detail the physical suffering that Traverse endures during prolonged sleep deprivation.

8. Leo Marx's *The Machine in the Garden* offers an in-depth reading of the contrast between the pastoral scene and technological advancement in nineteenth- and twentieth-century American literature.

9. Several authors have discussed the class distinctions that commonly mark important differences between literary realism and naturalism (see Bell; Campbell, *Resisting*; Dudley; Howard).

10. In the introduction to the 1986 critical edition of *Roderick Hudson*, Geoffrey Moore cites a preface to James's collected works, in which the author writes, "*Roderick Hudson* was my first attempt at a novel." Moore notes that James neglects to include his actual first novel, a serially published work titled *Watch and Ward*, which was featured in the *Atlantic Monthly* in 1871, four years before *Roderick Hudson* was published in the same journal (7–8).

11. The digital companion developed out of my postdoctoral fellowship for the Digital Humanities Initiative at the University of Illinois Chicago (2019–20), which was funded by a grant from the University of Illinois Presidential Initiative to Celebrate the Impact of the Arts and the Humanities. The digital archive was created in Scalar and is hosted by Reclaim Hosting.

Chapter 1. "The Most Restless of Mortals"

1. In this passage from the novel's 1907 preface, James quotes Shakespeare's play *The Tempest* (1610–11), in which Prospero encourages Miranda to recall her earliest memories, hoping that her heritage will direct her fate. In this way, Prospero implies that Miranda's outcome is predetermined, for her powerful lineage will protect her from environmental forces.

2. After seeing a photograph of Roderick's Thirst statuette at Rowland's dinner party, Sam Singleton concludes that Roderick "had only to lose by coming to Rome" (125).

3. The literal interpretation of Roderick's paternal family name, despite its southern origin in the novel, evokes the historical importance of the Hudson River. It also hints at the author's own lineage and his personal formation of inherited whiteness. In James's autobiography, he traces the "infusion" of English, Scottish, and Irish that encompassed his familial bloodline. He is most admiring of his grandmother Catherine Barber, whose Anglo-Saxon purity "represented for us in our generation the only English blood—that of both her own parents—flowing in our veins" (*Small* 5). He also takes pride in the industriousness of his forefathers, who settled on the banks of the Hudson River and profited from its proximity. Like Roderick, James synthesizes his diverse lineage into one image of prosperous whiteness.

Chapter 2. "A Monst'us Pow'ful Sleeper"

An earlier version of this chapter, entitled "Charles Chesnutt's 'Uncle Julius' Tales: Sleepy Subversions of Scientific Racism and the Master Clock," was featured in *Studies in American Fiction*, vol. 48, no. 1, 2021, pp. 1–26.

1. In this chapter, I follow the example of Heather Tirado Gilligan and refer to Chesnutt's short stories, commonly addressed as *The Conjure Woman* stories, as the "Uncle Julius" tales. I find this more fitting, as not all the stories discussed here were included in the original 1899 publication of the *Conjure* collection, and not all include elements of conjuration.

2. The National Sleep Foundation claims that individuals who suffer from post-traumatic stress disorder undergo flashbacks while sleeping (Newsom). These are often recalled much more vividly upon waking than other types of nightmares. Even enslaved women not suffering from immense trauma were still likely to experience lucid dreaming as a result of sleep deprivation. Additionally, a 2012 psychological sleep study (Kloet et al.) found that sleep deprivation contributed to symptoms such as "vivid fantasizing" and "waking dreams" that disorient sleepers upon waking.

Chapter 3. "A Great Blaze of Electric Light"

A condensed version of this chapter, entitled "Illuminating Sleeplessness in Edith Wharton's *The House of Mirth*," was featured in *Studies in American Literary Naturalism*, vol. 11, no. 2, 2016, pp. 1–22.

1. The War of Currents pitted Edison's concepts against those of George Westinghouse and Nikola Tesla. Their companies, Edison Electric Lighting Company and Westinghouse Electric Company, competed against each other in public demonstrations and tabloid debates from the late 1880s to the early 1890s (see Freeberg 174–214).

2. REM (rapid eye movement) sleep is a term that was coined in 1955 by Eugene Aserinsky to refer to a deep sleep state in which the body undergoes full muscle paralysis and the mind dreams vividly. Upon waking, a sleeper has no memory of the dreams experienced during REM sleep. Within the process of a night's uninterrupted rest, REM sleep begins after approximately two hours and, in the second half of the night, may extend to longer periods of time (see Horne 137–58).

3. Given both the success of William's 1890 publication and Wharton's closeness to Henry, it is likely that Wharton was aware of William's work prior to drafting *The House of Mirth*. In her study of Wharton's *The Custom of the Country* (1913), Cecelia Tichi writes that "ambivalent as she was about [William] James (perhaps, as R. W. B. Lewis suggests, resentful of Henry James's 'devotion' to his older brother), Wharton at some point was likely nonetheless to have perused *The Principles of Psychology*" (105). Patrick Mullen also reads gendered and capitalist embodiment in *The House of Mirth* alongside the elder James's theories of embodied intelligence.

References

AASM. *American Academy of Sleep Medicine,* aasmnet.org. Accessed 15 Jan. 2023.

Addington, Bruce. *Sleep and Sleeplessness.* 1915. Little, Brown, 1920.

Allen, Judith A. *The Feminism of Charlotte Perkins Gilman: Sexualities, Histories, Progressivism.* U of Chicago P, 2009.

Andrews, William L. *The Literary Career of Charles W. Chesnutt.* Louisiana State UP, 1999.

Aschoff, Jurgen. "Foreword." *Why We Nap: Evolution, Chronobiology, and Functions of Polyphasic and Ultrashort Sleep,* edited by Claudio Stampi, Springer Science and Business Media, 2013, pp. ix–xiii.

Banta, Martha. "Wharton's Women: In Fashion, in History, out of Time." Singley, pp. 51–86.

Bateson, William. *Mendel's Principles of Heredity.* Cambridge UP, 1909.

Baudelaire, Charles. *The Painter of Modern Life and Other Essays.* 1863. Edited by Jonathan Mayne, Phaidon, 1970.

Beard, George Miller. *American Nervousness: Its Causes and Consequences; A Supplement to Nervous Exhaustion (Neurasthenia).* G. P. Putnam's Sons, 1881.

———. *A Practical Treatise on Nervous Exhaustion (Neurasthenia): Its Symptoms, Nature, Sequences, Treatment.* William Wood, 1880.

Bederman, Gail. *Manliness and Civilization: A Cultural History of Gender and Race in the United States, 1880–1917.* U of Chicago P, 2008.

Bell, Michael Davitt. *The Problem of American Realism.* U of Chicago P, 1993.

Bellamy, Edward. *Looking Backward: From 2000 to 1887.* Houghton, Mifflin, 1888. *Internet Archive,* 30 May 2008, archive.org/details/lookingbackward01bellgoog/.

Ben-Joseph, Eli. *Aesthetic Persuasion: Henry James, the Jews, and Race.* UP of America, 1996.

Bentley, Nancy. *The Ethnography of Manners: Hawthorne, James and Wharton.* Cambridge UP, 2007.

———. *Frantic Panoramas: American Literature and Mass Culture, 1870–1920*. U of Pennsylvania P, 2012.

Bergman, Jill, editor. *Charlotte Perkins Gilman and a Woman's Place in America*. U of Alabama P, 2017.

Blair, Sara. *Henry James and the Writing of Race and Nation*. Cambridge UP, 1996.

Blansett, Bruce. "Swamp Doctor to Conjure Woman: Exploring 'Science' and Race in Nineteenth-Century America." *Southern Frontier Humor: New Approaches*, edited by Ed Piacentino, UP of Mississippi, 2013, pp. 86–103.

Bradford, Sarah Hopkins. *Harriet, the Moses of Her People*. Geo. R. Lockwood and Son, 1886.

Brodhead, Richard H. "Chesnutt's Negotiation with the Dominant Literary Culture." Chesnutt, *The Conjure Stories*, pp. 308–15.

———. *Cultures of Letters: Scenes of Reading and Writing in Nineteenth-Century America*. U of Chicago P, 1993.

Brown, Charles Brockden. "Somnambulism: A Fragment." *Literary Magazine and American Register*, vol. 3, 1805, pp. 335–47.

Brown, William Wells. *The Rising Son, or The Antecedents and Advancement of the Colored Race*. A. G. Brown, 1874.

Browner, Stephanie. *Profound Science and Elegant Literature: Imagining Doctors in Nineteenth-Century America*. U of Pennsylvania P, 2005.

Bruce, Philip Alexander. *The Plantation Negro as a Freeman; Observations on His Character, Condition and Prospects in Virginia*. G. P. Putnam's Son, 1889.

Call, Annie Payson. *Power through Repose*. Roberts Bros., 1891. *Internet Archive*, 1 Mar. 2008, archive.org/details/powerthroughrep02callgoog/.

Campbell, Donna M. "The 'Bitter Taste' of Naturalism: Edith Wharton's *The House of Mirth* and David Graham Phillips's *Susan Lenox*." Papke, pp. 237–59.

———. *Resisting Regionalism: Gender and Naturalism in American Fiction, 1885–1915*. Ohio UP, 1997.

Carpio, Glenda. "Black Humor in the Conjure Stories." Chesnutt, *The Conjure Stories*, pp. 329–38.

Carter-Sanborn, Kristen. "Restraining Order: The Imperialist Anti-Violence of Charlotte Perkins Gilman." *Arizona Quarterly: A Journal of American Literature, Culture, and Theory*, vol. 56, no. 2, 2000, pp. 1–36.

Cartwright, Samuel Adolphus. "Report on the Diseases and Physical Peculiarities of the Negro Race." *New Orleans Medical and Surgical Journal*, vol. 7, 1851, pp. 691–715.

Chesnutt, Charles W. *The Colonel's Dream*. Doubleday, Page, 1905.

———. *The Conjure Stories: Authoritative Texts, Contexts, Criticism*. 1899. Edited by Robert B. Stepto and Jennifer Rae Greeson, W. W. Norton, 2012.

———. *Frederick Douglass*. Small, Maynard, 1899.

———. *The House behind the Cedars*. Houghton, Mifflin, 1900.

———. *The Journals of Charles W. Chesnutt*. Edited by Richard H. Brodhead, Duke UP, 1993.

———. *The Marrow of Tradition*. Houghton, Mifflin, 1901.

———. "A Plea for the American Negro." *Critic*, vol. 36, Feb. 1900, pp. 160–63.

Chopin, Kate. *The Awakening*. Herbert S. Stone, 1899. *Internet Archive*, 12 Sept. 2006, archive.org/details/awakeningthe00choprich/.

Christophersen, Bill. "'Conjurin' the White Folks: Charles Chesnutt's Other 'Julius' Tales." *American Literary Realism*, vol. 18, no. 1/2, 1985, pp. 208–18.

Cralle, Terry, et al., *Sleeping Your Way to the Top: How to Get the Sleep You Need to Succeed*. Sterling, 2016.

Crane, Stephen. *The Red Badge of Courage*. Appleton, 1895. *Internet Archive*, 11 July 2007, archive.org/details/redbadgeofcourag00cranrich/.

Davis, Cynthia. *Charlotte Perkins Gilman: A Biography*. Stanford UP, 2010.

———. "His and Herland: Charlotte Perkins Gilman 'Re-presents' Lester F. Ward." *Evolution and Eugenics in American Literature and Culture, 1880–1940: Essays on Ideological Conflict and Complicity*, edited by Lois A. Cuddy and Claire M. Roche, Bucknell UP, 2003, pp. 73–88.

Derickson, Alan. *Dangerously Sleepy: Overworked Americans and the Cult of Manly Wakefulness*. U of Pennsylvania P, 2013.

Dijk, Derk-Jan, and Malcolm von Schantz. "Timing and Consolidation of Human Sleep, Wakefulness, and Performance by a Symphony of Oscillators." *Journal of Biological Rhythms*, vol. 20, no. 4, 2005, pp. 279–90.

Dimock, Wai-Chee. "Debasing Exchange: Edith Wharton's *The House of Mirth*." *PMLA*, vol. 100, 1985, pp. 783–92.

Dixon, Thomas. *The Leopard's Spots*. New York: Doubleday, Page, 1902.

Douglass, Frederick. *My Bondage and My Freedom*. Miller, Orton and Mulligan, 1855. *Internet Archive*, 19 June 2017, archive.org/details/DKC0119/.

———. *Narrative of the Life of Frederick Douglass, an American Slave*. Anti-Slavery Office, 1845.

Dreiser, Theodore. *Sister Carrie*. 1900. Penguin, 1994.

Du Bois, W. E. B. *The Souls of Black Folk*. Chicago: A. C. McClurg, 1903.

Dudley, John. *A Man's Game: Masculinity and the Anti-Aesthetics of American Literary Realism*. U of Alabama P, 2004.

Duquette, David. "Hegel: Social and Political Thought." *Internet Encyclopedia of Philosophy: A Peer-Reviewed Academic Resource*, iep.utm.edu/hegelsoc. Accessed 14 Jan. 2023.

Duquette, Elizabeth. "'Reflected Usefulness': Exemplifying Conduct in *Roderick Hudson*." *Henry James Review*, vol. 23, 2002, pp. 157–75.

Duvall, J. Michael. "The Futile and the Dingy: Wasting and Being Wasted in *The House of Mirth*." Totten, pp. 159–86.

Edelstein, Sari. "'A Crazy Quilt of a Paper': Theorizing the Place of the Periodical in Charlotte Perkins Gilman's *Forerunner* Fiction." Bergman, pp. 131–45.

Ekirch, A. Roger. *At Day's Close: Night in Time's Past*. W. W. Norton, 2005.

Elam, Charles. *A Physician's Problems*. Fields, Osgood, 1869.

Fama, Katherine A. "Domestic Data and Feminist Momentum: The Narrative Accounting of Helen Stuart Campbell and Charlotte Perkins Gilman." *Studies in American Naturalism*, vol. 12, no. 1, 2017, pp. 105–26.

Fienberg, Lorne. "Charles W. Chesnutt and Uncle Julius: Black Storytellers at the Crossroads." *Studies in American Fiction*, vol. 15, no. 2, 1987, pp. 161–73.

Fisher, Laura R. "Charlotte Perkins Gilman's Novel Aesthetics." *Modern Language Quarterly*, vol. 78, no. 4, 2017, pp. 491–515.

Fleissner, Jennifer. "Earth-Eating, Addiction, Nostalgia: Charles Chesnutt's Diasporic Regionalism." *Studies in Romanticism*, vol. 49, no. 3, 2010, pp. 313–36.

———. *Women, Compulsion, Modernity: The Moment of American Naturalism*. U of Chicago P, 2004.

Freeberg, Ernest. *The Age of Edison: Electric Light and the Invention of Modern America*. Penguin, 2013.

Galton, Francis. *Hereditary Genius*. 1869. New York: Macmillan, 1892.

Ganobcsik-Williams, Lisa. "The Intellectualism of Charlotte Perkins Gilman: Evolutionary Perspectives on Race, Ethnicity, and Class." *Charlotte Perkins Gilman: Optimist Reformer*, edited by Jill Rudd and Val Gough, U of Iowa P, 1999, pp. 16–41.

Gathercole, Michael. "The Use of Hypnosis for the Treatment of Hypnagogic Hallucinations." *Australian Journal of Clinical and Experimental Hypnosis,* vol. 36, 2008, pp. 169–75.

Gerard, Bonnie Lynn. "From Tea to Chloral: Raising the Dead Lily Bart." *Twentieth Century Literature,* vol. 44, 1998, pp. 409–27.

Gilligan, Heather Tirado. "Reading, Race, and Charles Chesnutt's 'Uncle Julius' Tales." *ELH*, vol. 74, no. 1, 2007, pp. 195–215.

Gilman, Charlotte Perkins. *Forerunner*. 7 vols., 1909–16. *Radical Periodicals in the United States, 1890–1960*, Greenwood Reprint Corporation, 1968. *HathiTrust Digital Library*, catalog.hathitrust.org/Record/000544186.

———. *The Home, Its Work and Influence*. McClure, Phillips, 1903. *Google Books*, books.google.com/books?id=Uc6MAAAAIAAJ. Accessed 13 Jan. 2023.

———. *The Living of Charlotte Perkins Gilman*. Madison: U of Wisconsin P, 1935.

———. "A Suggestion on the Negro Problem." *American Journal of Sociology*, vol. 14, 1908, pp. 78–85.

———. "Through This." 1893. Knight, pp. 299–302.

———. *The Yellow Wallpaper*. 1892. Feminist Press, 1973. *Internet Archive*, 25 Mar. 2010, archive.org/details/yellowwallpaper00gilm/.

Gleason, William. "Chesnutt's Piazza Tales: Architecture, Race, and Memory in the Conjure Stories." *American Quarterly*, vol. 51, no. 1, 1999, pp. 33–77.

———. *The Leisure Ethic: Work and Play in American Literature, 1840–1940*. Stanford UP, 1999.

Gleeson, David T. *The Irish in the South, 1815–1877*. U of North Carolina P, 2001.

Goel, Namni, et al., "Neurocognitive Consequences of Sleep Deprivation." *Seminars in Neurology*, vol. 29, 2009, pp. 320–39.

Golden, Catherine. "The Power of the Postal Service in Gilman's 'Turned': Exposing Adultery and Empowering Women to Find a Meaningful Place." Bergman, pp. 146–62.

Golden, Catherine, and Joanna S. Zangrando, editors. *The Mixed Legacy of Charlotte Perkins Gilman*. U of Delaware P, 2000.

Graham, Kellen H. "'To Work Is to Be Socially Alive': The Failed Promise of Domestic Service in Charlotte Perkins Gilman's *What Diantha Did*." *Women and Work: The Labors of Self-Fashioning*, edited by Christine Leiren Mower and Susanne Weil, Cambridge Scholars, 2011, pp. 188–205.

Graham, Wendy. *Henry James's Thwarted Love*. Stanford UP, 1999.

Grant, Madison. *The Passing of the Great Race, or The Racial Basis of European History*. Charles Scribner's Sons, 1916. *Internet Archive*, 17 Mar. 2008, archive.org/details/passinggreatrac01grangoog/.

Greaney, Michael. *Sleep and the Novel: Fictions of Somnolence from Jane Austen to the Present*. Palgrave Macmillan, 2018.

Green, Penelope. "Sleep Is the New Status Symbol." *New York Times*, 8 Apr. 2017.

Greven, David. "Hawthorne and the Gender of Jewishness." *Journal of American Culture*, vol. 35, no. 2, 2012, pp. 135–52.

Halberg, Franz, et al., "Transdisciplinary Unifying Implications of Circadian Findings in the 1950s." *Journal of Circadian Rhythms*, vol. 1, 2003, doi.org/10.1186/1740-3391-1-2.

Haralson, Eric. *Henry James and Queer Modernity*. Cambridge UP, 2003.

Harding, Jennifer Riddle. "A Mind Enslaved? The Interaction of Metaphor, Cognitive Distance, and Narrative Framing in Chesnutt's 'Dave's Neckliss.'" *Style*, vol. 42, no. 4, 2008, pp. 425–47.

Harris, Joel Chandler. *Uncle Remus: His Songs and His Sayings*. 1880. Hawthorn Books, 1921.

Hartman, Saidiya. *Scenes of Subjection: Terror, Slavery, and Self-Making in Nineteenth-Century America*. Oxford UP, 1997.

Hausman, Bernice L. "Sex before Gender: Charlotte Perkins Gilman and the Evolutionary Paradigm of Utopia." *Feminist Studies*, vol. 24, no. 3, 1998, pp. 488–510.

Hawthorne, Nathaniel. "The Birthmark." 1843. *Nathaniel Hawthorne's Tales*, edited by James McIntosh, W. W. Norton, 2013, pp. 152–66.

———. *The Marble Faun*. 1860. Oxford UP, 2008.

Hedge, Frederic Henry. "Characteristics of Genius." *Atlantic Monthly*, Feb. 1868, pp. 150–59.

Henke, Richard. "The Embarrassment of Melodrama: Masculinity in the Early James." *NOVEL: A Forum on Fiction*, vol. 28, no. 3, 1995, pp. 257–83.

Herndon, Jerry A. "Hawthorne's Dream Imagery." *American Literature*, vol. 46, no. 4, 1975, pp. 538–45.

Hersey, Tricia. *Rest Is Resistance: A Manifesto*. Little, Brown Spark, 2022.

Hild, Matthew, and Keri Leigh Merritt, editors. *Reconsidering Southern Labor History: Race, Class, and Power*. UP of Florida, 2018.

Hochman, Barbara. "Highbrow/Lowbrow: Naturalist Writers and the 'Reading Habit.'" Papke, 217–36.

Horne, James. *Sleepfaring: A Journey through the Science of Sleep*. Oxford UP, 2006.

Horst, Pieter W van der. "Pious Long-Sleepers in Greek, Jewish, and Christian Antiquity." *Tradition, Transmission, and Transformation from Second Temple Literature through Judaism and Christianity in Late Antiquity*, edited by Menahem Kister et al., Brill Press, 2011, pp. 93–111.

Howard, June. *Form and History in American Literary Naturalism*. U of North Carolina P, 1985.

Hubbs, Jolene. "Goophering Jim Crow: Charles Chesnutt's 1890s America." *American Literary Realism*, vol. 46, no. 1, 2013, pp. 12–26.

Huber, Hannah. "Charles Chesnutt's 'Uncle Julius' Tales: Sleepy Subversions of Scientific Racism and the Master Clock." *Studies in American Fiction*, vol. 48, no. 1, 2021, pp. 1–26.

———. "Illuminating Sleeplessness in Edith Wharton's *The House of Mirth*." *Studies in American Literary Naturalism*, vol. 11, no. 2, 2016, pp. 1–22.

———. "Selections from Charlotte Perkins Gilman's *Forerunner*." Huber, *Sleep Fictions*, updated 15 June 2021, sleepfictions.org/sleep/scalar/forerunner.

———. *Sleep Fictions: A Digital Companion*, sleepfictions.org. Accessed 15 Jan. 2023.

Hudak, Jennifer. "The 'Social Inventor': Charlotte Perkins Gilman and the (Re)Production of Perfection." *Women's Studies*, vol. 32, 2003, pp. 455–77.

Huffington, Arianna. *The Sleep Revolution: Transforming Your Life, One Night at a Time*. Harmony Books, 2016.

Jacobs, Harriet. *Incidents in the Life of a Slave Girl*. Self-published, 1861.

James, Henry. *The Bostonians*. Macmillan, 1886.

———. "Preface to the New York Edition." 1907. James, *Roderick Hudson*, pp. 35–48.

———. "Provocation." Chapter 8, *Roderick Hudson. Atlantic Monthly*, vol. 36, Aug. 1875, pp. 58–70.

———. *Roderick Hudson*. 1875. Edited by Geoffrey Moore, notes by Patricia Crick, Penguin, 1986.

———. *A Small Boy and Others*. Charles Scribner's Sons, 1913. *Internet Archive*, 29 Apr. 2011, archive.org/details/smallboyothers00jame/.

———. *The Two Magics: The Turn of the Screw, Covering End*, by Henry James, Macmillan, 1898, pp. 1–213.

James, William. *On Vital Reserves: The Energies of Men, the Gospel of Relaxation*. Henry Holt, 1911.

———. *The Principles of Psychology*, vol. 1. Henry Holt, 1890.

Jefferson, Thomas. *Notes on the State of Virginia*. 1785. David Carlisle, 1801.

Kassanoff, Jennie A. "Extinction, Taxidermy, Tableaux Vivants: Staging Race and Class in *The House of Mirth*." *PMLA*, vol. 115, 2000, pp. 60–74.

Kleitman, Nathaniel. *Sleep and Wakefulness*. 1939. U of Chicago P, 1963.

Kloet, Dalena van der, et al., "Fragmented Sleep, Fragmented Mind: The Role of Sleep in Dissociative Symptoms." *Perspectives on Psychological Science*, vol. 7, no. 2, 2012, pp. 159–75.

Knight, Denise. "The Reincarnation of Jane: 'Through This'—Gilman's Companion to 'The Yellow Wall-Paper.'" *Women's Studies*, vol. 20, 1992, pp. 287–302.

Kryger, Meir. *The Mystery of Sleep: Why a Good Night's Rest Is Vital to a Better, Healthier Life.* Yale UP, 2017.

Kytle, Ethan J., and Blain Roberts. *Denmark Vesey's Garden: Slavery and Memory in the Cradle of the Confederacy.* New Press, 2018.

Lanser, Susan S. "Feminist Criticism, 'The Yellow Wallpaper,' and the Politics of Color in America." *Feminist Studies*, vol. 15, no. 3, 1989, pp. 415–41.

London, Jack. "The Apostate." 1906. Charles H. Kerr, n.d. *HathiTrust Digital Library*, catalog.hathitrust.org/Record/002596642. Accessed 13 Jan. 2023.

Lutz, Tom. *American Nervousness, 1903: An Anecdotal History.* Cornell UP, 1991.

Maas, James B. *Power Sleep: The Revolutionary Program That Prepares Your Mind for Peak Performance.* Random House, 2012.

Maas, James B., and Haley A. Davis. *Sleep to Win! Secrets to Unlocking Your Athletic Excellence in Every Sport.* AuthorHouse, 2013.

Maas, James B., and Rebecca S. Robins. *Sleep for Success: Everything You Must Know about Sleep but Are Too Tired to Ask.* AuthorHouse, 2010.

Macnish, Robert. *The Philosophy of Sleep.* D. Appleton, 1830.

Marx, Leo. *The Machine in the Garden: Technology and the Pastoral Ideal in America.* 1964. Oxford UP, 2000.

Matheson, Neill. "Intimacy and Form: James on Hawthorne's Charm." *Henry James Review*, vol. 28, no. 2, 2007, pp. 120–39.

Mattis, Ann. "'Vulgar Strangers in the Home': Charlotte Perkins Gilman and Modern Servitude." *Women's Studies*, vol. 39, 2010, pp. 283–303.

McGrath, Charles. "Wharton Letter Reopens a Mystery." *New York Times*, 21 Nov. 2007.

McWilliams, Dean. *Charles W. Chesnutt and the Fictions of Race.* U of Georgia P, 2002.

Mendelssohn, Michèle. "Homosociality and the Aesthetic in Henry James's *Roderick Hudson*." *Nineteenth-Century Literature*, vol. 57, no. 4, 2003, pp. 512–41.

Merish, Lori. "Engendering Naturalism: Narrative Form and Commodity Spectacle in U.S. Naturalist Fiction." *Novel: A Forum on Fiction*, vol. 29, 1996, pp. 319–45.

Mitchell, David. *Cloud Atlas.* Random House, 2004.

Moody-Turner, Shirley. *Black Folklore and the Politics of Racial Representation.* UP of Mississippi, 2013.

Moore, Geoffrey. "Introduction." James, *Roderick Hudson*, pp. 7–32.

Motomura, Yuki, et al., "Sleepiness Induced by Sleep-Debt Enhanced Amygdala Activity for Subliminal Signals of Fear." *BMC Neuroscience*, vol. 15, 2014, article 97, doi.org/10.1186/1471–2202-15-97.

"Mr. Thomas A. Edison's Nonsense." *National Druggist*, vol. 24, no. 6, June 1894, pp. 166–67. *Google Books*, 30 Oct. 2015, books.google.com/books?id=MYtMAQAAMAAJ.

Mullen, Patrick. "The Aesthetics of Self-Management: Intelligence, Capital, and *The House of Mirth*." *Novel: A Forum on Fiction*, vol. 42, 2009, pp. 40–61.

Myers, Jeffrey. "Other Nature: Resistance to Ecological Hegemony in Charles W. Chesnutt's 'The Conjure Woman.'" *African American Review*, vol. 37, no. 1, 2003, pp. 5–20.

Nadkarni, Asha. *Eugenic Feminism: Reproductive Nationalism in the United States and India*. U of Minnesota P, 2014.

Nap Ministry. thenapministry.com. Accessed 13 Jan. 2023.

"Narcolepsy." *Mayo Clinic*, www.mayoclinic.org/diseases-conditions/narcolepsy /symptoms-causes/syc-20375497. Accessed 13 Jan. 2023.

Newman, Louise Michele. *White Women's Rights: The Racial Origins of Feminism in the United States*. Oxford UP, 1999.

Newsom, Rob. "How Trauma Affects Dreams." *National Sleep Foundation*, updated 15 Dec. 2022, www.sleepfoundation.org/dreams/how-trauma-can-affect-dreams.

Nicholls, Henry. *Sleepyhead: The Neuroscience of a Good Night's Rest*. Basic Books, 2018.

Norris, Frank, "The Puppets and the Puppy." 1897. *The Apprenticeship Writings of Frank Norris, 1896–1898,* vol. 1, edited by Joseph R. McElrath and Douglas K. Burgess, American Philosophical Society, 1996, pp. 268–71.

Northup, Solomon. *Twelve Years a Slave*. Sampson Low, Son, 1853. *Internet Archive*, 2 July 2008, archive.org/details/twelveyearslave00nort/.

Olsen, Hanna Brooks. "Homelessness and the Impossibility of a Good Night's Sleep." *Atlantic*, 14 Aug. 2014.

O'Malley, Michael. *Keeping Watch: A History of American Time*. Smithsonian Institution Press, 1996.

Otis, Laura. *Organic Memory: History and the Body in the Late Nineteenth and Early Twentieth Centuries*. U of Nebraska P, 1994.

Pacheco, Danielle. "Parasomnias." *National Sleep Foundation*, updated 8 July 2022, www.sleepfoundation.org/parasomnias.

Papke, Mary E., editor. *Twisted from the Ordinary: Essays on American Literary Naturalism*. U of Tennessee P, 2003.

Paravantes, Andrew James. "The Awakenings of Charlotte Perkins Gilman." *Utopian Studies*, vol. 30, no. 3, 2019, pp. 505–30.

Person, Leland S. "Falling into Heterosexuality: Sculpting Male Bodies in *The Marble Faun* and *Roderick Hudson*." *Roman Holidays: American Writers and Artists in Nineteenth-Century Italy*, edited by Robert K. Martin and Leland S. Person, U of Iowa P, 2005, pp. 107–39.

Poe, Edgar Allan. "The Facts in the Case of M. Valdemar." 1845. Poe, *The Works*, pp. 115–29.

———. "The Sleeper." 1831. *Poetry Foundation*, poetryfoundation.org/poems/48629/. Accessed 13 Jan. 2023.

———. "The Tell-Tale Heart." 1843. Poe, *The Works*, 352–59.

———. *The Works of Edgar Allan Poe*, vol. 2. Collier and Son, 1904. *Internet Archive*, 3 May 2009, archive.org/details/worksedgarallan09unkngoog/.

Popik, Barry. "Colored People's Time." *The Big Apple*, 12 Apr. 2016, www.barrypopik .com/index.php/new_york_city/entry/colored_peoples_time.

Rabinbach, Anson. *The Human Motor: Energy, Fatigue, and the Origins of Modernity*. U of California P, 1992.

Raynaud, Claudine. "'Mask to Mask. The "Real" Joke': Surfiction/Autofiction, or The Tale of the Purloined Watermelon." *Callaloo*, vol. 22, no. 3, 1999, pp. 695–712.

Reiss, Benjamin. *Wild Nights: How Taming Sleep Created Our Restless World*. Basic Books, 2017.

Resnick, Brian. "The Racial Inequality of Sleep." *Atlantic*, 27 Oct. 2015.

Restuccia, Frances L. "Edith Wharton's Feminism(s)." *Contemporary Literature*, vol. 28, 1987, pp. 223–38.

Roediger, David R. *The Wages of Whiteness: Race and the Making of the American Working Class*. Verso, 1999.

Rowe, John Carlos. "Hawthorne's Ghost in Henry James's Italy: Sculptural Form, Romantic Narrative, and the Function of Sexuality." *Henry James Review*, vol. 20, 1999, pp. 107–34.

Rucker, Mary. "Science and Art in Hawthorne's 'The Birth-Mark.'" *Nineteenth-Century Literature*, vol. 41, no. 4, 1987, pp. 445–61.

Sapora, Carol Baker. "Undine Spragg, the Mirror and the Lamp in *The Custom of the Country*." Totten, pp. 265–86.

Scharnhorst, Gary. "Historicizing Gilman: A Bibliographer's View." Golden and Zangrando, pp. 65–73.

Scrivner, Lee. *Becoming Insomniac: How Sleeplessness Alarmed Modernity*. Palgrave Macmillan, 2014.

Seitler, Dana. "Unnatural Selection: Mothers, Eugenic Feminism, and Charlotte Perkins Gilman's Regeneration Narratives." *American Quarterly*, vol. 55, no. 1, 2003, pp. 61–88.

Shackelford, Laura, and Bill Weinberg. *Our Appalachia: An Oral History*. UP of Kentucky, 2015.

Showalter, Elaine. "The Death of the Lady (Novelist): Wharton's *House of Mirth*." Wharton, *The House of Mirth*, pp. 357–72.

Singley, Carol J., editor. *A Historical Guide to Edith Wharton*. Oxford UP, 2003.

Smith, Mark. *Mastered by the Clock: Time, Slavery, and Freedom in the American South*. U of North Carolina P, 1997.

Sofer, Naomi Z. "Why 'Different Vibrations . . . Walk Hand in Hand': Homosocial Bonds in *Roderick Hudson.*" *Henry James Review*, vol. 20, 1999, pp. 185–205.

Southworth, E. D. E. N. *The Hidden Hand*. 1859. Feather Trail Press, 2009.

Stewart, Dugald. *Elements of the Philosophy of the Human Mind*. 1792. Revised, abridged, and notated by Francis Bowen, James Munroe, 1854.

Stiles, Percy G. "Theories of Sleep." *Popular Science Monthly*, vol. 63, 1903, pp. 432–38.

Summers-Bremner, Eluned. *Insomnia: A Cultural History*. Reaktion Books, 2008.

Sundquist, Eric. *To Wake the Nations: Race in the Making of American Literature*. Harvard UP, 1993.

Swift, John N., and Gigen Mamoser. "'Out of the Realm of Superstition': Chesnutt's 'Dave's Neckliss' and the Curse of Ham." *American Literary Realism*, vol. 42, no. 1, 2009, pp. 1–12.

Taylor, Matthew A. *Universes without Us: Posthuman Cosmologies in American Literature*, U of Minnesota P, 2013.

Teahan, Sheila. "Hawthorne, James, and the Fall of Allegory in *Roderick Hudson*." *Henry James Review*, vol. 12, no. 2, 1991, pp. 158–62.

Thrailkill, Jane F. *Affecting Fictions: Mind, Body, and Emotion in American Literary Realism*. Harvard UP, 2007.

Tichi, Cecelia. "Emerson, Darwin and *The Custom of the Country*." Singley, pp. 89–114.

Tillman, Lynne. "A Mole in the House of the Modern." *New Essays on "The House of Mirth*," edited by Deborah Esch and Emory Elliot, Cambridge UP, 2001, pp. 133–58.

Totten, Gary, editor. *Memorial Boxes and Guarded Interiors: Edith Wharton and Material Culture*. U of Alabama P, 2007.

Tourgee, Albion. *A Fool's Errand: By One of the Fools*. Fords, Howard, and Hulbert, 1879.

Trachtenberg, Alan. *The Incorporation of America: Culture and Society in the Gilded Age*. Hill and Wang, 2007.

Tuttle, Jennifer. "Rewriting the West Cure: Charlotte Perkins Gilman, Owen Wister, and the Sexual Politics of Neurasthenia." Golden and Zangrando, pp. 103–21.

Twain, Mark. *The Innocents Abroad*. 1869. Library of America, 1984.

Tyson, Lois. "Beyond Morality: Lily Bart, Lawrence Selden and the Aesthetic Commodity in 'The House of Mirth.'" *Edith Wharton Review*, vol. 9, no. 2, 1992, pp. 3–10.

US Congress. "An Act for Establishing Rules and Articles for the Government of the Armies of the United States." 10 Apr. 1806. *Acts of the Ninth Congress of the United States*, 1805–6, pp. 359–72.

Van Dongen, Hans, et al., "Sleep Debt: Theoretical and Empirical Issues." *Sleep and Biological Rhythms,* vol. 1, 2003, pp. 5–13.

Veblen, Thorstein. *The Theory of the Leisure Class*. Macmillan, 1899. *Internet Archive*, 19 Apr. 2008, archive.org/details/theoryleisurecl00veblgoog/.

Wallace, Nathaniel. *Scanning the Hypnoglyph: Sleep in Modernist and Postmodern Representation*. Brill, 2016.

Washington, Booker T. *The Future of the American Negro*. Small, Maynard, 1899.

———. *Up from Slavery: An Autobiography*. Doubleday, Page, 1901. *Internet Archive*, 23 May 2009, archive.org/details/upfromslaveryan09washgoog/.

Weinbaum, Alys Eve. "Writing Feminist Genealogy: Charlotte Perkins Gilman, Racial Nationalism, and the Reproduction of Maternalist Feminism." *Feminist Studies*, vol. 27, no. 2, 2001, pp. 271–302.

Wells, H. G. *The Sleeper Awakes*. Harper and Brothers, 1899. *Internet Archive*, 28 Dec. 2022, archive.org/details/whensleeperwakes0000hgwe/.

Wells, Mary Ellen, and Bradley V. Vaughn. "Poor Sleep Challenging Health of a Nation." *Neurodiagnostic Journal*, vol. 52, 2012, pp. 233–49.

Wharton, Edith. *The House of Mirth*. 1905. Edited by Elizabeth Ammons, W. W. Norton, 1990.

———. *Twilight Sleep. 1927.* Simon and Schuster, 1997.

Wharton, Edith, and Ogden Codman Jr. *The Decoration of Houses*. B. T. Batsford, 1898.

White, Jonathan. *Midnight in America: Darkness, Sleep, and Dreams during the Civil War*. U of North Carolina P, 2017.

Whitman, Walt. "The Sleepers." 1855. *University of Iowa Libraries*, bailiwick.lib.uiowa.edu/whitman/sleepers/poem1855.html. Accessed 13 Jan. 2023.

Wideman, John Edgar. "Charles Chesnutt and the WPA Narratives: The Oral and Literate Roots of Afro-American Literature." *The Slave's Narrative*, edited by Charles T. Davis and Henry Louis Gates, Oxford UP, 1985, pp. 59–78.

Winter, Chris. *The Sleep Solution: Why Your Sleep Is Broken and How to Fix It*. Penguin, 2017.

Wolf-Meyer, Matthew J. *The Slumbering Masses: Sleep, Medicine, and Modern American Life*. U of Minnesota P, 2012.

Wonham, Henry B. "Plenty of Room for Us All? Participation and Prejudice in Charles Chesnutt's Dialect Tales." *Studies in American Fiction*, vol. 26, no. 2, 1998, pp. 131–46.

Woods, Gregory. "The Art of Friendship in *Roderick Hudson*." *Henry James and Homo-Erotic Desire*, edited by John R. Bradley, St. Martin's Press, 1999, pp. 69–78.

Worth, Aaron. "Edith Wharton's Poetics of Telecommunication." *Studies in American Fiction*, vol. 36, 2008, pp. 95–121.

Index

Note: Page numbers in *italics* denote figures.

Addington, Bruce, 60
Affecting Fictions. See Thrailkill, Jane F.
agency: *Forerunner* (Gilman), 149, 150; *The House of Mirth* (Wharton), 99, 107, 110; *Roderick Hudson* (James), 28–29, 44, 47, 52, 55; social, 2, 4, 5, 20, 151, 154; "Uncle Julius Tales" (Chesnutt), 69
Allen, Judith A., 124
American Academy of Sleep Medicine, 96
American Journal of Sociology, 17
American Nervousness. See Beard, George Miller
American Nervousness, 1903. See Lutz, Tom
Andrews, William L., 65, 90
"Ant and the Grasshopper, The," 95
Antebellum period, 2, 16, 19, 148
"Apostate, The." *See* London, Jack
Articles of War (1806), 11
Atlantic, 161
Atlantic Monthly, 28, 34, 164n10
awakening, 1, 11, 13, 123, 132, 136
Awakening, The. See Chopin, Kate

Banta, Martha, 94
Bateson, William, 95
Baudelaire, Charles, 33, 34
Beard, George Miller: Black hysteria, 17, 81; neurasthenia, 7, 14, 81, 96, 103–4; sleep paralysis, 101; social degeneration, 31, 18, 51, 96
Becoming Insomniac. See Scrivner, Lee

Bederman, Gail, 10, 45, 121
Bell, Michael, 164n9
Bellamy, Edward, 136, 137
Ben-Joseph, Eli, 55
Bentley, Nancy, 98, 102, 121–22
Birth of Venus, The. See Botticelli, Sandro
"Birthmark, The." *See* Hawthorne, Nathaniel
Blair, Sara, 45
Blansett, Bruce, 65–66, 67, 76
Botticelli, Sandro, 109
Bradford, Sarah Hopkins, 78, 80
Brodhead, Richard H., 65, 70, 89
Brown, Charles Brockden, 2, 4
Brown, William Wells, 80
Browner, Stephanie, 163n2
Bruce, Philip Alexander, 64

Call, Annie Payson, 126–27, 159
Campbell, Donna, 94
Carpio, Glenda, 76
Carter-Sanborn, Kristen, 168
Cartesian dualism, 9, 36
Cartwright, Samuel Adolphus, 17, 59–60, 71, 75
"Characteristics of Genius." *See* Hedge, Frederic Henry
Chesnutt, Charles, 4, 8, 15–19, 22, 151, 155, 156–57; *The Colonel's Dream,* 76, 88; *The House Behind the Cedars,* 62, 83, 85; *The Marrow of Tradition,* 75, 84; "Superstitions and Folk-Lore of the South," 79; "Uncle Julius Tales" (*see* "Uncle Julius Tales")

Chopin, Kate, 1–2, 133–34
Christophersen, Bill, 68, 76
chronobiology, 7
circadian rhythm, 7, 156, 160
Civil War, 10, 20, *21*, 65
Cloud Atlas. See Mitchell, David
compulsion: *The House of Mirth* (Wharton), 8, 106, 109–10, 112, 115; social 9, 20, 151
Codman, Ogden, Jr. *See* Wharton, Edith: *The Decoration of Houses*
conspicuous consumption, 28, 39, 42, 98. *See also* Veblen, Thorstein
Cralle, Terry, 160
Crane, Stephen, 10
critical sleep studies, 2
culture: aesthetic, 27, 41, 51; industrial or time-oriented, 8, 9, 18, 27–28, 31–32, 50, 147; Jim Crow, 63; leisure class, 98; modern, 20; print, 21, 22; sleep, 2, 25, 158; southern US, 61, 69, 79, 82, 87; white, 16

Dangerously Sleepy. See Derickson, Alan
Dante's *Inferno,* 109
Davis, Cynthia, 124, 138, 139, 140
degeneration, 12, 18, 124, 131
Derickson, Alan, 88, 93, 126, 152. *See also* "heroic wakefulness" and "manly wakefulness"
determinism, 19, 99, 133
digital companion, 21, *23,* 132, *155,* 164n11
Dimock, Wai-Chee, 93, 94, 102, 116
Dixon, Thomas, 86, 87
Douglass, Frederick, 19, 72, 74, 75, 77–78, 81, 85
Dreiser, Theodore, 13–14, 15
Du Bois, W. E. B., 16–17, 39, 64–65, 67
Dudley, John, 164n9
Duquette, David, 56
Duquette, Elizabeth, 27
Duvall, Michael J., 112
Dysæsthesia Æthiopis. See Cartwright, Samuel Adolphus

Edelstein, Sari, 140
Edison, Thomas: lightbulb, 6, 29–30, 32, 92; productivity, 16, 18, 47, 89, 126; War of Currents, 165n1 (chap. 3)
efficiency: American ethos, 94; artistic, 36; concerns, 152; cult of, 70, 89; cultural demand for, 18, 29, 30; industrial, 7, 12, 142; overlords, 154; science,

125–27, 136–37; sleep, 4–5, 160. *See also* Taylorism
Ekirch, A. Roger, 5–6, 12
Elam, Charles, 7, 34–35, 59–60, 72, 149
electricity, 5–6, 36, 48, 91–95, 100
Elements of the Philosophy of the Human Mind. See Stewart, Dugald
Endymion myth, 33
Ethnography of Manners, The. See Bentley, Nancy
eugenics, 17, 51, 60, 125, 139–41
exhaustion: "The Apostate," 11–12; *The Awakening* (Chopin), 2; *Forerunner* (Gilman), 121, 122–23, 125, 130, 144; in Google Ngram, 20; *The House of Mirth* (Wharton), 16, 19, 97, 100, 105, 108, 111–15; *Roderick Hudson* (James), 31, 40, 43, 45, 51, 57; *Sister Carrie* (Dreiser), 13; study of, 7; "Uncle Julius Tales" (Chesnutt), 8, 65, 75, 84, 89

"Facts in the Case of M. Valdemar, The." *See* Poe, Edgar Allan
Fama, Katherine A., 159
Fienberg, Lorne, 82
Fisher, Laura R., 94
Fleissner, Jennifer, 10, 82, 107, 120, 129; "biological clock," 108; compulsive behavior, 14, 99, 100
Fool's Errand, A. See Tourgee, Albion
Ford, Henry, 13
Forerunner: brain power, 124–25, 132, 136; collective social energy, 136–38, 141, 150; *The Crux,* 131, 132; domesticity and atavism, 18–20, 121, 124–25, 128, 131, 140–42, 149; "Dr. Clair's Place," 130–33, 152, 159; exploitation of immigrant and Black women, 124–25, 138–139, 141–42, 145–49, 150; "Her Housekeeper," 121, 122, 143, 144–46, 152, 159; *Herland,* 125, 132, 138–39, 140, 142; "His Crutches," 135; "How Little Time," 136; "Improved Methods of Habit Culture," 129; "Improving on Nature," 23, 134, 135; "Making a Change," 144, 145, 149, 155; "A March for Women," 136; Mother Nature, 23, 134–35; *Moving the Mountain,* 124, 135–39, 141, 150, 159; "Morning Devotions," 131, 132; "Mrs. Merrill's Duties," 134, 152, 159; nativism, 122, 123, 125, 142; natural or diurnal sleep, 131, 132, 134, 135, 139; *Our Brains and What Ails Them,*

124, 125; "The Power of the Farm Wife," 147–48; "Rest and Power," 124, 126, 130, 150; "The Sanctity of Human Life," 141; scientific management of sleeping hours, 123, 126–29, 132, 138, 142, 146–48; Silas Weir Mitchell's rest cure, 129–30; sleep as privilege, 124, 125, 144; sleep as social currency, 122, 127, 128, 135; social evolution, 121, 123–26, 129, 132, 141–42, 149–50; "Studies in Social Pathology," 128, 134, 141; "A Summary of Purpose," 150; "Three Thanksgivings," 129; "Turned," 122; "Two Callings," 148–49; utopian novels, 18, 19, 124–25, 131, 136–38, 147, 159; *What Diantha Did*, 8, 143, 145–50, 152, 159–60; "When I was a Witch," 140, 141; "While the King Slept," 135; *Won Over*, 128; "World Rousers," 135, 136
Franklin, Benjamin, 5
Freeberg, Ernest, 95
freneticism, 37, 38, 50, 57, 58, 120
Fuseli, Henry, 157
Future of the American Negro, The. See Washington, Booker T.

Galton, Francis, 18, 30, 40
Ganobcsik-Williams, Lisa, 124, 141
genetics, 95, 156–59
Gerard, Bonnie Lynn, 106, 110, 111
Gilbert, J. A., 7
Gilded Age, 15, 19, 61, 95, 98, 119
Gilligan, Heather Tirado, 85, 165n1 (chap. 2)
Gilman, Charlotte Perkins, 4, 8, 151, 158–59; *Forerunner* (see *Forerunner*); *The Home, It's Work and Influence*, 142; "A Suggestion on the Negro Problem," 17; "Through This," 144; "The Yellow Wall-Paper," 120, 144
Gleason, William, 27, 42, 66, 82, 83
Gleeson, David, 39
Godey's Lady's Book, 126
Golden, Catherine, 122
Google Ngram. *See* visualization (in digital humanities)
Graham, Kellen H., 126, 144, 146, 148, 149
Graham, Wendy, 27, 52
Grant, Madison, 139
Greaney, Michael: "geography of sleep," 90, 93; "history of sleep," 163n1; "human significance of sleep," 150; insomnia, 6; "politics of sleep," 152–53; sleep and

social agency, 5; sleep as assertive act, 12; on "The Sleepers" (Whitman), 3
Green, Penelope, 160
Greven, David, 55

Halberg, Franz, 7
hallucinations, 80, 97, 101, 158
Haralson, Eric, 27, 47
Harding, Jennifer Riddle, 69
Harris, Joel Chandler. *See* Uncle Remus
Hartman, Saidiya, 74
HathiTrust Digital Library, 21
Hausman, Bernice L., 138
Hawthorne, Nathaniel, 2–3, 47–48, 55, 163n2
Hedge, Frederic Henry, 34
Hegel, Georg Wilhelm Friedrich, 56
Henke, Richard, 40
Hereditary Genius. See Galton, Francis
Herndon, Jerry A., 163n2
"heroic wakefulness" 5, 16, 89. *See also* Derickson, Alan
Hersey, Tricia, 161, 162
Hidden Hand, The. See Southworth, E. D. E. N.
Hild, Matthew, 39
Hochman, Barbara, 94, 100, 101
Horne, James, 95, 113, 163n3
House of Mirth, The: biological impulses, 94, 100, 107, 112, 113, 115; chloral hydrate, 95, 112–13, 115–16; compulsive behavior, 8, 99, 100, 108, 120, 156; degeneration, 12, 131, 133–34, 152, 156; fragility of whiteness, 15; Gus Trenor as sleepwalker, 100, 154; indulgent rest, 102–3, 110; Lily as naturalist New Woman, 15, 108; marginality, 99, 119, 122; sleep debt, 19, 94, 96–97, 99, 103, 107, 125; physiological experience of sleep, 18, 97, 128, 157–58; social debt, 16, 94, 98, 102, 107–8, 118; stimulants, 111–13, 116; time slippage, 103–8, 111, 115; Veblen's conspicuous consumption, 93, 98
Howard, June, 164n9
Hubbs, Jolene, 64
Hudak, Jennifer, 124, 138, 140
Huffington, Arianna, 160
hysteria, 17, 47, 60, 81, 82

idleness, 40, 42, 54, 82, 98, 149
Incidents in the Life of a Slave Girl. See Jacobs, Harriet

industriousness, 19, 29, 40, 96, 164n3
insomnia: *The House of Mirth* (Wharton), 9, 104–5, 118, 158; in Google Ngram, 20, *21*; medical terminology, 22; Progressive-Era zeitgeist, 6; "The Yellow Wall-Paper" (Gilman), 120–21
Insomnia. See Summers-Bremner, Eluned

James, Henry, 4, 12, 29, 151, 164n3; *The Bostonians*, 86, 130; *Roderick Hudson* (see *Roderick Hudson*); *The Turn of the Screw*, 58; *Watch and Ward*, 164n10
James, William, 37, 165n3; "The Energies of Men," 35; "The Gospel of Relaxation," 35, 36; *On Vital Reserves,* 36; *The Principles of Psychology*, 105, 165n3
Jacobs, Harriet, 19, 78, 85, 143
Jefferson, Thomas, 17, 60

Kassanoff, Jennie A., 94
Kinnicutt, Francis, 116
Kleitman, Nathaniel, 156
Knight, Denise, 144
Kryger, Meir, 6, 158, 160

labor: artistic, 18, 31, 38, 42–43, 46, 49–50, 54–55; convict, 64, 88; enslaved, 59–60, 70, 72, 75, 78; exploitative, 71, 84, 87–88, 112, 159; forced, 60–61, 64, 65; frenetic, 41; hierarchies of, 124; industrial, 4, 6, 12, 27, 126; minoritized and Black, 16–17, 19, 145, 159, 162; non-Anglo domestic workers, 121, 125, 128, 142–43, 146–50; productive, 28, 29, 30, 34–35; racialized delegation of, 122; time, 16, 52, 63, 137–38, 152
Ladies' Home Journal, 126
Lanser, Susan S., 124
Lear, Edward, 23, 123
Leopard's Spots, The. See Dixon, Thomas
Looking Backward. See Bellamy, Edward
London, Jack, 11–12, 13
Lutz, Tom, 10, 15, 17

Maas, James B., 160
Macnish, Robert, 3
Mamoser, Gigen, 157
Manliness and Civilization. See Bederman, Gail
"manly wakefulness," 47. *See also* Derickson, Alan

Marble Faun, The. See Hawthorne, Nathaniel
Marx, Leo, 164n8
master-slave dialectic. See Hegel, Georg Wilhelm Friedrich
Mattis, Ann, 124, 142, 147, 148–49
McGrath, Charles, 116
mechanization, 4, 9, 18, 29, 46
McWilliams, Dean, 80
medicine, 124: mid-nineteenth-century, 3; modern, 3, 101; sleep, 7, 19, 96, 152, 156; twenty-first-century, 8; white, 66, 70, 89. *See also* sleep science
Mendelssohn, Michèle, 38, 41, 43, 44, 51
Merish, Lori, 94
Merritt, Keri Leigh, 39
Mexican-American War, 11
Mitchell, David, 159, 162
modernity: constraints on restorative rest, 10, 20, 108, 121, 151; dangers posed, 30, 162; environmental forces, 15, 102, 106, 115; haste of, 9, 11, 120, 158; industrialized, 12; machinelike rhythms of, 94; permeation of, 4
Moody-Turner, Shirley, 71
Moore, Geoffrey, 164n10
Mullen, Patrick, 112, 165n3
My Bondage and My Freedom. See Douglass, Frederick
Myers, Jeffrey, 88
Mystery of Sleep, The. See Kryger, Meir

Nadkarni, Asha, 122, 124, 138, 141
Nap Ministry, The. See Hersey, Tricia
narcolepsy, 8, 66, 80, 157
National Druggist, 126
National Sleep Foundation, 165n2 (chap. 2)
Naturalism, 9, 12, 14, 19, 164n9
Newman, Louise Michele, 122, 124, 142, 147
New Woman: George Miller Beard, 14; Jennifer Fleissner, 14, 108; *Forerunner* (Gilman), 16, 19, 121, 130, 143, 152, 159; *The House of Mirth* (Wharton), 15, 108; *Sister Carrie* (Dreiser), 13
New York Tribune, 29
neurasthenia: Beard, 14, 17, 96; "Dr. Clair's Place" (Gilman), 130; "The Goophered Grapevine" (Chesnutt), 81–82; in literary scholarship, 10; in medicine, 7, 120; "The Yellow Wall-Paper" (Gilman), 129
Nicholls, Henry, 157–58, 160

Nightmare, The. See Henry Fuseli
Norris, Frank, 110
Northup, Solomon, 72
Notes on the State of Virginia. See Jefferson, Thomas

Olsen, Hanna Brooks, 161
O'Malley, Michael, 50, 51, 61, 63
Otis, Laura, 94

Pacheco, Danielle, 101
Painter of Modern Life and Other Essays, The. See Baudelaire, Charles
parasomnia, 22, 101, 104, 105, 112, 113
Paravantes, Andrew James, 124
Passing of the Great Race, The. See Grant, Madison
Patrick, G. T. W., 7
Person, Leland S., 38
Philosophy of Sleep, The. See Macnish, Robert
Physician's Problems, A. See Elam, Charles
Plantation Negro as a Freeman, The. See Bruce, Philip Alexander
Poe, Edgar Allan, 2–4
Poor Richard's Almanack. See Franklin, Benjamin
Popik, Barry, 62
Popular Science Monthly, 7
Power Sleep. See Maas, James B.
Power Through Repose. See Call, Annie Payson
Progressive Era, 2, 17, 22, 60
Project Gutenberg, 21
Protestant work ethic, 9, 38, 54
pseudoscience, 4, 8, 22, 65, 89, 152, 157
"Puppets and the Puppy, The." *See* Norris, Frank

Rabinbach, Anson, 9, 12, 31
racism: Chesnutt on racism of white medicine, 70, 89; Chesnutt on scientific racism, 19, 61; digital companion theme tag, 22; Gilman's eugenics, 139; Gilman's vision of domestic industrialization, 16; institutional, 161; pseudoscience, 4
Raynaud, Claudine, 66
realism, 9, 18, 164n9
Reconstruction, 61, 62, 70, 87, 88, 89
Red Badge of Courage, The. See Crane, Stephen

Reiss, Benjamin, 13, 60, 74, 75, 83, 154
REM sleep, 7, 80, 101, 113, 158, 165n2 (chap. 3)
Resnick, Brian, 161
Rest is Resistance. See Hersey, Tricia
restlessness: *The Awakening* (Chopin), 1; Gilman, 120; *The House of Mirth* (Wharton), 19, 104, 113; *Roderick Hudson* (James), 18, 26, 29, 32–46, 50, 56–58; study of, 4
restorative rest: "The Apostate" (London), 12; *The Awakening* (Chopin), 2; biological necessity of sleep, 9; *Forerunner* (Gilman), 20, 125, 126, 130–31, 143–45; *The House of Mirth* (Wharton), 102, 113; modernity's constraints, 20, 151; New Woman, 13; paradox of sleep as social privilege and essentiality, 20; *The Red Badge of Courage* (Crane), 10; *Roderick Hudson* (James), 34, 46, 56; sleep hygiene, 160; "Uncle Julius Tales" (Chesnutt), 82
Restuccia, Frances L., 94–95
Rising Sun, The. See Brown, William Wells
Roderick Hudson: artistic genius, 17–18, 26, 30, 43–44, 96; artistic masculinity, 47, 49; Baudelaire and the flaneur, 32–33; cultural demand for efficiency, 29; Hawthorne and feminine energy, 48; Hedge and the genius-somnambulist, 34–35; indulgent rest, 46, 102, 115, 131; kinesis, 31, 34–37, 40, 47, 49; labor supply and withdrawal, 16; objectification of Christina Light, 50–51, 98; patronage and class, 27–29, 32, 41–42, 93; racial otherness, 55; restlessness and Rowland Mallet, 56–58, 154; Roderick as broken-down clock, 8, 51–53, 107, 127, 156; Roderick as energy source, 36–37; Roderick as son of enslaver, 45; Roderick's degeneration, 12, 57–58, 152; Roderick's internalized whiteness, 15, 38–39, 83; Sam Singleton's working-class methodology, 54; sleep deprivation and class, 15, 23; social Darwinism, 44; stasis, 18, 31–38, 40–41, 47, 49, 54, 57
Roediger, David R., 39
Roosevelt, Theodore, 15, 17, 60
Rucker, Mary, 163n2

Index   183

Sapora, Carol Baker, 93

Scalar, 22, *23*, *24*, *25*, 164n11

Scanning the Hypnoglyph. See Wallace, Nathaniel

Scharnhorst, Gary, 122, 124, 146, 147

scientific management, 6, 8, 126, 129, 137, 145, 148, 159

scientific racism, 19, 22, 61, 139

Scrivner, Lee, 5, 35, 104–5, 120–21, 124, 163n3

sedatives, 113, 134. *See also* soporifics

Seitler, Dana, 122, 124, 131, 145, 147

Sister Carrie. See Dreiser, Theodore

Shakespeare, William, 164n1

Showalter, Elaine, 112

slave narratives, 19, 90

sleep aid, 95–96, 136. *See also* soporifics

Sleep and Sleeplessness. See Addington, Bruce

Sleep and the Novel. See Greaney, Michael

Sleep and Wakefulness. See Kleitman, Nathaniel

sleep deprivation: "The Apostate" (London), 11–12; and wakefulness, 8–9, 152; digital companion theme tag, 22, 23, 24, *25*; *Forerunner* (Gilman), 123, 131, 143, 144, 155; *The Hidden Hand* (Southworth), 10–11, 163n7; homelessness, 161; *The House of Mirth* (Wharton), 95–101, 112, 118, 156; medical science, 4, 7, 160, 165n2 (chap. 2); *Roderick Hudson* (James), 156; Thomas Jefferson on Black labor, 60; "Uncle Julius Tales" (Chesnutt), 61, 62, 70, 72, 76–82, 87–90

sleep discipline, 19, 89, 125–26, 130

sleep divide, 152, 153, 155, 158, 160–62

"Sleeper, The." *See* Poe, Edgar Allan

Sleeper Awakes, The. See Wells, H. G.

"Sleepers, The," *See* Whitman, Walt

Sleep for Success. See Maas, James B.

Sleeping Beauty: *The Awakening* (Chopin), 1; digital companion theme tag, 22, 23, *24*; *Forerunner* (Gilman), 23, 123, 134, 135, 148; *Roderick Hudson* (James), 33, 49; "Uncle Julius Tales" (Chesnutt), 66

sleep paralysis, 4, 9, 101, 157–58, 165n2 (chap. 3)

sleep phenomena, 7, 8, 18, 20, 95

Sleep Revolution, The. See Huffington, Arianna

sleep science, 156, 163n3, 165n2 (chap. 2)

Sleep Solution, The. See Winter, Chris

sleep studies, 19, 96, 161, 138

Sleep to Win! See Maas, James B.

Sleeping Your Way to the Top. See Cralle, Terry

sleeplessness: across class divides, 5, 154; *Forerunner* (Gilman), 149; *The House of Mirth* (Wharton), 18, 19, 95–97, 99–101, 106–7, 110–12, 118, 156; pharmacological treatments, 7; neurasthenia as diagnosis, 10; "sleepless" in Google Ngram, 20; "Uncle Julius Tales" (Chesnutt), 75, 82, 87

sleepwalker, 34, 99–100, 123, 124, 136, 148

Sleepyhead. See Nicholls, Henry

Smith, Mark, 62, 63–64

Sofer, Naomi Z., 41, 45

somnambulism, 7, 33–35, 59–60, 71–72, 149, 163n4

"Somnambulism: A Fragment," *See* Brown, Charles Brockden

soporifics, 9, 22, 96, 111, 135, 152

Souls of Black Folk, The. See Du Bois, W. E. B.

Southworth, E. D. E. N., 10–11, 163n7

Stewart, Dugald, 60

Stiles, Percy G. See *Popular Science Monthly*

"Story of the War, A." *See* Uncle Remus

Stowe, Harriet Beecher, 83

suicide: *The Awakening* (Chopin), 1, 2, 133; *Forerunner*, (Gilman), 130, 133, 144, 155; *The House of Mirth* (Wharton), 116, 117, 133; race, 15; *Roderick Hudson* (James), 15; "Uncle Julius Tales" (Chesnutt), 76–77

Summers-Bremner, Eluned, 6, 32

Sundquist, Eric, 72

surveillance: *Forerunner* (Gilman), 146, 148; *Roderick Hudson* (James), 42, 46, 50; "Uncle Julius Tales" (Chesnutt), 61, 72, 74, 78–79, 85

Swift, John N., 157

Szymanski, J. S., 7

Taylor, Frederick Winslow, 6, 125

Taylor, Matthew A., 69–70

Taylorism, 84, 147

Teahan, Sheila, 48

"Tell-Tale Heart, The." *See* Poe, Edgar Allan

Tempest, The. See Shakespeare, William
Theory of the Leisure Class, The. See
   Veblen, Thorstein
"There Was an Old Man of Jamaica." *See*
   Lear, Edward
Thrailkill, Jane F., 3, 9, 10, 36, 129
Tichi, Cecelia, 165n3
Tillman, Lynne, 116
"Tortoise and the Hare, The," 95
Tourgee, Albion, 86, 87
Trachtenberg, Alan, 30
Tubman, Harriet, 78–80, 157
Turner, Nat, 86
Tuttle, Jennifer, 130
Twain, Mark, 157
Twelve Years a Slave. See Northup, Solomon
two sleeps, 6
Tyson, Lois, 116

"Uncle Julius Tales": Black lethargy stereo-
   type, 16, 18–19, 60–62, 64–69, 71, 89;
   Black railroad porters, 87–89; Colored
   People's Time (CPT), 62, 63, 65, 84;
   "Conjurer's Revenge," 87, 140; "Dave's
   Neckliss," 73, 76–77, 157; "A Deep
   Sleeper," 8, 19, 65–69, 70, 73, 79, 90,
   156–57; dialect, 67; enslaved women and
   dreamworld, 79, 80; enslavement and
   surveillance, 61, 72, 74, 78, 79, 85; "The
   Goophered Grapevine," 63, 65, 76, 81,
   82; "The Gray Wolf's Ha'nt," 74; "Hot-
   Foot Hannibal," 85; "Mars Jeems's Nightmare," 22, 69, 70–74, 89, 90, 112; master
   clock time, 61–66; plantation fiction,
   64, 69–70, 82–83, 87; "Po' Sandy," 65,
   75, 84; "Sis' Becky's Pickaninny," 80–82;
   twinned deprivations of food and sleep,
   61, 76, 89; vagrancy, 88–89; "Victim of
   Heredity, A," 76–77; white anxieties
   about sleep, 61, 86–87
Uncle Remus, 69
Up from Slavery. See Washington, Booker T.

Veblen, Thorstein, 28, 39, 42, 93, 98. *See
also* conspicuous consumption

visualization (in digital humanities):
   Forerunner (Gilman), 132, *133*; Google
   Ngram, 20, *21*; *The House of Mirth*
   (Wharton), 115, 117–18; *Roderick Hudson*
   (James), 53, 56, 115; Scalar, 22–25; sleep-
   related terms, 22–23; "Uncle Julius
   Tales" (Chesnutt), 68, 72, 73; Voyant
   stopwords, 21; work and time, 152, *153,*
   154, 155
Voyant Tools. *See* visualization (in digital
   humanities)

wakefulness: *The Awakening* (Chopin), 1;
   Black uplift, 16; *Forerunner* (Gilman),
   121, 126; Gilded Age class oppression, 19;
   The House of Mirth (Wharton), 92, 93,
   95–97, 101, 112–13, 156, 158; industrial-
   ized labor; 12, 152, 162; neurasthenia,
   14; obsession, 4; *The Philosophy of Sleep*
   (Macnish), 3; *Roderick Hudson* (James),
   34, 36, 43, 47; sleep deprivation, 8–9;
   universal, 5; "Uncle Julius Tales" (Ches-
   nutt), 75, 84, 89; *See also* Derickson,
   Alan.
Wallace, Nathaniel, 163n6
War of Currents, 95, 165n1 (chap. 3)
Washington, Booker T., 16, 19, 64, 77, 85,
   89
Weinbaum, Alys Eve, 122, 124, 138, 147
Wells, H. G., 136
Wharton, Edith, 4, 12, 151; *The Custom
of the Country,* 165; *The Decoration of
Houses,* 91, 92, 118, 126; *The House of
Mirth* (see *The House of Mirth*); *Twilight
Sleep,* 118–119
White, Jonathan, 80
Whitman, Walt, 2, 3, 10
Wideman, John Edgar, 66
Wild Nights. See Reiss, Benjamin
Winter, Chris, 160
Wolf-Meyer, Matthew J., 5, 6, 163n6
Women, Compulsion, Modernity. See
   Fleissner, Jennifer
Wonham, Henry B., 70, 71
Worth, Aaron, 100, 111, 115

Index   185

HANNAH L. HUBER is an adjunct professor
of English and the Digital Technology Leader
and Project Administrator for the Center for
Southern Studies at The University of the South.

Topics in the Digital Humanities

From Papyrus to Hypertext: Toward the Universal Digital Library
   Christian Vandendorpe, translated from the French by
   Phyllis Aronoff and Howard Scott
Reading Machines: Toward an Algorithmic Criticism   *Stephen Ramsay*
Macroanalysis: Digital Methods and Literary History   *Matthew L. Jockers*
Digital Critical Editions   *Edited by Daniel Apollon, Claire Bélisle,*
   and Philippe Régnier
Teaching with Digital Humanities: Tools and Methods for Nineteenth-Century
   American Literature   *Edited by Jennifer Travis and Jessica DeSpain*
Critical Digital Humanities: The Search for a Methodology   *James E. Dobson*
Technology and the Historian: Transformations in the Digital Age
   Adam Crymble
Sleep Fictions: Rest and Its Deprivations in Progressive-Era Literature
   Hannah L. Huber

The University of Illinois Press
is a founding member of the
Association of University Presses.

University of Illinois Press
1325 South Oak Street
Champaign, IL 61820-6903
www.press.uillinois.edu